Library of Congress Cataloging-in-Publication Data
Sheimo, Michael D., 1944–
    Stock market rules : 70 of the most widely held investment axioms
explained, examined and exposed / by Michael D. Sheimo.—2nd ed.
      p. cm.
    ISBN 0-07-134096-3
    1. Investments—Miscellanea.   2. Stock exchanges—Miscellanea.
I. Title.
HG4521.S519   1999
332.63'22—dc21   98-45658
                                                              CIP

McGraw-Hill

A Division of The **McGraw·Hill** *Companies*

1 2 3 4 5 6 7 8 9 0   DOC/DOC   9 0 4 3 2 1 0 9

ISBN 0-07-134096-3

> *As a rule . . .*
> *Always*
> *for*
> *Linda*

The sponsoring editor for this book was Roger Marsh, the editing supervisor was Scott Amerman,
and the production supervisor was Suzanne Rapcavage. It was set in ITCCentury Light by Lisa M.
Mellott through the services of Barry E. Brown (Broker—Editing, Design and Production).

Printed and bound by R.R. Donnelley & Sons Company.

CONTENTS

PREFACE

Axioms about the market have been around as long as stock trading. The stock market, with its continuous buying and selling, attracts clever sayings or words of wisdom about what to do or what not to do in different situations. Why are these axioms important? Because they are based on real market experience. Experience is often the seasoning that makes investors richer or poorer.

Many axioms are still true, while others that were once true have changed. "Buy on Monday, sell on Friday" (Chapter 39) is well known by investors, but many aren't aware that the pattern has changed. Statistically, the axiom is not as good a strategy as it was prior to 1990. "Good companies buy their own stock" (Chapter 5) might be good for the company, but is it always good for the investor? Bellwethers—that is, stocks that turn before the rest of the market—have been kicked around for decades. Part of the problem with bellwethers is their tendency to be inconsistent, turning ahead of the market sometimes and after the market other times. As shown in Chapter 56, "Watch the Bellwethers," they are frequently on the money when viewed in a short time frame.

Although many of the time-honored sayings are helpful, knowledge of the axiom alone is not enough; it is essential to understand the meaning behind the saying. If it is better to "Sell the losers and let the winners run" (Chapter 1), how does an investor determine which stock is a loser and which one is a winner? Is price the only determining factor, or should other factors be considered? If the investor continually sells the losers, how and when does profit taking become an event? Answers to questions like these can give the investor a strong understanding of the full meaning behind the axiom. These are only a few of the concepts covered in this book. A review of the table of contents will quickly give the full picture.

A look at the list of illustrations shows the depth of coverage of this comprehensive work. The book contains more than a hundred charts of stock market indexes, primarily the Dow Industrial and Transportation Averages and the Standard & Poor's 500 Index, as well as many charts of stock price trends for individual companies. Although the analysis is relevant to the time of the charts, things change. In today's market, things change quickly. The price charts and analysis are not meant to be current buy or sell recommendations. Rather, the charts show real-world examples of the concepts presented in this book.

The "rules" presented in this book are axioms based on investing in and trading stocks of publicly held corporations. The concepts are explained, examined, and exposed in order to bring about an understanding of the many fine points of stock trading. The investor's understanding of these concepts will improve his or her decision-making process and help him or her with the buying and selling of stocks. Greater knowledge can lead to greater profits.

Some words of wisdom from stock market notables follow:

You are neither right nor wrong because the crowd disagrees with you; you are right because your data and reasoning are right.

—Benjamin Graham

All the sales growth in the world won't produce the right type of investment vehicle if over the years, profits do not grow correspondingly.

—Philip Fisher

To succeed in the market, you must have discipline, flexibility—and patience. You have to wait for the tape to give its message before you buy or sell.

—Martin Zweig

The truth is that, while spot news can affect some or all of the market on a day-to-day basis, the underlying trend is what matters—and that takes a little more perspective than daily deadline pressures can permit.

—Louis Rukeyser

Why must you learn about investing? You can hire a financial planner or manager to make the decisions, cash your dividend checks, and try to forget about the whole business. But no matter how much responsibility you delegate, and how much help you receive, the fate of your portfolio rests in your hands. Think of it this way: You're the CEO of an important enterprise called "Your Financial Future."

—Peter Lynch

In a majority of cases this method of choosing the time to buy, founded upon clear perception of value in the stock chosen and close observation of the market swings underway will enable an operator to secure stock at a time and at a price which will give fair profits on the investment.

—Charles Henry Dow

The future is never clear; you pay a very high price for cheery consensus. We simply attempt to be fearful when others are greedy and to be greedy only when others are fearful.

—Warren Buffett

CHAPTER 1

Sell the Losers and Let the Winners Run

The title of this chapter is one of the oldest sayings in the stock market. In the late 1800s, Daniel Drew had a slightly different version:

Cut your losses and let your profits run.

The concept is sound; in fact, it is one of the most important understandings an investor can have about the stock market. It is prudent for an investor to sell stocks that are losing money, stocks that could continue to drop in price and value. It makes equally good sense to stay with stocks that show significant gains, as long as they remain fundamentally strong.

But just what is a loser? Is it any price drop from the high? Is a stock a loser only if the investor is actually in a loss position? (That *position* is with the current price below the original purchase price.)

Any price drop is a losing situation. Price drops cost the investor money. They are a loss of profits. In some circumstances the investor should sell, but in other situations the investor should take a closer look before reaching a sell decision.

The determination of whether a stock is still a winner depends on the cause of the price correction. If the cause of a price drop appears to be a weakness in the overall market situation or is the result of a "normal" daily fluctuation of the stock price, it can still be a winner.

If the cause has long-term implications, it could be time to take the loss and move on to another stock. Long-term implications could be any of the following:

Declining sales

Tax difficulties

Legal problems

An emerging bear market

Higher interest rates

Negative impacts on future earnings

Any event that has a negative impact on the long-term picture of earnings or earnings growth can quickly turn a stock into a loser. Many long- and short-term investors will sell out their positions and move on to a potential winner.

VALUE IN EARNINGS GROWTH

Value, in terms of growth potential, is based on earnings and earnings growth. Analysis of earnings and news about a company can give some insight into the quality of earnings. If earnings have been increased by management's firing half the company's personnel or closing several facilities, the quality of the earnings' increase is not as high as it would be if the earnings had increased due to improved sales. Slash-and-burn strategies can lead to a further decline in productivity, resulting in additional weakness in earnings and eventually lower prices for the stock. On the positive side, drastic cuts can force companies to become more efficient, thereby increasing the quality of earnings, which may lead to higher stock prices.

The investor must analyze the company's growth and observe the stock price in action. From the analysis the investor can reach an investment decision after determining whether the value of a stock is more likely to increase, remain flat, or begin to decline. The analysis can be difficult at times because a winner can temporarily take on the appearance of a loser.

Three situations—daily price fluctuations, market declines, and price advances followed by weaknesses—can make a winner appear to look weak, but they are not necessarily a signal to begin selling. These are usually temporary situations and are therefore exceptions to the sell-the-losers rule.

Exception 1: Daily Price Fluctuations

Stock prices fluctuate up or down in day-to-day trading. A glance at any daily price chart will show what may be considered normal daily fluctuations for any individual stock (Figure 1–1). Stock prices also move from one trading range to another. For example, a stock price could have a daily fluctuation of $30 to $35, but it could occasionally move to $40, then drop back to the $30 to 35 range. The trading range would be considered $30 to $40. When the stock moves up and begins fluctuating between $40 and $55, it is trading in a new, higher range.

The stock of NCR Corp. traded in a narrow range between $26 and $28 a share during January 1998. In February, it moved up to a range between $31 and $32. In March and April the price climbed to a range between $32 and $34; then in late April it showed a nice rally to $37 a share.

The trading ranges and daily fluctuations can be readily observed on a price pattern chart. The investor should take the time to become familiar with these trad-

FIGURE 1–1

Trading range, NCR Corp. (NYSE: NCR), 1997-1998.

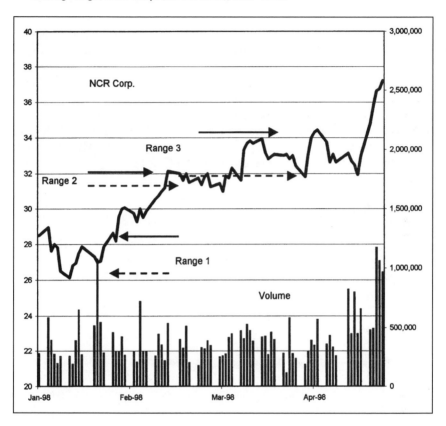

ing ranges and fluctuations from the preceding few months. Many Internet sources provide daily price charts for a 12-month time period at no charge. The charts can be saved to a computer hard drive or printed (where allowed). Becoming familiar with price movements will help the investor differentiate between what may be a normal fluctuation and what might be a breakout to a new trading range. If a lower stock price is within the normal range, it may still be a winner, even if the investor is experiencing a small loss—assuming that the initial analysis showed the stock to be a winner in earnings and growth. Therefore, the kind of weakness seen in a normal fluctuation is not the time to sell out and take a loss.

Exception 2: Market Decline

A significant drop in the overall stock market can force the price of a winner to lower levels. All stocks can eventually look like losers or become losers. Most often these severe market corrections are a time for concern, but not for panic. As we have seen in recent years, the stock market can drop 100, 200, or more than 500 points and recover quickly. Stocks that were winners before the correction will likely be winners again when the market recovers.

In October 1997, the Dow Industrials dropped more than 554 points. Take a look at Figure 1–2 to see what that biggest one-day drop in history— October 27—did to Merck. Merck & Company had already been showing some weakness, but on the sharp correction it dropped $8⅜, a significant amount (Figure 1–3). This correction was an overall market reaction in fear of higher oil prices. When one considers how quickly the market recovered, it's fair to say that the market overreacted. For Merck, the weakness of October 27, 1997, was an excellent buying opportunity. By April 1998, MRK was trading between $123 and $132 a share. That's up $47 a share, a gain of more than 55 percent.

FIGURE 1–2

Market correction, Merck (NYSE: MRK), October 1997.

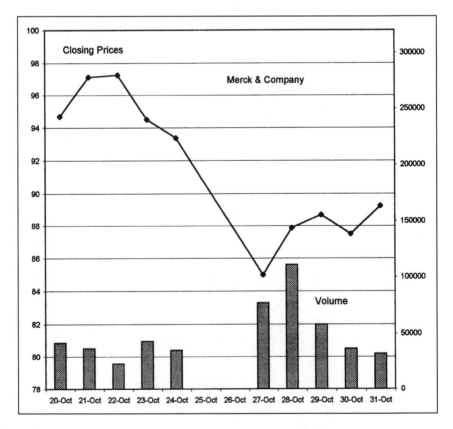

FIGURE 1-3

Merck & Company (NYSE: MRK), April 1997-1998.

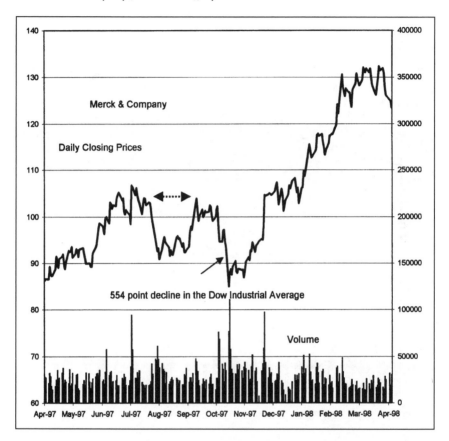

If a market decline continues, the investor should consider selling and moving the funds to the sideline. September 1997 (October was too late) would have been excellent timing for this strategy. If the market correction is sudden and appears to stabilize in just a few days, it can be best to hold a position and even consider buying more shares of the same stock. This strategy could have been effective in the October 1989 correction and more recently in the October 1997 correction when the Dow Industrial Average dropped 554 points and then stabilized quickly (see Figure 1–4). Many investors recognized the severe correction as a buying opportunity, and the industrials rose more than 300 points the following day. Although the Dow remained volatile, it reached new highs in early 1998.

Unless they are severe and extend over a few weeks and months, market corrections do not necessarily turn winners into losers. Extended market corrections are bear markets where stock prices decline and interest rates rise.

FIGURE 1–4

Dow Industrial Average, October 1997 through February 1998.

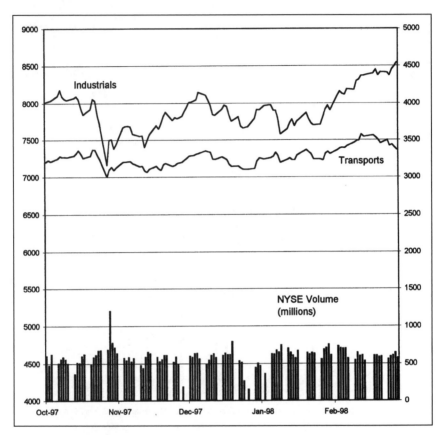

Exception 3: Price Advance Followed by a Weakness

A significant upward move to a new trading range, followed by some price weakness, is a fairly normal occurrence. As a stock price makes a major upward movement, many investors will begin to take profits. Although there is nothing wrong with taking profits, the upward price movement might have only just started. Even so, it is inevitable that some profit taking will occur, and the stock price that has risen to new highs will show some downward price correction (Figure 1–5). Again, this correction doesn't make the stock a loser.

In 1996 to 1997, Intel showed a couple of price consolidations, where the price traded sideways and occasionally corrected (circled areas). In mid-1996, the price traded between $34 and $37, and in 1997, between $65 and $83 a share. Notice that in 1997, the trading range was much wider than it was back in 1996. There was obviously some deep concern about the price dropping through the up trend line in February 1997. The concern led to a rather sharp correction to support at $65 to $70.

A signal is given if a stock begins to fall lower than its daily trading range and the overall market is unchanged or advancing. If a stock price that normally trades between $45 to $50 a share drops to $43 and then to $40, it is time to be concerned. The signal is even stronger if the stocks of comparable companies are not showing a similar weakness. It is a signal to either sell the stock or find out the reason for the price decline.

CONSISTENT GROWTH

Winners are the stocks of those companies showing consistent growth in revenues (sales), earnings, and price. They are the leaders in their industry and have continual new product developments for new or existing markets. Their products

FIGURE 1–5

Price consolidation, Intel Corp. (NASDAQ: INTC), 1996-1997.

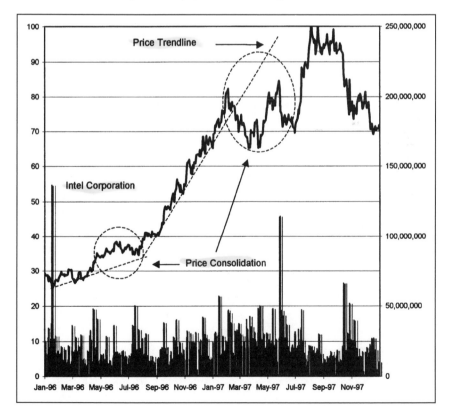

are not passing fads. Even though a product may have created a tremendous demand, how likely is it that this demand will remain strong in the next three to five years? Pet Rocks, wall walkers, and Cabbage Patch dolls can have strong sales for a year or two, but seldom are these types of products able to build enduring demand that will last over the years. Although faddish products can be earnings boosters for well-established companies, they are usually not a firm enough foundation on which to build an entire company.

FUNDAMENTALS

Winners should be held until the fundamentals that make them winners begin to weaken or until the price runs too far ahead of the earnings, causing a decline in value. Stocks trade on the anticipation of future growth. At times the anticipation vastly outpaces the growth and even the growth potential. Add the news of weaker earnings to that anticipation and the stock price gets hammered down hard. The winner stock becomes a loser.

Losers are taking money from the investor and should be sold and forgotten until they stabilize and rebuild the fundamental strength necessary to be winners.

CHAPTER 2

Make Winners Win Big

It was Jessie Livermore, known for his aggressive investing at the turn of the century, who indicated the importance of winning big. When the investor's conclusions, based on analysis, are correct, it's time to win big. Livermore did this when he sold short shares of Union Pacific (railroad) just before the 1906 San Francisco earthquake. At first the price did not drop. The company was strong and the price held. After all, it was one of the best companies on Wall Street. Livermore believed it would take a few weeks for the news to spread and the implications of the news to be realized, but he believed he was right, and he put his fortunes on the line. Eventually, Livermore was proven right and his fortunes multiplied significantly. He believed in winning big when he knew he was right.

VALUE

Winning stocks are a special situation. Although it is prudent to establish a price objective for a winning stock, value also needs to be considered before selling. *Value* is the price appreciation in relation to the fundamental growth of the company (e.g., earnings and revenues). The momentum of anticipation can cause a company's stock price to run ahead of earnings potential. Sometimes the earnings potential backfills the price growth, and sometimes it doesn't.

More than one investment advisor is guilty of saying, "When you make 100 percent or 200 percent on a stock, sell and take the profit. Leave something for the next investor." Livermore didn't believe in such a strategy, most institutional investors surely do not follow that practice, and it's a cinch that Warren Buffett doesn't sell because of the amount of profit in a stock. So why should anyone else sell, just when the action gets interesting?

PROFITS LEFT ON THE TABLE

The 1995 through 1998 time period illustrates the lack of wisdom in selling just to take profits. The track records of the stocks of two large corporations, General Electric (GE) and Caterpillar, show how an investor who sold shares in these companies because the price had doubled or tripled would have left serious capital gains "on the table"—gains that would have been lost forever.

Tables 2–1 and 2–2 list the closing prices for the two companies on specific annual dates. The prices illustrate the incredible strength of the stock market advances for the 1995 through 1997 time period.

An investor purchasing 100 shares at $16.00 per share ($1,600 total) had a market value of $7,431.20. There would have been $2,306.20 less if the stock had been sold in December 1996, and considerably less in 1995.

One way to win big is to buy a larger quantity of shares. As you can see in Figure 2–1, an investment of $16,000 for 1,000 shares had a market value of $74,312, a capital gain of $58,312. Obviously, the amount would have been considerably less if profits had been taken the previous December—that's serious money.

T A B L E 2–1

General Electric (Prices Adjusted for Any Splits)

Date	Market Price	
12/92	$16.00	
12/93	$26.125	
12/94	$25.50	
12/95	$36.00	↔ Doubles the original investment
12/96	$51.25	↔ Triples
12/97	$74.312	↔ More than quadruples (365%)

T A B L E 2–2

Caterpillar

Date	Market Price, Adjusted	
12/91	$10.968	
12/92	$13.406	
12/93	$22.25	↔ Doubles the original investment
12/94	$27.562	
12/95	$29.375	↔ Triples
12/96	$37.625	
12/97	$48.50	↔ Quadruples (342% gain)

FIGURE 2-1

Win big, General Electric (NYSE: GE), 1992-1998.

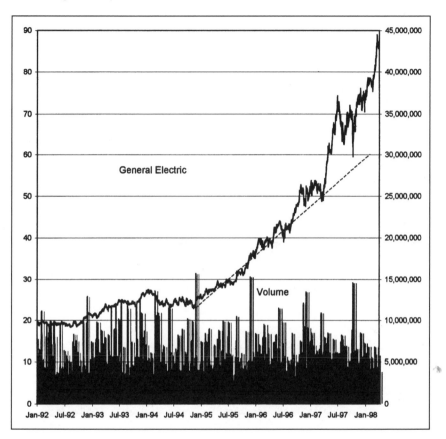

The chart for GE shows a steady uptrend during 1995 and 1996, with the sharpest acceleration appearing after the February 1997 secondary downtrend. A trend like this would have been ideal for averaging up. Averaging up, even buying additional shares every 6 or 12 months, would have enabled the investor to win big. Now look at Table 2–2 for another example.

The 342 percent gain in price would be a total of $3,753.20 on 100 shares or $37,532 on 1,000 shares. Those are significant gains (see also Figure 2–2).

Caterpillar shows a similar uptrend, with acceleration starting in April 1997. Some might call this "the buying frenzy at the top," but many said the same thing back in 1996. Obviously it takes more than a buying frenzy to indicate a market top. The overall investment climate, primarily interest rates, is usually the strongest determiner of a top. As inflation returns and interest rates rise, the market eventually turns. The timing of a market turn is often difficult to foresee, as it is possible for interest rates and the stock market to rise at the same

FIGURE 2–2

Win big, Caterpillar, Inc. (NYSE: CAT), 1992-1998.

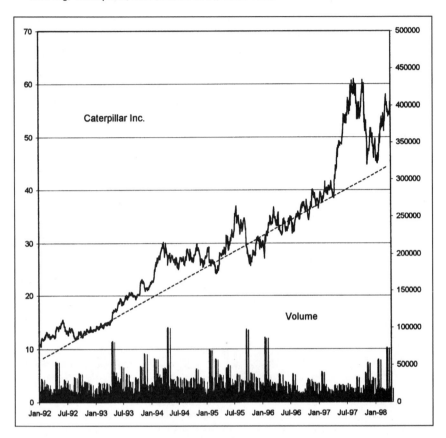

time. Eventually rising interest rates force the market to turn. Other times they can create a sensitive market that reacts to the mere suggestion of higher interest rates.

PROTECTING GAINS

Many investors, institutional and individual, would use protective stop-loss orders to protect these gains. Stop-loss orders for exchange-listed stocks frequently appear at support levels (see Figure 2–3). There were likely several stops triggered as the price rose, consolidated, then rose higher. Chart prices are adjusted for splits and dividends.

Although the placement of stop-loss orders is personal preference, a stop price should be placed so that it is not likely to be activated by daily fluctuations in price. It is essential to examine a price chart to select a stop price based on trading ranges, rather than depending on a set formula of 10 percent (which often dooms a portfolio to 10 percent losses) or $2 below the current market price (which can be too tempting for the specialist).

The April through August 1979 rally had three main support levels. Stop-loss orders placed on or just under these levels would have been executed. An investor being stopped out would have had until February 1998 to buy back the stock.

The view here is looking back at what happened. Skeptics can say that it's easy to look back and say what would have been a good strategy. But the fact is there are many traders using these kinds of strategies, as evidenced by sharper and deeper corrections once a support level is penetrated. Stop orders are triggered automatically and cause the price to fall even farther. Those placing these stop orders did not have the advantage of looking back. Sell stop orders placed under a rapidly rising stock price are part of a shorter-term strategy and considered speculative by many.

FIGURE 2–3

Support levels, Caterpillar, Inc. (NYSE: CAT), 1997-1998.

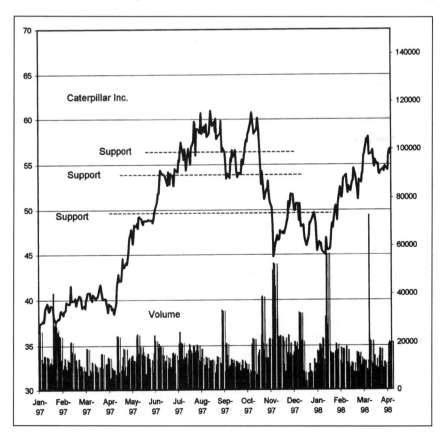

OTC NO STOPS

Most broker-dealers won't accept stop orders on over-the-counter (OTC) stocks, so the investor has to decide what level to sell at when the price declines, thereby setting a mental stop-loss order. If you believe a stock price will decline soon and desire to protect profits, sell the stock and don't enter a sell stop order.

Price Objective

When the price of a stock is at, say, $30 a share and the price-earnings (p/e) ratio of 16 reaches $40 a share and a p/e ratio of 20 (with no increase in earnings), it will be sold. The price objective should be adhered to and the stock sold, except when an unusual situation warrants an increase in the price objective.

Buyers and Sellers

The only activity that makes a stock price rise is the presence of more buyers than sellers. Buyers are attracted because they believe the price of the stock will rise higher. Buyers might be attracted to the value of the stock, or they could be attracted to an even higher anticipated value (sometimes referred to as *perceived value*). There are three situations that tend to bring buyers to the market and make a stock price rise:

- Increase in earnings or earnings manipulation (e.g., closing plants or firing people)
- General market move upward
- Takeover rumor or manipulation[1]

If any of these conditions occur and a stock price does not rise in price, there could be something wrong with either the value or perceived value. If the problem with the price is in the perceived value, it can be an "undervalued" situation.

Improved high-quality earnings can be caused by the following:

- New large contracts
- Lowered interest rates
- A favorable legal judgment
- Lending confidence inspired by a strong bull market

These are sound reasons to raise a price objective and make the winners win big. The emergence of a buyout offer can be another good reason to carefully raise a price objective. Corporate acquisitions need careful attention. The arrival of more than one suitor can create bidding wars, which drive the price to unusually high levels, sometimes too high.

---

1. Manipulation is included with takeover rumor because the two tend to go together, although it is certainly possible to have manipulation without a takeover rumor.

Flat or Bearish Markets

Raising a price objective in a flat or bearish market should be done with a great deal of caution. Stock prices tend to move as a group. The market can pull an individual stock price down during a bearish move. Rather than raise a price objective, this could be a good time to increase the holding of winning stocks. Bearish moves create on-sale prices for good stocks. The situation is one of opportunity emerging from crises.

Averaging Up

In the example below, there are five purchases of stocks of the same company. Each purchase is for 100 shares. The per share price for each transaction increases with each purchase (because the stock price is rising), but the cumulative average price per share is below each purchase price.

1. Buy 100 shares at $30.00 each:
   Average cost: $30.00
   Total shares owned: 100

2. Buy 100 shares at $35.00 each:
   Average Cost: $32.50
   Total shares owned: 200

3. Buy 100 shares at $40.00 each:
   Average Cost: $35.00
   Total shares owned: 300

4. Buy 100 shares at $45.00 each:
   Average Cost: $37.50
   Total shares owned: 400

5. Buy 100 shares at $50.00 each
   Average Cost: $40.00
   Total shares owned: 500

Average cost per share = $40.00

Average profit per share = $10.00
(current price $50.00, less the average cost per share of $40.00)

Built-In Profit

Each share of the last group of 100 had a $10 profit built in at the time of purchase. Owning a stock with profit built into the purchase is an enviable position.

As the price continues to advance and the investor continues to make purchases, the per share cost is lowered and the potential profit increases. Averaging up is a strategy frequently used by institutional investors and investment advisors. It requires planning and calculation, but it is a sound investment practice.

So when does one sell and take profits? The question is difficult, even for professionals. The time to sell for profits can be determined by any one of the following conditions:

TIME TO SELL

Price Objective Related to Earnings Potential

The attainment of a price based on the value comparison between the current price and current earnings growth (not necessarily the p/e ratio) can determine a sell. If a company has experienced an annual growth rate of 20 percent over the preceding five years and that rate has now slipped to 10 percent, the investment value is declining.

If the price is continuing to increase and the earnings remain the same, the inherent value of the stock is falling. Obviously, when earnings backfill or increase with the price, the inherent value is also increasing. One of the complications in evaluating this situation is the anticipation factor. When the price continues to climb without an increase in earnings, it means that others are anticipating an improvement in future earnings.

Stopped Out

Being *stopped out* means that a protective stop order has been executed.[2] This can be a time to buy an alternative stock that better fits the objective. However, if the price of a stopped-out stock drops low enough, consider a repurchase. Although it is difficult to repurchase a stock just sold, if the investor believes the price weakness to be temporary, it is a valid strategy. If the price falls low enough on an exchange-listed stock, a buy stop order might be appropriate. Catch that stock on the recovery.

Better Opportunity

"The time to sell a stock is when you find a better one to buy." Finding a better growth opportunity can be a valid reason to sell. Selecting a new stock can be a difficult decision requiring time and research. Therefore, new opportunities should be selected in advance. Ideally, they should be similar to the stock sold unless the investor's strategy has changed. The investment theme or play can change, but the value basics of selection should be similar.

---

2. See Chapter 16 for more information.

Need the Money

When the money is needed to fulfill an objective larger than successful investing, it's time to sell the stock:

- Financing a child's college education
- Buying a new house
- Retiring
- Providing for other large cash need

The purpose of investment is to make money. Money targeted for a special need should be made available at the proper time. Sell the stock, pay the taxes, and use the money for its intended purpose.

Let 'em Run

Letting the winners run is a solid, basic concept, but it is also possible to let them run until they drop. Eventually, the price of the stock might outpace earnings growth. If the price continues to rise, it does so on anticipation. At some point skepticism appears and profit taking occurs. Although the turning point can be difficult to anticipate, it is the price at which many investors begin to take profits, profits that are reinvested in other opportunities. When you're right, win big; then go elsewhere and win big again.

CHAPTER 3

Losers Demand Careful Strategy

The strategy for managing underperforming stocks can become as important as the strategy for winners. Although the usual strategy is to sell the losers at the earliest possible moment, sometimes this is not so simple. Researching and planning strategy take time, as does selecting new stock targets. At times the price of the loser slips away all too quickly, and the price drops so low that selling would not yield significant assets to reinvest.

It is also possible to have a stock price hit hard and still remain a fundamentally good company. A failed takeover attempt, unfavorable report, or other temporary situation can hammer the stock price until it becomes undervalued. Within a few weeks or months, the price climbs back up to former levels. Some of these situations can be ideal for portfolio building at cheap prices. These situations call for specific strategies rather than a general approach.

SELL OUT AND REPOSITION

If stocks are turning into losers, a great deal of time might pass before they recover. Time is important as it means lost profit potential. The stock can be sold and the assets reinvested elsewhere, thereby making up the loss and bringing new gains.

When a decision is made to sell a stock, it should be sold immediately. The timing is crucial. The stock should usually be sold at the "market" price as opposed to placing it as a limit sell order. Using a limit sell order can cause delays and loss of profits if the limit order is not executed. Timing is usually more important than trying to squeeze out an extra eighth of a dollar.

Here are some important factors to consider before you sell stock:

- *Can the assets be better invested elsewhere?* Although implementing this strategy might not be possible in a declining market, the funds could be parked in a money market fund. Ideally the investor should have new stocks targeted for inclusion in the investment portfolio.

- *Are the stocks underperforming?* Selling underperforming stocks in a bull market makes sense. If other investors like the stock, it will grow as well or better than the market. It should not be difficult to find better stocks.

- *Is the market flat?* In a flat to bearish market, the investor might consider other alternatives, such as placing the funds in a temporary investment such as a good dividend-paying stock or the money market.

- *Are there other considerations involved in addition to a 10 percent decline in value?* Many investors claim to follow a strategy of "take a loss at 10 percent." Be careful that this strategy doesn't doom the portfolio to a 10 percent loss. Rather than basing a sell on an amount, it might be better to base it on what's happening in the market and the individual stock. The 10 percent or less measure could be used as a signal for a closer look at what's going on with the company. Use that information to determine a sell.

Once the strategy has been planned, it should be implemented immediately. Waiting to see what happens can be dangerous. Few investors have the luxury to sit and watch the stock market during trading sessions.

TAKING AN INVESTMENT POSITION

Situations can arise in which selling might not be the preferable strategy. Although it is speculative to do so, an investor can take a larger position rather than selling. In these situations, the investor is looking for a turnaround in corporate earnings and in the price recovery. Although the wisdom of this strategy is often debated, it can be effective especially when the investor has a deep understanding of the financial strength of the company and its ability to improve.

LOSS TO PROFIT

Taking an investment position has its risk, but it can be a strategy for turning a loss into a profit. This strategy is best used with companies that have been around for many years and have a diversified product line. These companies tend to be more stable and have the capability to weather financial difficulties and market swings.

The investor should have some fundamental reasons for believing company earnings will recover, remain stable, and continue to grow. Asking questions such as these can help the decision:

- Why is the stock currently losing?
- Has the stock recovered from former difficult times?
- Are there good reasons to keep the stock and add to the position?
- How much time will it take for recovery?

Of course, the decision to sell is less complicated. In many situations, a sell is the best course of action, with a possible repurchase on recovery.

HOLDING FOR RECOVERY

Another alternative is to simply hold the stock and wait for the price to recover. It could take some time, but if the initial investment is of a considerable size and the price drop is severe, the proceeds from selling might not be enough to reinvest. If a $10,000 position is now worth less than $1,000, you might just as well hold on and hope for the best. Although tax loss potential should be considered, there just isn't much that can be done with less than a thousand dollars.

CAUTION ON HOLDING

A word of caution on the hold strategy: Some companies will decline in price and be bought out by another company who sees the price as a bargain. This situation creates an automatic loss for the investor who purchased the stock at a price higher than the takeover. So what about Apple Computer—think anyone's interested?

CAREFUL STRATEGY

The decision to buy, sell, or hold depends on the individual investor's situation. Many active investors would take the loss at the 10 to 15 percent level and move on to other opportunities. Serious consideration should be given to the strategy best suited to risk tolerance and previously established investment strategies.

Losing stocks demand a careful analysis. Whether the strategy is to sell the stock and buy another, or build an investment position in the losing stock, the investor should always act quickly. If the stock is thoroughly researched and the action planned ahead of time, it will be easier to implement.

CHAPTER 4

It Is Better to Average Up Than to Average Down

Price averaging is a prudent strategy with the right stock and situation. There are two ways to lower the average cost of a stock purchase. One is *averaging up* (discussed earlier) and the other is *averaging down* (buying more stock as the price declines). When faced with a dropping share price, when the longer-term outlook is believed favorable, it can be worthwhile to hold the current shares and let the price hit bottom. When the price turns and begins to increase, the investor can begin a program of buying at various price levels.

AVERAGING DOWN

Averaging down, though frequently suggested, is often not the best course of action. It can work in some situations, but it doesn't fit well into most investment plans. Many describe this aggressive strategy as "throwing good money after bad." The problem with averaging down is that it is impossible to know where the price decline will stop.

Implementation of averaging down can also be difficult. Few investors have the discipline to buy more stock at regular intervals as the price continues to drop. The first couple of buys might be acceptable, but continuing to buy becomes more difficult.

AVERAGING UP

The results of averaging up can be similar to successful averaging down, but there may be less risk involved. Earlier a method of averaging up was examined as a strategy to enhance the profits on an advancing stock price. Here we look at averaging up with a stock price in a losing position.

When an investor's stock price suddenly takes a turn for the worse and the price declines significantly due to bad news, the investor holds the position. The investor knows the company and believes the price decline to be a temporary situation. Eventually the stock price will reach a support level, and buyers will stop the fall. The investor then plans to average up as the price recovers.

Take a look at Dayton Hudson stock as shown in Table 4–1. If an investor had purchased 100 shares at $63 per share in October 1987, holding the position for the rest of the month would have been difficult. As the bottom dropped out of the market, Dayton Hudson's price also plunged. But the investor who believed the weakness was in the market and not in the stock could hold the stock and prepare to buy more.

The investor could buy additional shares at the bottom. Finding the bottom is not easy. Bottoms often do not become evident until some time after the event. Buy stop orders can be used instead of trying to pick the illusive bottom. A *buy stop order* is an order to buy stock as soon as the stop price is traded on or through. When triggered by the stop price, a buy stop order becomes a *market order* (best available price). Buy stop orders are placed above the current trading price, with the idea that they will be filled only if the price is recovering. If the market and stock price continue to fall, the buy stop can be lowered.

Will Rogers might have had this stock in mind when he said, "only buy the stock that goes up. If it don't go up, don't buy it."

T A B L E 4–1

Original Purchase of Dayton Hudson at $63.00 = $6,300

Trade	Buy Stop Price, $	Quantity New/Total, $	Fill Price, $	Average Price, $	Total $ Invested, $
Original	63	100/100	63.00	63.00	6,300
1	25	100/200	25.25	44.13	8,825
2	30	100/300	30.00	39.41	11,825
3	35	100/400	35.00	38.31	15,325
4	40	100/500	40.75	38.80	19,400
5	45	100/600	45.00	39.83	23,900

Note: Notice the average price drops in transactions 1, 2, and 3. It then rises, but it is still significantly below the current market price, which is the fill price.

The belief is that the stock and the market will recover. The strategy of buying only if the stock price rises and the action of placing buy stop orders are in line with each other.

For Dayton Hudson, the high price for all of 1988 was 45.5 dollars. If the investor sold the 600 shares at $45 a share, he or she would have had a profit of $3,100. If the investor waited until the summer of 1989 and then sold at $60 a share (that's still $3 less than the original purchase price), the investor would have had a profit of $12,102. On an initial investment of $23,900, that is a return of more than 50 percent, a reasonable return on any investment portfolio security:

Average cost per share	$39.83
Sell price	60.00
Profit per share	$20.17

Profit per Share ÷ average cost per share = Total gain

$$\$20.17 \div \$39.83 = 50.6\%$$

Averaging up enables the investor to make a move based only on the price recovery of the stock. It is more comfortable to add money to a stock position when the price is rising instead of declining.

THAT WAS THEN, THIS IS NOW

It happened again. There is a saying that "history repeats itself, but does it differently." The 554-point Dow Industrial correction in October 1997 pulled Dayton Hudson's price down, which was similar to the 1987 situation (see Figure 4–1 and Table 4–2).

In the October 1997 correction, the price of Dayton Hudson dropped from 65¼ to 52⅜, then immediately started to recover. Averaging up could have started at this point and continued into 1998, as long as the price continued to climb. The weakness in April 1998 could cause some hesitation, but it was likely caused by a general market weakness. A look at these kinds of historic prices can help the investor select candidates for averaging up.

BE CAREFUL WITH BUY STOPS

Buy stop orders need to be fully understood before making this type of move. Protection limits can be added and should be considered. The strategy makes sound investment sense, and an investor is more likely to stay with the strategy. Obviously, if the market or individual stock's price falls, the buy stop is not triggered and can be lowered. In the Dayton Hudson example, the results would have yielded even greater profits if the purchase of 400 shares had been filled at the low price, but the strategy would have had higher risk. If the company's earnings had tumbled after the price drop, recovery could have taken a long time.

Although buying stock is anticipating uncertain future results, it is prudent to set a strategy that limits risk whenever possible. By averaging up with a strategy using buy stops and limits, the investor has some control over this risk. Effectively, the investor is buying shares only on price recovery or on a price advance. It's buying the stock that goes up.

FIGURE 4–1

Averaging up, Dayton Hudson (NYSE: DH), 1997-1998.

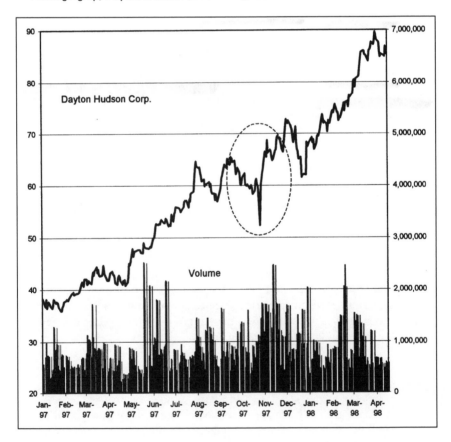

T A B L E 4–2

Financial Data Dayton Hudson (NYSE: DH)

	Growth Rates			
	1 Year	3 Years	5 Years	
Sales, %	9.40	9.21	9.14	
EPS, %	71.09	23.11	16.49	
Dividend, %	4.76	5.63	5.15	
Year	1995	1996	1997	1998
Annual revenues, millions of U.S. dollars	21,311	23,516	25,371	27,757
	Earnings per Share, U.S. Dollars			
Quarters	1995	1996	1997	1998
April	0.079	0.015	0.085	0.275
July	0.104	0.055	0.220	0.306
October	0.144	0.090	0.255	0.395
January	0.635	0.515	0.475	0.830
Totals, U.S. dollars	0.962	0.675	1.035	1.806

CHAPTER 5

Good Companies
Buy Their Own Stock

"XYZ Company has announced a purchase of 2 million shares of their own stock. The stock must be a good buy if the company itself is willing to buy."

It's still a common belief. The stockbroker tells a client, the client tells a friend, and so on, until a stock price begins to move upward. Many of these and other investors who heard the good news rush out to purchase more of the stock. The price continues to rise for the next few days and weeks. But is it really a good sign when a company announces a stock buyback?

Actually, company stock buybacks are often a "mixed bag" with some good and some not so good effects. Matthew Schifrin, writing for *Forbes*, had this to say about the November 1997 stock buyback announcements:

> Will buybacks repair the damage after the 1997 selloff? IBM has already thrown another $3.5 billion into its buyback hopper.[1]

It's been done before: After the 508-point Dow Industrials correction in 1987, more than 700 companies announced stock buybacks. The immediate effect of companies' buying their own stock is to reduce the supply of available shares, thereby increasing demand. Obviously increased demand exerts an upward pressure on stock prices.

In terms of soothing the nerves of investors, announcements of buybacks after the 554-point 1997 drop in the Dow Industrial Average helped the market a great deal. They gave investors a sense of confidence in the economy and in the stock market.

---

1. Matthew Schifrin, "The Buyback Monster," Forbes.com, November 17, 1997.

GOOD NEWS AND BAD NEWS

Companies often use buybacks when they have bad news to report. Obviously, the well-timed positive announcements are intended to soften the blow. It's the "we've got good news and bad news" situation. "We're going to buy back 8 percent of our stock . . . and, oh, by the way, our earnings are down 3 percent." The company is hopeful that the good news will outweigh the bad, and therefore the price impact will be neutral to positive. The good news–bad news technique is often used, even by some of the larger corporations. It can be quite effective.

It's not just small companies; megacorporations like General Electric, IBM, and General Motors continue to use the stock buyback strategy in 1998. When General Motors announced a program in January 1998, it boosted the stock price another 4 percent, more than $16 a share in just over a month. A significant increase indeed. Take a look at the price chart for GM shown in Figure 5–1.

FIGURE 5–1

Stock buyback, General Motors Corp. (NYSE: GM), 1998.

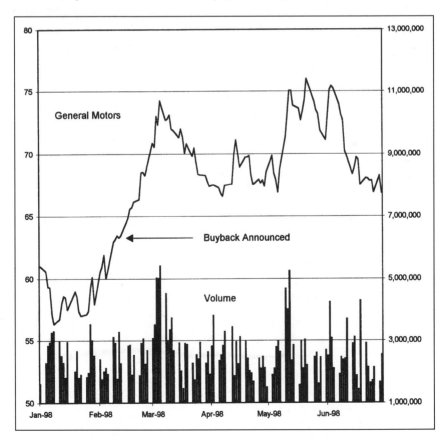

Granted, there were probably other factors in the GM price increase; however, the buyback news certainly helped. But some skepticism began to appear in April 1998, as the price dropped back to the mid-60s. The stock market was generally showing some weakness at this point, and the pullback of GM's stock can partially be attributed to what was happening in the overall market.

DOES IT SHOW CONFIDENCE?

Sometimes companies will boldly announce their buyback intention with the statement that the stock has investment value at the current price. But considering the price impact of all that good publicity, one wonders. Is the announcement just more window dressing, or is the company sincere?

Short-term speculators have a great time with stock buyback announcements. To have a price rise several percentage points in just a few days is one of their dream selections.

Interesting—good for the speculators in the short-term but not necessarily helpful to investors in the long term. So what's the problem? Are companies dumb enough to pay prices that are actually too high? Peter Russ seems to think so. The following comments on stock buybacks are from *US News & World Report*:

> The hitch. What could be wrong with this picture? Simply this: Many companies' shares are selling at or near record prices and may not be worth buying by anyone.[2]

Many analysts calculate a company's intrinsic value based on business potential rather than on the actions of excited buyers. When companies buy their own shares at or below the "intrinsic value," they effectively create added value for the other shareholders. When they buy significantly higher than intrinsic value, they push the price up temporarily, but the value has to catch up in support. Paying that high price can cause problems:

> "But the minute that you start paying a premium to buy back your stock," says Russ, "You are probably destroying value—using company money in a way that's not going to earn a great rate of return."[3]

SHOULD WE BE WARY TODAY?

It's always good to be wary about the stock market. Historically, companies with too much money would either expand or return some money to shareholders in the form of dividends. The problem with dividends is that they are taxed. In fact,

2. Steven D. Kaye, "A Buyback Binge," *US News Online* (http://www.usnews.com), February 17, 1997.
3. Kaye, "A Buyback Binge."

they are taxed twice; first as corporate income and second as investor dividends. Therefore, dividends aren't as popular as they once were.

Companies still like to show growth. They like to announce the opening of 200 additional retail outlets or the opening of a new plant to employ 2,000 workers. It's the kind of publicity that creates a warm feeling in the company's investors and customers. But what does it mean when the company is not expanding but is buying back its own shares? Don't they have anything better to do with the money? Have they run out of ideas? If they really think the company is undervalued, shouldn't they be investing the money in preparation for the new growth? These are real concerns the long-term shareholder and potential stock buyer should have.

Stock buybacks don't necessarily add significant value to a company's stock. The p/e ratios are too high and companies have too much cash, the cash being the reason they're willing to overpay. There's less risk in buying back their own shares than in new corporate growth or at least less risk in how the actions are perceived by investors.

ONLY AN ANNOUNCEMENT

Some stock buyback announcements are just that—announcements. Following the announcement, either the buyback never occurs, or fewer shares are repurchased. Possibly the company originally intended to repurchase the shares, but things change and they are later unable to do so because the economics have changed. The financing became unavailable. Although companies are occasionally accused of trumpeting a stock buyback for the purpose of supporting or accelerating the price, in reality that practice is unusual. The large majority of stock buyback activities are sincere.

WHAT HAPPENS TO THE STOCK?

Much of the stock is effectively retired, clearing up some of the dilution problems. Other shares are used for employee retirement and stock option plans. Obviously, this is a good effect if the shares have true value but a negative effect if they are overpriced. Are there other negative effects from this action?

> When a company buys a share of its stock on the open market for $80 to sell to an employee who has an option to buy at $20, the statisticians count that as a net equity issuance of negative $60—even though the actual supply of stock on the market is unchanged."[4]

Stock buyback announcements have many implications. In some cases it is a positive move for the company and its shareholders, even if only temporary. It

---

4. Justin Fox with Lenore Schiff, reporter associate, "The Hidden Meanings of Stock Buybacks," *Fortune*, September 8, 1997.

improves the earnings per share since there are often fewer shares outstanding. A stock price will often rise after a buyback announcement, especially in a rising market, but the price can weaken and fall if negative news follows. An understanding of the company's announcement and the current true value of the stock can help an investor decide whether to buy or sell the stock.

Price Doubling Is Easy at Low Prices

Many "boiler room" sales representatives have touted this questionable idea more than once; there are times that it is at least partly correct. Although it can be easy for some low-priced stocks to double in price. However, it can also be easy for high-priced stocks to double in price. Price doubling usually depends on factors other than the current price level. For example, it generally depends on changes in efficiency, restructuring, revenue growth, and earnings growth potential. The stocks can be new companies or older companies that have recently had some earnings problems, companies that are showing signs of a turnaround. Like Apple Computer—see Figure 6–1.

As shown in Figure 6–1, Apple slid from $35 a share in 1996 to just over $13 a share at the end of 1997. Although there were several significant rallies on the way down, none were strong enough to stop the price decline. It finally hit bottom at the end of 1997. There was similar support for $13 back in the June to July 1997 time period. This time the support held. Technically, the earlier support, followed by support at the identical level, was a strong indicator that this was a good time to buy shares of Apple. Those who bought shares between the prices of $13.00 and $15.50 a share saw their money double by the middle of May 1998. A 100 percent gain in less than six months is an excellent return.

So, what happened?

Apple lost market share to IBM-compatible personal computers for years until finally adapting a similar clone-friendly strategy. But then it ditched the Mac clone makers.[1]

---

1. Rick Aristotle Munarriz, "Apple Computer," The Motley Fool, Daily Double, Monday, June 8, 1998: http://www.fool.com/DDouble/1998/DDouble980608.htm.

FIGURE 6–1

Price doubling, Apple Computer, Inc. (NASDAQ: AAPL), 1996–1998.

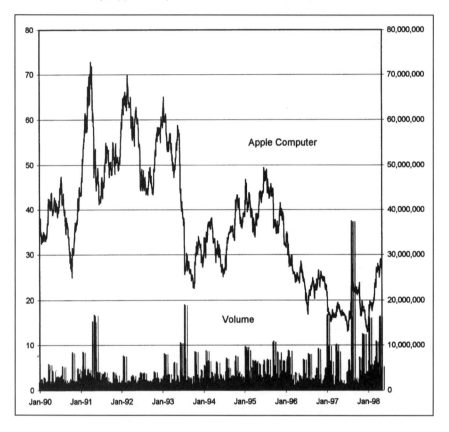

Apparently the reason Apple made this decision was a combination of margins and their desire to centralize operations, so it got out of Circuit City, Best Buy, and many other retailers. The retail presence became reestablished when Apple set up shops inside Comp USA stores. Obviously this gave Apple more control over sales.

Apple Computer reorganized, restructured, streamlined and brought back one of the founders, Steven Jobs. This strategy, combined with new product (the G3 Macintosh line), brought back some investor anticipation. Additionally, there is new product for release in the future. Apple is bringing out the iMac, a monitor-encased unit that could be a good seller to be priced attractively below $1,000 by year end if rumors prove true.

The price performance shown by Apple Computer is the type of turnaround investors look for, to find the company that has gone through difficult times but is on the road to recovery. Although a turnaround strategy is risky, it can be quickly profitable.

WHAT ABOUT A HIGHER-PRICED STOCK?

After cycling back and forth between $30 and $35 a share in 1996, the number 2 home improvement store,[2] Lowe's, finally broke through resistance and rallied to $42.75 (Figure 6–2). From that point it slowly floated back to $32.25 between October 1996 and February 1997. New resistance formed at $40, with support in the mid-30s. In September 1997, Lowe's began a new rally, this time with force.

    The price ran into some minor resistance at $40, but it did not fall back to the mid-30s. It began to accelerate upward. Six months later it encountered resistance at the $70 level. Possibly this was profit taking by those who bought at 35, since they had now doubled their money. The price then ran from $70 to $83 a

FIGURE 6–2

Price doubling, Lowe's Companies, Inc. (NYSE: LOW), 1996–1998.

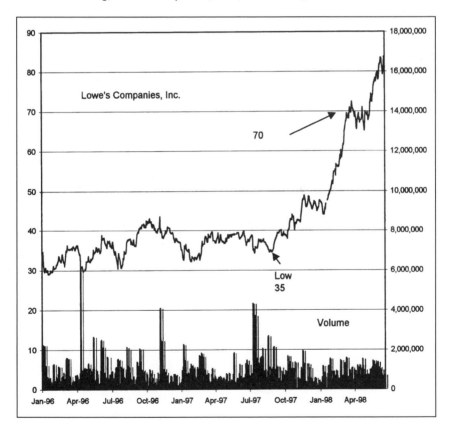

---

2. Number 1 was Home Depot.

share without much resistance, partly due to an earnings surprise, consisting of a 32 percent improvement on earnings per share. Also, the company announced a 2-for-1 stock split payable in June.

WHERE'S THE GROWTH?

Lowe's stronger following among professional building contractors means it is somewhat more affected by changes in the economic climate. In a strong economic situation, bolstered by growth in new housing starts, an investor can easily become interested in Lowe's. Lowe's had double-digit sales gains in the preceding three years (16 percent in 1995, 22 percent in 1996, and 18 percent last year) with the opening of new stores. It had reportedly larger store formats, and mid-single-digit same-store sales gains. Furthermore, Lowe's also exceeded quarterly estimates and received a number of upgrades from stock analysts in late 1997 and early 1998.

Lowe's is now moving from the smaller-town concentration into some of the bigger cities. They also have served as supplier to building contractors and are thereby linked to the economic climate for new housing starts. Although much of the good news is now discounted by the market price, continued growth in earnings and sales could add up to a bright future for the stock.

OTHER FACTORS

Whether or not a share price will double is dependent on factors other than the current price. Again, it's earnings or earnings growth potential that investors are anticipating. They are all trying to buy the stock ahead of the earnings growth. The risk is always whether or not the earnings growth will occur.

Many times the stock likely to have its price double soon is the one whose price most recently doubled. This also has little if anything to do with the current market price. One might even say, forget the price, and look at growth, growth potential, and anticipation.

CHAPTER 7

Look for Insider Trading

Insiders of a corporation are the decision makers and the strategy formulators. They are the directors, the officers, and the high-level "line" personnel. If anyone knows what's going on in a company, it is the managers who are directly involved in the upper-level decision-making process.

ILLEGAL VERSUS LEGAL

In a broad sense, it is illegal for anyone to buy or sell shares of stock in the United States based on information not yet available to the public:

> In general, Section 10(b) of the Exchange Act, 15 U.S.C. 78j(b), proscribes the use of any "deceptive device" in connection with the purchase or sale of securities in contravention of the rules prescribed by the Securities and Exchange Commission. The pertinent rule, known as Rule 10b-5, similarly prohibits any device, scheme, artifice, act, practice or course of business to defraud or to deceive in connection with the purchase or sale of any security.[1]

The basic idea of *insider trading* is simple: if a person has important information that will influence the price of a company's shares, the law is broken if that person uses the information for buying or selling stock.

---

1. Carl Peckinpaugh, *What Constitutes Insider Trading?* Washington, D.C.: FCW Government Technology Group (http://www.fcw.com), 1998. Peckinpaugh is a member of the government contracts section of the law firm of Winston & Strawn.

FAIR AND ORDERLY MARKET

Disallowing trades based on inside information is important. It is part of the *fair and orderly market concept* being adhered to by all the world's stock exchanges. If such activities were allowed or ignored by the authorities, the public securities market would lack integrity, without which they could not function. Why trade stocks or other securities if others have this distinct advantage? Stock market prices are driven by anticipation based on information. Making trades based on privileged information, ahead of the public, amounts to fraud. Individual investors need to have the same information as the professional investors in order for the public markets to be a level playing field for all.

INSIDERS MUST REPORT

However, at times corporate employees are privy to inside information, and they want to legitimately buy and sell their company's stock. For various reasons, such information cannot be immediately released to the public. In fairness, the insiders are allowed to trade, but they must report transactions, holdings, and other information. A sense of fairness is maintained because the public is able to view and assess such transactions.

SEC INSIDER FORMS

According to the Securities Exchange Act of 1934, an insider is defined as an officer or director of a public company, or an individual or entity owning 10% or more of any class of a company's shares. The definition in all its legal speak is given in Section 16 of the 1934 Act; there are further words sparred on how more specifically to define an "officer" and "beneficial owner" in Rule 16a-1 of the Code of Federal Regulations.

For all the legal definitions of *titles* and *share owners*, what the rule is saying is that anyone who is involved in the inner workings of a publicly traded company is an insider. The concern is that this person could gain an unfair advantage over the rest of the public when trading company shares. Therefore, an insider must register by making a statement of holdings (SEC Form 3) within 10 days. Changes in ownership must be filed by the tenth day of the month following the transaction (SEC Form 4)

At the end of the fiscal year, an insider or former insider must file Form 5 within 45 days. Its intent is to prevent people from moving in and out of insider status.

Obviously Form 4 gives the most useful information to investors. It answers the question of what the insiders are doing, whether buying or selling, as well as their current holdings in the company. Information on insider trades, available on the Internet and through several newsletters, is usually based on this SEC form.

FORM 144 STOCK

Form 144 used by the SEC to track insider information is for those currently holding securities that are not registered. The form is the last step, allowing the shares to be sold on the open market and be publicly traded. The form allows the shares to be sold but ensures that the number is relatively small and the seller isn't an underwriter bringing a new issue to market.

The form tells how many shares will be sold within the following three months. If they are not sold, the form must be amended. In the real world, by the time the 144 form information is seen by the investor, the shares have been sold. Many will file the 144 and Form 4 at the same time.[2]

SIGNIFICANT TRADES

Those who follow insider transactions claim that buys are usually more significant than sells. Some people also argue that corporate insiders tend to avoid making transactions because they know the public is watching. Instead, they rely on their stock option benefit to supply them with company shares. Another side to this suggests that an insider or group of insiders could influence the share price by buying stock on the open market. These considerations are some of the reasons the value of watching insider transactions is often debated.

Two Situations

Rise in the Number of Insider Buys

Some people view an increase in the number of insider buys as an additional reason to buy a stock. They believe that a sudden flurry of insider buys is a positive statement of growth potential for the company. It is important to keep in mind, however, that sometimes companies lend money to their employees to buy stock, with the intention of having the public see the buys. Such corporate strategies suggest a manipulation of public interest; therefore it is important to view the presence of insider trades in relation to other information about a company.

Media Attention

If the insider's trading has been significant enough to be discussed in the financial news media, it calls additional attention to the activity. The extra attention from the news appearance can affect the stock's price. However, the impact follows right on the heels of the announcement. If an investor plans to take action based on the news, he or she must do so quickly. Waiting even a day or two can be too late.

---

2. InsiderTrader, downloaded May 9, 1998. Original source: Securities and Exchange Commission.

PART OF THE PICTURE

Obviously, an investor can follow insider trading as an investment strategy by itself. However, investment professionals recommend the use of additional analysis to form a conclusion before taking action. Corporate insiders can have any one of several reasons or motives for buying and selling their company's stock. Therefore, it is prudent to use information on insider trades as part of the picture of a company rather than as a sole indicator.

SELLS VERSUS BUYS

Unless there are several insiders selling the same stock, sells are generally not meaningful as an indicator. Insiders are often selling stocks to raise cash to purchase items other than the company's stock. A new car, boat, or a down payment on a lake cabin are frequently motivators for the insider.

Buys can have significance, although again, they should not be the only consideration for selecting a stock. Does it work? The answer is mixed, but one can find evidence of successful situations based on insider buys. Going back to an article from April 1997, we find some specific stocks recommended. Let's see what happened.

The following information came from *Online Money News, Money Daily,* Weekend, April 19 to 20, 1997, in an article by Michael Brush. A few specific companies were named for insider trading activities. We will list them and analyze the results.

FIRST THE OBLIGATORY CAUTION

Results can vary when the activities of others are used as a forecasting tool. What works on one occasion might be a dismal failure on the next. All stock market analysis systems are capable of sending false signals. The investor needs to be aware of this and not rely too heavily on any one system of analysis.

Insider Trading Companies[3]:

Apache Corp. (NYSE: APA), oil and gas exploration

Santa Fe Energy Resource (NYSE: SFR), oil and gas exploration

Barnes & Noble (NYSE: BKS), retail bookseller

Borders Group (NYSE: BGP), retail bookseller

Morningstar Group (NASDAQ: MSTR), a milk products and food company

---

3. Michael Brush, "Stock Buying by Corporate Insiders on the Rise," *Online Money News, Money Daily,* April 19–20, 1997.

Mobile Telecomm Tech (NASDAQ: MTEL), in wireless
communications

CKS Group (NASDAQ: CKSG), in marketing communications

Oakley (NYSE: OO), which makes sunglasses and goggles

Sodak Gaming (NASDAQ: SODK), which distributes slot machines

Take a look at Table 7–1 to see what happened.

Virtually all of these had potential for a short-term gain. The gains were not
huge, but they were consistent. A year after the article, nearly every stock remained ahead except for CKS Group, which was flat, and Sodak Gaming, which
showed a $3 loss. Actually, that's an excellent record for using insider trading as
an indicator.

The dollar amounts of the gains were not particularly impressive, but these
were essentially low-priced stocks. The highest potential gain was CKSG at a
possible $23, and the lowest was SODK with a possible $6 a share. But take a
look at CKSG, (see Figure 7–1); timing was everything.

T A B L E 7–1

Results of Insider Trading, April 1997 through April 1998

Stock	Buy Range before the Article, Dollars	Ideal Quick-Sell Range, Dollars	Price a Year Later, April 1998, Dollars
Apache Corp. (NYSE: APA)	32–35	40–44	36
Barnes & Noble (NYSE: BKS)	17–18	25–31	34
Borders Group (NYSE: BGP)	19–21	25–29	33
CKS Group (NASDAQ: CKSG)	21–27	30–44	21
Mobile Telecomm Tech (NASDAQ: MTEL)	6–8	12–18	25
Morningstar Group (NASDAQ: MSTR)*	N/A	N/A	N/A
Oakley (NYSE: OO)	9–12	10–14	14
Santa Fe Energy Resource (NYSE: SFR)	8–9	11–14	12
Sodak Gaming (NASDAQ: SODK)	10–11	10–16	7

* Information not available for MSTR.

FIGURE 7–1

Insiders trading, CKS Group (NASDAQ: CKSG), 1997–1998.

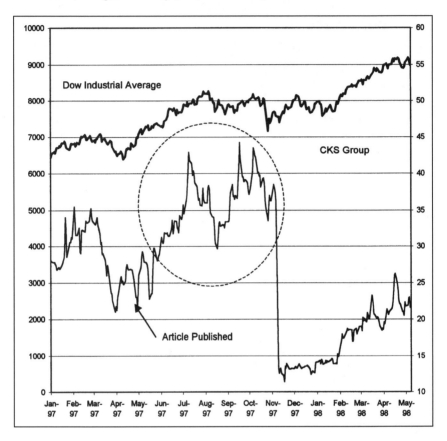

Anyone who was not out of the stock by November 1997 got clobbered. The price went into a free fall and dropped from just over $36 a share to a little more than $11 a share. Getting out at the wrong time here could have resulted in a $10 loss per share or more.

Check the sad news with SODK in the price chart shown in Figure 7–2.

Sodak Gaming turned in September 1997 and kept heading south. Granted, it didn't fall far, but then, it didn't have far to fall. Many of the stocks on this list fall into the growth-speculative category. They should always be approached with great caution, as they are frequently traded just for the short-term hit. Once it's over, the price falls back to former levels or lower.

The best long-term potential appears to be in the established trend of
Barnes & Noble. Take a look at the excellent long-term uptrend established by the
stock price (see Figure 7–3). If this can be sustained and backfilled with earnings
and revenue growth, it could be an excellent stock.

From March 1997 to March 1998, the price doubled from just under $20 to
nearly $40 a share. That's a 100 percent gain in one year's time—an excellent re-
turn by anyone's standard. But that trend line is running at a near 45-degree angle. It's consistent for more than a year. The weakness in April through May 1998
could make a buying opportunity. This shows what can come out of the study of
stock prices.

FIGURE 7–2

Insiders trading, Sodak Gaming (NASDAQ: SODK), 1997–1998.

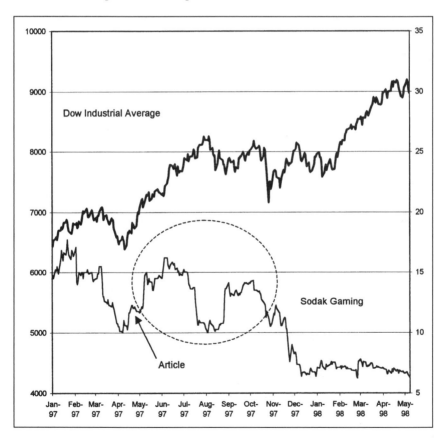

FIGURE 7-3

Insiders trading, Barnes & Noble (NYSE: BKS), 1997–1998.

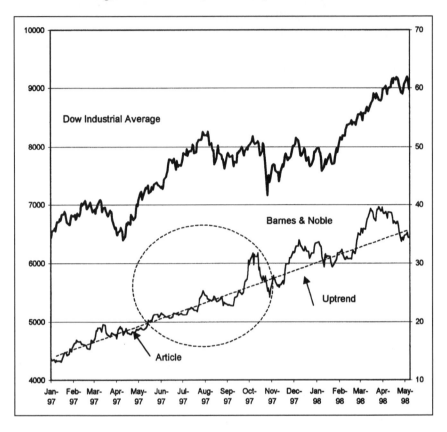

INTERNET SOURCES

There are many Internet sources for information on insider trading. Here are just a few:

> http://www. insidertrader.com
>> quote.com/info/vickers.html
>> fedfil.com/industry/insiders.htm
>> bloomberg.com/bbn/sec/sec1.html
>> cda.com/investnet/welcome.html
>> the-wiz.com/insideindex.html

CHAPTER 8

Buy Low, Sell High

Back in the early days of Wall Street, it was stated, "Buy that which is cheap and sell that which is dear." Charles Dow, one of the founding fathers of Dow Jones & Company and the first managing editor of *The Wall Street Journal,* might have put it this way: "Buy a stock that has value in earnings and value in the dividend paid out. As this stock rises in price and the value of earnings and dividends declines, sell the stock."

Although the methods of evaluating stock "of value" may have changed, the basic idea is still sound. The anticipation of value and value growth are what make a stock price rise. The value is not the price alone. However, it is one of the factors in determining value. Another important factor of value is earnings past and earnings forecast. Stock prices move in anticipation of future earnings growth.

OLD IDEA

The idea of "buy low, sell high" is as old as trading ownership of properties. It is the basis of all business. Buy a property at one price and sell it at a higher price. The difference between the buy and sell transactions is *profit*. To make a profit is the reason to buy and sell stock.

It is the one axiom most everyone understands but many have trouble implementing. An investor hears that Company ABC is buying out XYZ Company. The stock had been trading at $35 a share, but the buyout is expected to be at $60. The investor knows there is some risk involved and so decides to think about buying a hundred shares. The following afternoon, the investor calls the broker and learns that XYZ Company is now trading at $54.50. A feeling of panic overcomes the investor because the price is nearly up to $60 already.

Better place that buy order. An order to buy 100 shares of XYZ Company is placed and filled at $55 a share.

The following week the investor calls the broker to check on XYZ Company and learns that it is now trading at $50. That's a $5 loss per share. Even more frightening is that it's a 10 percent loss. Trying to restrain the feeling of panic, the investor gives instructions to sell the 100 shares of XYZ Company at the market. The order is entered and executed at 50.

A few weeks later the investor decides to look at the price quote in the newspaper and is shocked to find the stock closed yesterday at $56.50 a share. The investor feels disappointed and exasperated about investing. Sound exaggerated? It isn't really. In fact, this scenario could have occurred with Digital Equipment in early 1998, when Compaq Computer bought them out (Figure 8–1).

FIGURE 8–1

Buy low, sell high, Digital Equipment (NYSE: DEC), 1997–1998.

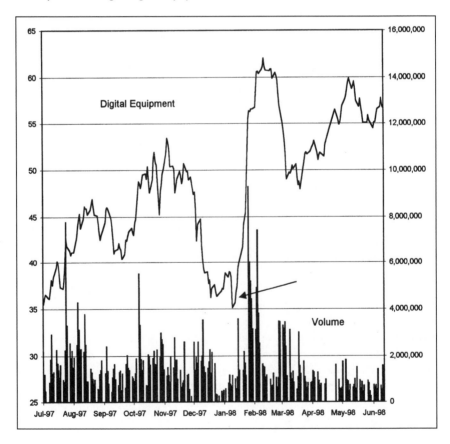

SO WHAT WENT WRONG?

Several things:

- When the investor first heard about the takeover, it was already late in the game to make a play. Thinking for a day or two about buying or selling can sometimes be disastrous.

- The investor sold out the position without learning the details. Compaq was having some earnings difficulties, but it still planned to proceed with the takeover. Once a strategy is put in play, an investor should not be too quick to change.

- The investor should have checked the background on the two companies. Then the decrease in earnings wouldn't have been such a surprise and could have been viewed as a buying opportunity.

- The 10 percent loss strategy is just that, a 10 percent loss. It has nothing to do with how a price will perform in the next few days. Some professional investors look for stocks that are down 10 to 15 percent and consider them buying opportunities, if the fundamentals are reasonable. They know the 10 percenters (with weak hands) will be bailing out and the stock prices can become bargains. These investors will allow a 10, 15, or even 20 percent (sometimes more) drop because the majority of buyers did not buy at the top. Weak hands in Digital caused a drop of nearly 30 percent. It's not possible to control these corrections, and sometimes sellers overreact.

- If an investor is going to speculate on takeovers, it is important that he or she realize that the prices will tend to be volatile until the actual takeover occurs.

- The axiom "buy low, sell high" should not be followed in reverse by the investor.

CYCLICALS

If an investor wants to buy low and sell high on the same stock, why not go to the cyclicals, such as automobile stocks? When they cycle down, buy. When they cycle up, sell. The only trick is to understand when the change is coming. Take a look at General Motors in Figure 8–2.

If an investor had bought at the top of the down cycle, the stock would have cost $58.75 a share. Selling at the bottom of the up cycle would have netted $65.00. A total gain of $6.25, and, on a hundred shares, that's a $625 gain in six months. Not bad.

Irritating surprises can come along, however, and skew the neat cyclical patterns that make these stocks so fun to trade.

FIGURE 8–2

Cyclical, General Motors (NYSE: GM), 1997–1998.

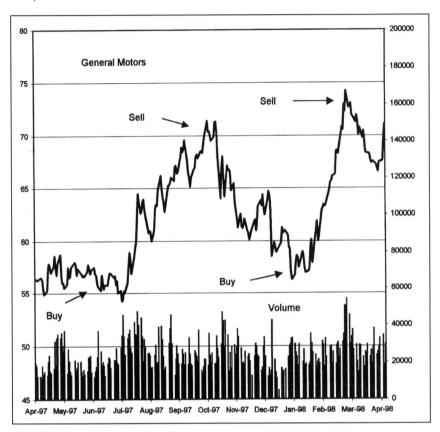

Car companies are simple. You build a car, you sell a car. Build too many, and there are problems. Don't sell enough, and there are problems. But the basic business is not complicated; it's a simple commodity. As a manufacturer, you have only two concerns: the competition and the old "beater" the consumer is now driving. Sales bounce back and forth depending on who has the greatest bells and whistles or occasionally who has the best knock-your-socks-off warrantee, which the manufacturer will regret.

In the past decade of the nineties, car manufacturers have done an excellent job of attracting customers with stock features: the safety items, air bags, and antilock brakes. They have also invested in appearance items such as cool colors, mag wheels, and wide tires (remember white walls). They have made available all sizes of pickups and sports utility vehicles (probably the most effective marketing).

Megadollars have been spent to encourage the consumer to buy the latest and best vehicle from Ford, General Motors, and Chrysler. These companies have all consistently done well at bringing in the dollars. The public has benefited by having better cars. The companies have benefited by having greater profits. The stock buyer has benefited by owning a winning stock. So, who lost? Well, there were a few thousand workers put out of work by consolidation and automation. In some cases this was catastrophic, but in most it was recoverable. Change is inevitable, and our society is gradually waking to the knowledge that it can be a good thing.

In using the simple buy low, sell high trading strategy, if the companies are carefully selected as fundamentally good companies, the rewards from stock ownership can be good and sometimes great. It may take some time and patience for the stock to perform well, but it is often worth the wait. Some companies have income and earnings growing with or ahead of the price. In these situations the axiom buy low, sell high might be changed to "buy low, buy high, and don't sell."

CHAPTER 9

Buy High, Sell Higher

Many individuals are attempting to "buy high and sell higher" when they buy a stock that is on the move. In fact, professional traders frequently use the strategy. Soaring prices are attractive to investors, who believe the prices will keep moving. As long as the momentum of the price swing attracts new buyers, the soaring stock price will continue to climb. It might run up for a couple of days, weeks, or even months. Eventually, however, there is a hesitation, followed by a turn as the profit taking begins. The last buyers not only have the smallest gains from the run up, they will obviously also have the biggest losses. It's somewhat like a pyramid scheme where the losers are the last to join.

A severe market decline creates lower prices and large cash positions even though the earnings of stocks can remain unchanged (meaning that their value is increasing as prices decline). The bargains can be resisted for only a limited time. In a severe market decline, the climb back to former levels could take a few months or longer, but the recovery will come in time.

WHERE ARE THE PLAYS?

Individual investors can seek out stocks that are either in play by the institutions or are likely to come into play. Often they are stocks with strong fundamentals in earnings and revenues, found in industries with good growth potential. In the late 1990s, computer software companies with products related to the Internet show great potential. Medical products and devices can be exciting fast-growth companies. Sometimes older medical products companies with strong growth records do well.

Medtronic, Inc.

Take a look at the price movement of Medtronic stock. A glance at the price chart shows strong price growth, in line with the stock market. Growth was especially strong in the March 1997 through April 1998 time frame. The price nearly doubled in the same time by climbing $28 a share. Volume increased, but not by much. There were just more buyers than sellers.

Between the first price in January 1996 and June 12, 1998, the price increased 120 percent, just over $31 a share. The p/e ratio back in 1996 averaged 28.3, so the price wasn't exactly cheap then. In 1997, the p/e ratio averaged 31.2, and it stood at a big 59.6 (for 12 months, with preliminary data) on June 12, 1998. Obviously a great deal of anticipation and momentum have carried the price of this stock high. If the market stays strong and earnings backfill that high p/e ratio, it could keep going. But if the stock market weakens or earnings come out less than expected, things could become difficult.

There Were Dips

On the way up, there were several weakness areas, dips in price that turned out to be excellent buying opportunities. In 1996, there was an opportunity at about the $25 level in June and even below that in August. The following year had a good opportunity in March when the price dipped below $30. Then it was the October 1997 correction that provided a small window at just under $45 a share.

ENHANCEMENTS

The strategy of buy high, sell higher, can be enhanced by anticipated increases in earnings or by corporate takeover situations. Although anticipation of higher earnings creates unusually high p/e ratios, when the earnings do increase, the ratios return to normal levels. If the earnings do not cause a return to normal levels, sellers will eventually force the return. As the price drops, so will the p/e ratio.

TAKEOVERS

Corporate takeovers create a different situation. Professional arbitrageurs go on search missions in which they look specifically for companies likely to be bought out by some other company. In the late 1980s there were several large leveraged buyout (LBO) situations. The LBO takeover can become a classic buy high, sell higher, situation. In 1988 and 1989, it seemed as though cash-heavy corporations would rather invest in the market by purchasing an entire company than by just buying some of the stock. For those companies who could arrange the deals, there was less risk with greater profits.

The late 1990s continued to have takeovers and mergers. Early 1998 started with Compaq Computer taking over Digital Equipment, announced in late January. May saw the giant merger announced by Chrysler and Daimler:

> "The world's largest industrial merger is set to go ahead after the boards of the German and US car giants, Daimler-Benz and Chrysler, approved a $US35 billion ($55 billion) deal which could create a global shake-out in the industry. The merger was confirmed by a joint statement from Daimler-Benz chairman Mr. Juergen Schrempp and Chrysler chairman Mr. Robert Eaton, in which they said: "This is an historic merger that will change the face of the automotive industry." They said it was "a perfect fit of two [market] leaders."[1]

According to the report, the new trans-Atlantic corporation Daimler-Chrysler will be second only to Toyota in market capitalization. The company will employ more than 400,000 in Germany and the United States and will have total sales of 4 million vehicles.

Merger and takeover activities in computers, automobiles, and banking— the "urge to merge" is still with us. In the long term such activities are not necessarily good for investors, but the short-term gains make them attractive to many. Caution is prudent as deals can quickly become shaky and fall through.

COMPAQ AND DIGITAL

In a time when computer companies had been having troubles with oversupply, this takeover came as good news to many investors. The business community, including customers and vendors looked at the merger positively:

> Big mergers in the computer industry are usually nail biters for users of the companies' technologies. But Compaq's proposed acquisition of Digital Equipment could spell good news for customers of both companies and for users of competitive vendors' products, too, analysts said Tuesday.[2]

If it's good for customers and the companies involved, it's good for investors. Takeovers viewed as positive will often cause significant price increases in both of the companies involved (Figure 9–1).

Compaq's price had been declining since the fall of 1997. Notice the turn came just slightly ahead of the announcement, suggesting there was something floating around in the rumor mill. February 1998 had a couple of hesitations, showing some indecisiveness on the part of investors. No doubt there was con-

---

1. Geoff Kitney, "Record Industrial Marriage," Berlin, Friday, May 8, 1998,
    http://www.smh.com.au/daily/content/980508/business/business5.html.
2. Mitch Wagner, "Compaq-Digital Merger: Customers May Actually Win This Time," *InternetWeek*,
    January 28, 1998, 2:31 P.M. EST.

FIGURE 9–1

Takeover, Compaq Computer Corp. (NYSE: CPQ), 1997–1998.

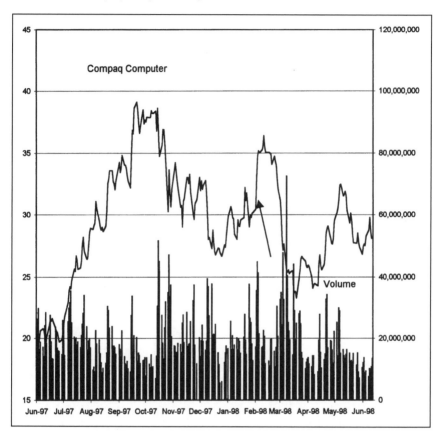

cern over a general weakness in the computer industry. At least part of the initial price surge was likely due to short sellers' closing out their positions.

In mid-February, concern over weakness in the computer industry became more clearly defined when Compaq announced an earnings problem:

> NEW YORK (Reuters)—Compaq Computer Corp. said Wednesday earnings fell 96 percent in the first quarter as it slashed prices because of weak demand and that the next quarter would not be much better. The world's biggest personal computer maker said net income fell to $16 million, or 1 cent a diluted share, in the quarter, from $414 million, or 27 cents a diluted share, a year earlier.[3]

Just the kind of news Wall Street doesn't like to hear, even when it's expected. The price went into a near free fall to July 1997 levels. The price hit bottom

---

3. Richard Melville, "Compaq Ekes Out Profit, Matches Low Estimate." April 1998.

at 23¼ and began to climb. The bumpy ride suggests that a number of investors were indecisive about Compaq's future prospects.

However, as it often does, anticipation and confidence returned to rally the price once again. Notice the rally halted once again between $32 and $33 a share. The area has a history of resistance back in January, as well as the autumn of 1997.

Take a look in Figure 9–2 at a similar price pattern with Digital. Digital's rally on the takeover announcement was probably good news to several stock-holders—all the way up to $62 a share. It's easy to see where some early profits were taken. When the news of Compaq's earnings disappointment came out, the takeover of Digital became a big concern. See how the price stopped near the $50 level, a support level established back in October and November of 1997.[4] Both

F I G U R E   9–2

Takeover target, Digital Equipment Co. (NYSE: DEC), 1997–1998.

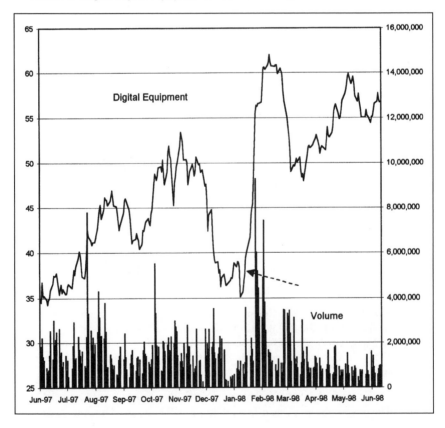

---

4. The October and November areas were resistance levels at the time, but once resistance is
   penetrated, it becomes support.

of these stocks have had a lot of play in both directions. Although money can be made from these swings, it's also easy to see how an investor can get whipsawed on both sides of the price moves. Few investors have the patience to hang on to stocks that suddenly drop $2, $3, or $4 a share.

LONG-TERM INTENTION

Buying high and selling higher can be a viable way to make money in the stock market, but it is not without risk. The strategy usually calls for the intention of a longer-term hold—for example, when the earnings cannot catch up with the price or, in a takeover, when the deal is finalized. Although it is possible to trade in and out during volatile times, the whipsaw effects of being on the wrong side can be devastating.

Corporate takeovers that fail to materialize are a different story. If a buyout does not occur, the stock price will probably fall to previous levels or below. Most often, investors would be prudent to sell and take the loss quickly, rather than hang on and hope for a recovery. Failed buyouts can be frustrating and costly for the individual investor.

A prudent play after selling out can be to attempt bottom fishing once the price gets hammered. Such activity should be based on the individual's belief that the stock can weather the storm and that the company is still capable of generating good earnings.

It would not be unusual for institutional or other experienced stock traders to play these stocks for small profits. They might sell short at the peaks and attempt to buy long at the lows. Such actions often end up to be momentum oriented. They watch the trades minute by minute to see if there is any strength as shown by volume. If strength is indicated by larger volume, then they hold their position. If the volume declines, they close out their positions and plan their next strategy. Obviously, timing is everything in these speculative strategies.

LONG- OR SHORT-TERM

Buy high, sell higher, can work for either the conservative long-term or speculative short-term strategy. But what either strategy needs is a stock that has a solid reason to go higher in price. Two of the main reasons for a stock price to go higher are anticipated higher earnings or a takeover plan.

CHAPTER 10

Buy on the Rumor, Sell on the News

An old saying that usually accompanies the buy high–sell higher strategy is to "buy on the rumor, sell on the news." This can be an effective strategy in many ways, but the investor must be willing to accept certain conditions. For instance, the rumor might have been fabricated with the intent of pushing the stock price up.

Financial consultants, whether advisors or stockbrokers, tend to discourage those who would buy any stock based on rumor alone. False rumors frequently appear regarding corporate takeover situations. The share prices advance, but then suddenly retreat to former levels. In most situations it is best to leave the rumor alone. In fact, buying "on the news" can be appealing.

LOOK BACK TO CPQ AND DEC

In January 1998, Compaq Computer Corp. (CPQ) released details concerning the acquisition of Digital Equipment Corp. (DEC). As shown in the chart in Figure 10–1, Digital's price had fallen from $52.50 to just above $35, a decline of $17.5 a share. When the news came out, the stock went up to more than $60 a share. It even took a few days to get there. Plenty of time to buy? Note the gap of nearly $10 (a reason to be careful with any buy stop orders).

WHERE WAS THE RUMOR

It is impossible to see from looking at the chart where the rumor started. Digital's price in the June through July 1997 uptrend was coming off a low of just over $25 a

F I G U R E 10–1

Takeover, Digital Equipment Corp. (NYSE: DEC), 1997–1998.

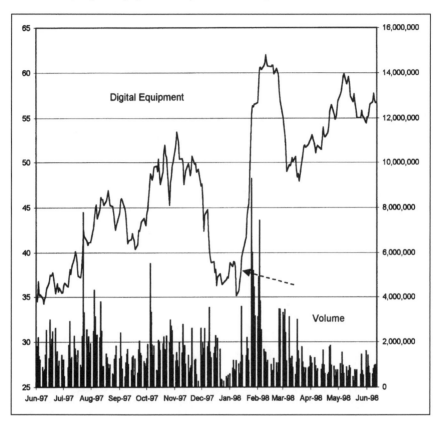

share back in April 1997. Each upward surge in price could have been due partly to rumor. The surge after the takeover announcement is due largely to the market price's coming in line with the takeover offer and investors' believing the deal might be sweetened. Another suitor could appear and start a bidding war for Digital.

Such moves are not unusual. Back in the 1980s, the tire company Firestone had a takeover offer at $40, which was sweetened to $70 by a new suitor. Northwest Airlines (NWA) had a takeover offer increased by a new suitor. Selling on the news can be selling too soon.

Digital's price decline in March 1998 was due mostly to an earnings weakness announced by Compaq Computer. The news of earnings weakness created uncertainty. Many investors sold their shares of Digital because of fears that Compaq might not be able to complete the takeover.

Compaq's price trend was similar to that of Digital's. The price advanced on news of the acquisition and fell on an unfavorable earnings report (see Compaq chart in Figure 10–2).

News of Compaq's acquisition intentions was obviously viewed favorably by investors. Equally obvious was their concern over Compaq's announcement of weaker earnings.

TARGET PRICE

When takeover details are announced, the market price of the target company will usually rise to or close to the new market value, the value of the acquisition. Many investors sell their holdings at this point instead of waiting for the actual

F I G U R E 10–2

Takeover, Compaq Computer Corp. (NYSE: CPQ), 1997–1998.

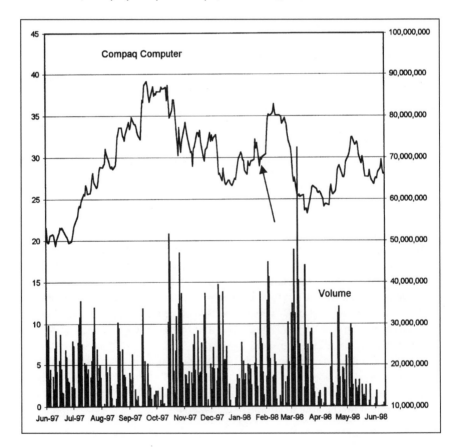

takeover. Although they might not receive the full acquisition value, their assets aren't tied up while waiting for the deal to be completed.

SPECULATIVE STRATEGY

Buying on rumor and selling on or after news is high speculation. Things change, and takeovers can fail to occur. Rumors reach the news media after the action has started. Many times this is too late for the individual investor. Many sophisticated investors avoid rumor investing because of the uncertainty. It is more prudent to look for companies that might become attractive takeover candidates and have other desirable traits. If these companies are not taken over, the investor still has a quality stock at a good price.

CHAPTER 11

Sell High, Buy Low

Sell short at a high price and buy back at a lower price. Wonderful. An investor can make money in a falling market. If XYZ Corporation has trouble breaking through price resistance at $50 a share, chances are that many speculators are going to be selling short between $45 and $49, higher if possible. If the price of XYZ falls back to $36 and the investor who sold short at $46 buys it back, that's a profit of $10 a share when the short is closed. The strategy can be profitable in the right situation; however, there are considerations to be aware of to protect a short position.

LIMITED GAIN

A short position can profit only to the amount that a price drops (obviously, a stock price cannot drop below zero dollars). But in a short position, there is virtually unlimited risk because there is no limit as to how high a stock price can go. Eventually, the shares must be bought back or, if the investor currently owns the shares, delivered to cover the short position. The potential problem is that, if the price doesn't fall, it might rise higher than the investor can afford to pay. Perhaps a verse attributed to Daniel Drew, in the late 1800s, states the risk more clearly: "He who sells what isn't his'n,/Buys it back or goes to prison."

MARGIN CALL

There exist some controls over short selling because a margin call can be issued when the price rises to a certain level. A *margin call* is a brokerage firm's request for money or other marginable securities to be deposited immediately. The call helps to control the risk of the investor and the brokerage firm. Risk can be seriously escalated if a takeover announcement appears relating to the company in which an investor has a short position.

Since a short seller of a stock has an obligation to buy back the stock at some point, the broker does not normally permit the short seller to withdraw proceeds. In fact, the firm could require the short seller to deposit a further sum of money or marginable securities in case the stock price rises and additional funds are needed to buy back the stock. All of this is determined by the situation existing in the investor's margin account.

BORROWED STOCK

In order to prevent a situation in which more shares are sold short than exist, shares must be "borrowed" by the brokerage firm to cover a short sale. If the shares can't be borrowed from within the firm, an attempt is made to borrow the stock from another firm. Sometimes there is a shortage of stock to borrow and the investor is unable to sell short.

Lenders of stock for short positions can call back the stock at any time. If stock cannot be borrowed elsewhere, the position can be closed out by the brokerage firm, no matter what the current profit or loss situation looks like. The short seller is notified, though not necessarily before the stock is repurchased. The borrowing situation means that it is good to select a candidate with a fairly large number of outstanding shares.

Although shares for borrowing can become scarce with any company, the more shares that are outstanding, the more shares there are available for borrowing.

PRICE IMPLICATIONS

All short selling (except "short against the box," where the investor owns the same stock being sold short) is considered to be risky speculation. There are usually more forces at work trying to push the price higher than lower. It becomes very high speculation with low-priced stock. Although the lower prices attract many investors, the risk is often much higher than the potential reward. A stock price can drop only to zero, so a $5 or even $10 price doesn't have much further to go. Even though the volatility is often higher in the low-priced stocks, the return potential is quite limited.

It makes sense, especially for someone new to selling short, to start with stock that has a price with some room to fall, although the price will depend partly on the investor's funds available to meet the margin account requirements.

AT&T SHORT SELECTION

Looking at a one-year chart of AT&T (Figure 11–1) shows one of the situations many investors would look for as a short sell. After a rather dramatic rise in 1997, the price of AT&T stock seemed to run into a brick wall in the mid-$60 area. It

F I G U R E 11–1

Selling short, AT&T (NYSE: T), 1997–1998.

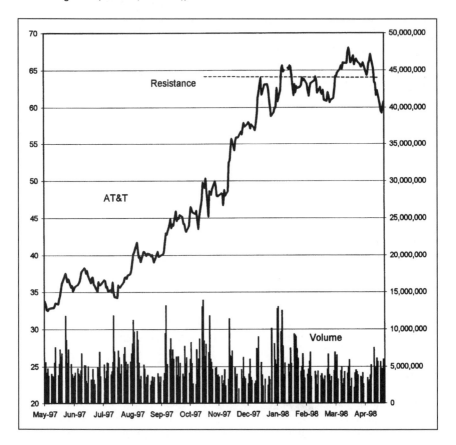

had trouble rising higher in January and February 1998. Finally in March 1998, the price moved up to just over $67. But look at the weakness in volume for the same time period. The March rally had some volume increase, but it was still lower when compared to the advances of 1997. It's a safe bet that a considerable amount of short selling took place with AT&T stock in January and February 1998. In fact, it did—see the short interest figure given in Tables 11–1 and 11–2.

STRONG MARKET, SLOWER ECONOMY

Selling short tends to increase when the markets are rising rapidly but the national economy isn't growing in a similar manner. Under such conditions, sooner or later there will be a correction, a sudden drop, in the market. One can find the volume of short selling in most financial periodicals (especially *The Wall Street*

Journal) under "Short Interest Highlights." *Short interest* refers to shares that have been sold short. Many investors use the information as a sentiment indicator of strength or weakness in the stock prices.

SHORT INTEREST ON THE INTERNET

Information on short interest can be obtained from various sources on the Internet. Using a search engine, just typing in the words "short interest" will bring up several pages. The following is an example of a short interest report from the New York Stock Exchange. Over-the-counter short interest can also be obtained on the Internet at nasd.com, which makes the data available on a monthly basis.

SHORT INTEREST INFORMATION

Tables 11–1 and 11–2 give some of the data released monthly by the New York Stock Exchange. Data are normally released four to five days after mid-month. Notice that the short interest on AT&T appears both on the largest-amount list and on the largest-increase list. Did AT&T's appearance on this list indicate a weakness in the stock price? Take a look at the chart in Figure 11–2 showing the price of AT&T from March through April 1998.

T A B L E 11–1

Largest Short Positions, New York Stock Exchange Data, from March 13 to April 15, 1998

Company Name	Symbol	April 15, 1998	March 13, 1998	Change, +/–
Compaq Computer	CPQ	74,898,545	70,911,764	3,986,781
Micron Technology	MU	39,250,741	44,559,076	–5,308,335
Columbia/HCA Healthcare	COL	36,708,295	38,238,428	–1,530,133
AT&T Corp.	T	35,817,537	30,010,522	5,807,015
Cedant Corp.	CD	34,476,363	36,058,134	–1,581,771
Wal-Mart Stores, Inc.	WMT	33,767,631	35,312,303	–1,544,672
Kmart Corp.	KM	33,319,622	30,024,097	3,295,525
US West Media Group	UMG	29,941,513	29,920,321	21,192
First Union Corp.	FTU	25,209,189	22,185,318	3,023,871
Walt Disney Hldg.	DIS	24,381,863	23,645,695	736,168
News Corp. ADS	NWS	23,215,679	23,676,895	–461,216
CBS Corp.	CBS	22,521,306	22,858,968	–337,662
Bank One Corp.	ONE	22,148,373	23,859,832	–1,711,459
SBC Communications	SBC	22,042,656	9,628,157	12,414,499
Nike, Inc.	NKE	21,785,190	23,563,098	–1,777,908

T A B L E 11-2

Largest Changes, New York Stock Exchange Data, from March 13 to April 15, 1998

Company Name	Symbol	April 15, 1998	March 13, 1998	Increase
SBC Communications	SBC	22,042,656	9,628,157	12,414,499
Perusahan Pt. Telekom	IIT	12,987,830	3,319,301	9,668,529
America Online	AOL	18,874,537	9,968,730	8,905,807
Haliburton Co.	HAL	19,111,007	11,699,938	7,411,069
AT&T Corp.	T	35,817,537	30,010,522	5,807,015
Iomega Corp.	IOM	20,382,053	14,851,538	5,530,515
Conseco Inc.	CNC	18,395,556	13,819,957	4,575,599
USA Waste Services	UW	17,357,005	12,791,913	4,565,092
Lucent Technologies	LU	12,977,429	8,506,488	4,470,941
Safeway, Inc.	SWY	21,368,821	17,007,885	4,360,936
Company Name	Symbol	April 15, 1998	March 13, 1998	Decrease
Williams Cos.	WMB	9,890,426	28,261,640	−18,371,214
Allegheny Teledyne	ALT	5,329,714	14,391,013	9,064,299
National City Corp.	NCC	3,965,709	9,589,956	−5,624,247
Lockheed Martin Corp.	LMT	7,869,050	13,300,575	−5,431,525
Laidlaw Environmental	LLE	3,935,387	9,336,453	−5,401,066
Micron Technology	MU	39,250,741	44,559,076	−5,308,335
Sealed Air Corp.	SEE	7,579,437	12,798,726	−5,219,258
Loral Space & Comm.	LOR	11,405,486	16,527,744	−5,122,258
Advanced Micro Devices	AMD	10,026,389	14,492,780	−4,466,391
Fred Meyer, Inc.	FMY	6,569,191	10,589,682	−4,020,491

Selling short between $65 and $66 a share would have done well as a strategy if the investor had been able to buy back in the $59 to $60 range at the end of April. A profit of $6 or $7 a share is often attractive to the speculator, but problems can arise with selecting a stock based on high levels of short interest.

SHOULD HEAVY SHORT INTEREST BE AVOIDED?

Knowing how short a stock has been sold can be a factor in deciding on a strategy to implement. If too many people short a stock and all attempt to cover their position at the same time, the flurry of buying activity will drive the price up—making it difficult for the individual investor to cover the short position. It is interesting to see the high level of AT&T short interest that appears to be driving the price back up, likely due to short covering at the end of April 1998.

Sometimes too much short activity can attract large buyers. Buyers know that the short positions will be covered if the stock price rises enough and that the covering will push the price even higher. Such actions are commonly referred to as a *short squeeze*; if they happen, it's more often by accident than intent. Intentional short squeezes are considered a form of price manipulation and are technically illegal, but it is difficult to prove an intent like this in a bull market.

SHORT INTEREST AS AN INDICATOR

Many investors use the changes and amounts of short interest as a sentiment indicator. As was seen with AOL, it's not always correct, but many times, when considered with other indicators, short interest does show approaching weakness.

F I G U R E 11–2

Short interest, AT&T (NYSE: T), March through April 1998.

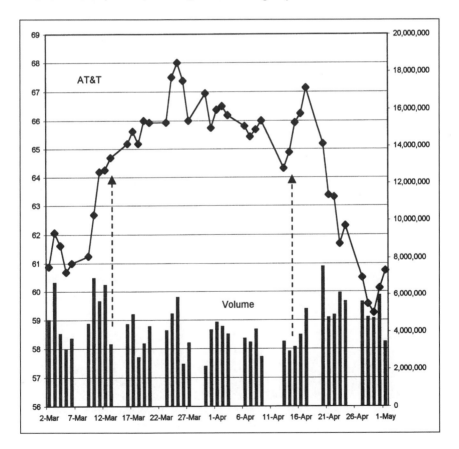

This situation appeared to be the case with AT&T, when the stock price dropped from a high of $68 to a low of $59¼ a share.

SBC Communications was also on the list of large short interest increases. Take a look at Figure 11–3 to see what happened. After a correction in early fall of 1997, the price of SBC climbed steadily upward. Some price volatility occurred in November and December, but still it climbed higher. After breaking through $40, it rather suddenly shot up to $46 a share. Although there appears to be a volume spike on the advance, it didn't hold up—the short sellers apparently didn't trust the price level. It fell back to just over 43, stayed flat for a few days, then collapsed. Compare the lack of volume in February through April 1998 to the volume levels of October through December (ignore the holidays) and into January. It appears that the short interest in this situation clearly reflected the changing sentiment regarding the price of SBC Communications.

FIGURE 11–3

Short interest increase, SBC Communications (NYSE: SBC), 1997–1998.

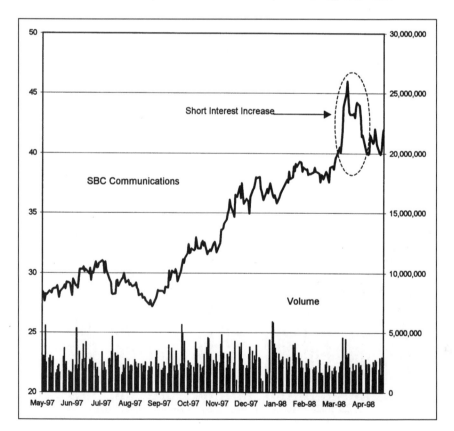

UP-TICK RULE ON EXCHANGES

An additional word of caution to the short seller: Short sells on a stock exchange can be executed only on an "up tick" (price higher than the previous trade) or "zero-plus tick" (price the same as the last trade, if the last trade was an up tick). The purpose of this rule is to make short selling difficult when a stock price or the market is falling. At the present time, over-the-counter (NASDAQ) stocks are not bound by this up-tick rule.

CHAPTER 12

The Perfect Hedge Is Short against the Box

Selling short "against the box" means to take a conservative position. It is a position with no loss potential and no gain potential. If an investor owns (long) 100 shares of IBM and sells (short) 100 shares of IBM, the investor's position is short against the box. The strategy is often called the "perfect hedge." If the price of IBM drops, there is no loss. Conversely, if the price rises, there is no gain.

Long 100 IBM at $110 = $11,000

Short 100 IBM at $115 = $11,500

If both positions are closed out, the profit is $500. If the stock price declines, the profit remains $500. If the stock price rises and both positions are closed out, the profit remains at $500.

A short against the box position can be closed by selling the long position and buying back the short position or by delivering the long shares to close the short. Physically delivering stock to close a short might require a letter of instruction to the broker. No orders are written on delivering, and generally no commission is charged.

The perfect hedge can be useful in a situation in which the investor currently owns the stock but does not have physical possession. This strategy can benefit the investor who is receiving stock from a corporate purchase plan but will not receive the certificate for a few days or weeks. Margin requirements must be fulfilled (Regulation T, which currently requires a deposit of 50 percent, and all margin maintenance calls must be met if the stock continues to rise in price), but the strategy does lock in the price with the short sell. When the investor receives the stock, it can be delivered to close out the short position.

Short selling can be a useful and profitable strategy in the proper situation, but it should be used with caution. The short seller must be aware of the rules and the risks. Obviously, the main risk is the nonparticipation in any future gains. The perfect-hedge short sell can be a useful tool in the right situation.

CHAPTER 13

Never Short a Dull Market

A *dull market* is a *sideways market*, sometimes also referred to as a *trendless market*. Movement is slow, with an occasional advance, followed by a small correction. During dull or balanced markets, institutional investors are all waiting (if they can) for a good reason to get back into the market. The slightest good news (sometimes bad news that is not as bad as expected) can cause a strong rally to develop. The rally can cause the price of the short stock to rise sharply, resulting in margin calls and eventually a loss. The proof of market strength is shown by the stability creating the dullness. If there were no underlying strength, the market would obviously be falling.

All lethargic markets have occasional rallies and corrections, although the price swings are generally not severe. If an investor can identify where the heaviest volume occurs, it is possible for him or her to determine whether the sentiment is bullish or bearish. If the volume on a correction (downward movement) is consistently and significantly greater than the volume on a rally, the sentiment tends to be bearish.

During the year after the crash 1987, investors were overly cautious (Figure 13–1). Much of 1988 had a dull, lethargic market that tended to have heavier volume on rallies and lighter volume on corrections. Most of the rally action was caused by *dividend capture*, which is the buying of a stock just for the purpose of receiving the dividend.

Looking at Figure 13–1, we can see various dull markets over a 10-year period. In this chart only the 1989 through 1990 market had a sharp drop at the end of the dullness, and even that was followed by a resumption of the uptrend. Other years show corrections, but they do not show a change in trend. After a short-lived

FIGURE 13–1

Dull markets, Dow Averages, 1987 through 1998.

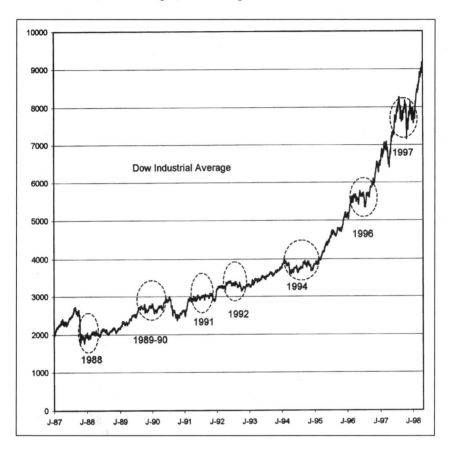

correction, they resume the uptrend. Rallies at the end of these brief corrections are usually started by short sellers covering their short positions.

A more recent dull market in 1994 showed the market holding position. There were two downtrends, but the uptrend continued at the end of the year. A few areas offered short selling opportunities, but they followed a downward penetration of the short-term uptrend. The opportunities were small and quickly over. They would have been difficult to trade on the short side.

A real danger in shorting a dull market is where the Dow Industrial Average makes a *double bottom* (Figure 13–2.) The confirmed double bottom marked the beginning of a strong bull market uptrend that more than doubled the industrial average by 1998.

FIGURE 13-2

Dull market, Dow Averages, 1994.

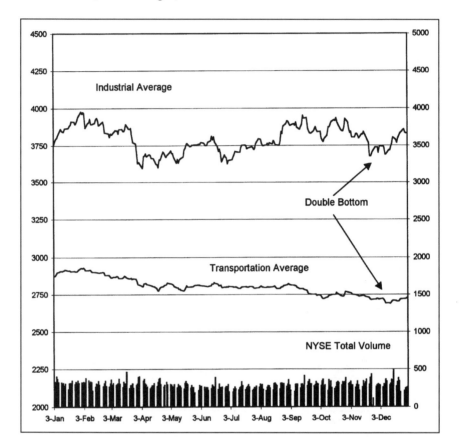

LOOK OUT FOR A SQUEEZE

Selling short is a speculative strategy, requiring timing, patience, and skill. Dull markets are notorious for sudden rallies that put the "squeeze" on short sellers. In fact, traders usually refer to these rallies as being a "short squeeze" or "squeezing out the shorts." A short seller caught in the squeeze runs the risk of receiving a margin call for additional cash or marginable securities to be deposited or the risk of being forced to sell at a loss.

"Never short a dull market" means to be careful with the underlying strength of stock prices in a market that has become lethargic, with no clear trend. As shown by the past 10 years, the underlying strength can turn to buying activity on the slightest positive news. The ensuing rally and resumption of the uptrend creates a high-risk situation for the short investor.

CHAPTER 14

Never Short the Trend

S*horting the trend* refers to selling short when a new high is reached in the stock market or by an individual stock price when the trend has been definitely upward. The investor is making a large gamble that the market will turn and decline.

LOOK FOR THE TURN

Stock prices tend to move as a group, and trends continue until they violate the trend and turn. Shorting a stock at the "top" is generally an exercise in futility and can become costly if an uptrend continues. For individual stocks, a top might be the beginning of a takeover that will push the price even higher. Although it is usually not a good idea to short the trend, shorting the turn can be profitable.

Unocal (see Figure 14–1), showed some instability in mid-October 1997, then fell with the rest of the market on October 27 (Dow Industrials' biggest one-day drop—554 points). Unocal had an uptrend starting in mid-August 1997. The price rose steadily, with some increase in volume. In early October, the price began to falter and broke through the trend line. A short sell at the turn could have been an excellent strategy. It could have been possible to sell short at $43½. The October 27 correction came along and forced the price down to $39. Some would have closed the short position as Unocal appeared to stabilize, giving $450 per 100 shares. Keeping the short open could have allowed the investor to close out the short position at $35 or less, a profit of $8, $9, and maybe $10 a share in less than three months' time.

FIGURE 14–1

Short sell, Unocal Corp. (NYSE: UCL), 1997–1998.

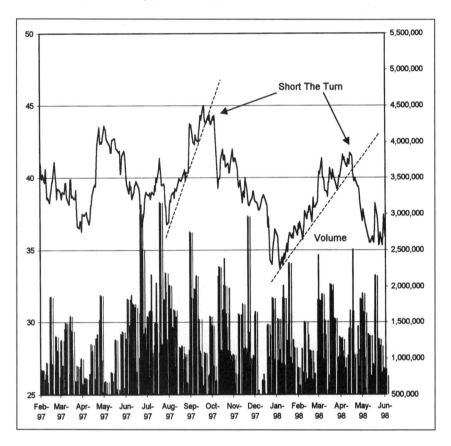

WEEKLY CHART

Look at Eastman Kodak on a weekly chart. In weekly charts a lot of important detail can be lost, but if they are compared to daily charts, they can also give a better idea of the strength and duration of a trend.

On the weekly chart (Figure 14–2), we see a long-term uptrend for Eastman Kodak (EK). Although there was some volatility and a couple of trend penetrations, the turn didn't appear until 1997. The trend violation in February was severe.

In the weekly chart EK had a well-defined turn in the trend in February through March 1997. The hesitant recovery couldn't break through the resistance at $93, and the price started to go lower. It's a fairly safe bet that considerable short selling occurred after the February 1997 turn. The following rally was likely due to upticks for short selling (see Figure 14–3).

Looking at a daily chart for EK (Figure 14–3) shows a much more detailed picture of that period from March through December 1997. The best short selling opportunity was when the uptrend turned (point 1). Another opportunity appeared when a short-term uptrend turned at point 2 on the chart.

Even a short sell as low as $78 (point 2) wouldn't have been difficult to obtain, and it would have dropped more than $20 by mid-December. Were there any scary moments? No, not really. A rally in August showed that the volume declined as the price advanced. Volume increased significantly on the mid-September drop. October 27, the Dow Industrials' drop (554 points) had barely an effect on Kodak. Even the volume in the December rally wasn't very exciting. The $54 level has a history of support as resistance back in 1994, and again in 1995, but that was a long time ago. The price wanted to find support, but it was

F I G U R E 14–2

Trend, Eastman Kodak (weekly) (NYSE: EK), 1997–1998.

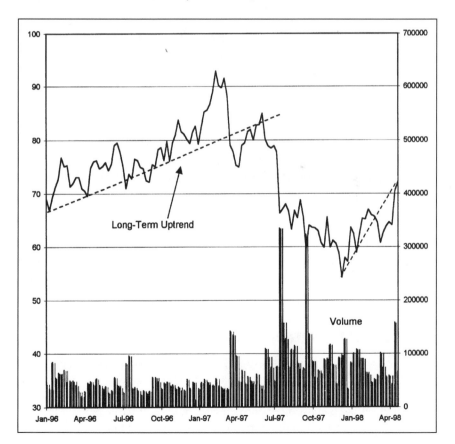

FIGURE 14–3

Trend, Eastman Kodak (daily) (NYSE: EK), 1997–1998.

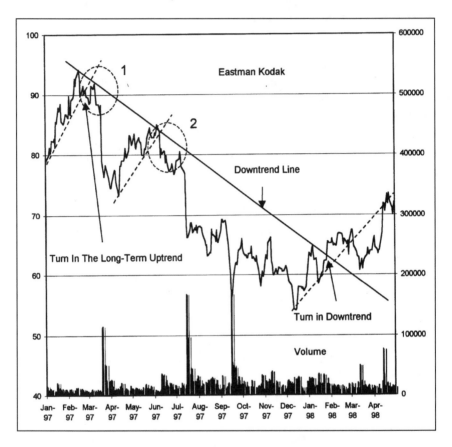

having trouble finding interested investors. Was it still a short sell in February 1998? No, or at least not a good one. The rally from $54 penetrated the downtrend line on its way to recovery. The short selling opportunity wasn't as good as points 1 and 2 on the chart.

NEVER SHORT THE TREND—SHORT THE TURN

Selling short is a risky way of investing. It should be approached with caution and a knowledge of the company and its price trend. Buy stop orders can be used for upside protection, but they cannot substitute for vigilance in study and observation. Short selling is most often pursued on a short-term basis, before the stock drops low enough to become attractive to buyers or another company with takeover plans.

CHAPTER 15

Never Buy a Stock Because It Has a Low Price

Buying a stock just because it has a low price is often a risky strategy. It's especially risky if the investor doesn't find out why the price is so low. Many times investors are attracted to low-priced stocks that pay a dividend. The lower price pushes the dividend percent higher. The yield on the dividend might be 10, 15, or 20 percent or higher. Sometimes the companies that own the stocks are about to severely reduce or even eliminate the dividend. When they do so, the stock price plummets even further. The investor is then left with an extremely low-priced stock and no dividend.

HOW CAN A STOCK BE OVERSOLD?

Some analysts and investors don't believe an "oversold" situation can actually exist because the term implies that investors sold more shares than they intended to sell. Actually, *oversold* refers to that price at which a significant number of buyers come to the stock, believing it is worth more than the current market price reflects. It can be accompanied by higher trading volume. On the other end, *overbought* is the price at which volume decreases and investors start selling because they believe the current market price is too high. Technical analysts frequently use the two terms *overbought* and *oversold*. Fundamental analysts might use the terms *overvalued* or *undervalued*. They would tend to look at the price in relation to earnings and revenues.

6 7211

FIGURE 15–1

Oversold, Toys 'R' Us, Inc. (NYSE: TOY), 1996–1998.

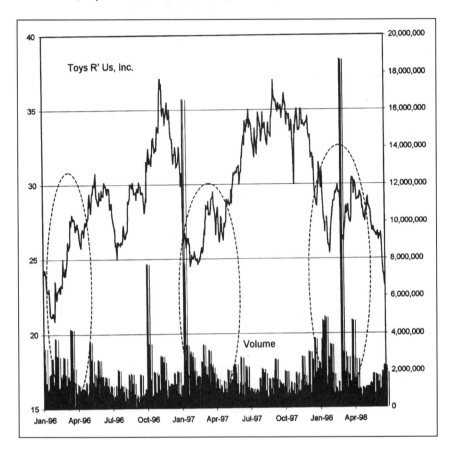

Toys 'R' Us, Inc.

Notice the three areas in the price chart in Figure 15–1 that show an increase in volume after a price decline. Following the volume increase, in each of the three circled areas is an increase in price. One would expect a certain amount of volume increase on a price decline. When that increase extends beyond the bottom, it shows positive anticipation coming into the stock.

December is the busiest month of the year for all toy retailers, and January is also the fourth quarter for Toys 'R' Us. Thus, at least part of the rally is due to anticipation of a good year-end for earnings. When this stock declines $10 to $15 a share, it also lowers the p/e ratio significantly and becomes attractive to value investors. When the p/e drops with the price as shown in the chart below, the stock becomes attractive to value investors, who buy it and consequently push the price and p/e ratio back up:

TABLE 15-1

p/e Ratio Averages, Toys 'R' Us

1993	1994	1995	1996	1997	12 Months (June 98)
26.2	22.4	15.8	41.5	16.2	14

These are some fundamental reasons for the price stabilizations and turnarounds.

Eastman Kodak

The price chart of Eastman Kodak as shown in Figure 15–2 looks quite technical. There is a well-formed (technical analysis) "head-and-shoulders" pattern that

FIGURE 15-2

Oversold, Eastman Kodak (NYSE: EK), 1996–1998.

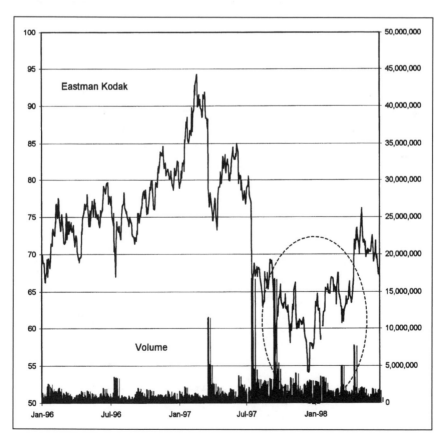

formed between late 1996 and mid-1997. The head-and-shoulders pattern says the price will drop an amount equal to or greater than the distance from the top of the head to the shoulder line, at the breakout point. The stock price did achieve this minimum measurement.

Look at the volume. It increased significantly as the price began to drop. The volume continued to be high as the price hit bottom and started back up. Only with the sell-off in late May to early June did the volume start to show some steady decline.

Fundamentally, Eastman Kodak went from earnings of $3.82 a share in 1996 to a penny per share in 1997. That was obviously enough earnings weakness for many investors, who bailed out of the stock in 1997. But investors have liked Kodak for a long time. Anticipation of better times spread throughout the market and captured the imagination and anticipation of other investors. It's one of the 30

FIGURE 15-3

Dow Industrial Average and Eastman Kodak, 1996–1998.

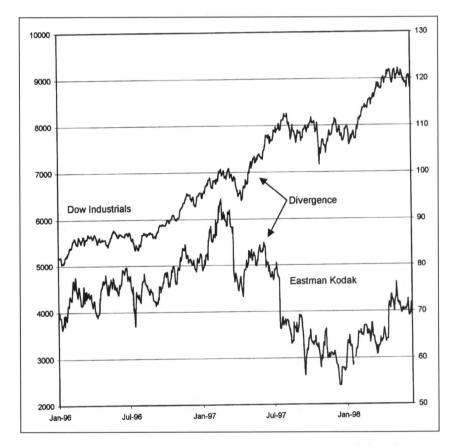

Dow Industrial Average stocks that has been considered a bellwether for many years.

If we examine in Figure 15–3 the price of Eastman Kodak as compared to the Dow Industrial Average, something interesting appears. Note the obvious divergence. After tracking the Dow Industrial Average for many years, Eastman Kodak came out with some weak earnings and lost a lot of investor confidence. But look how closely the price of Kodak tracks the Industrials. In fact, it often turns before the Dow. As with many bellwethers, it's not always ahead of the market, and there are a few times it goes off on its own. The strong divergence gave investors a reason to sell, and the later oversold condition gave them reason to buy. (See Chapter 49 for more discussion of this phenomenon.)

Undoubtedly Eastman Kodak needs to have significant improvement in earnings to rebuild anticipation in its price. Whether it returns to acting as a bellwether or not, at least a significant number of investors believe it to be a good investment.

LOW PRICE

"Never buy a stock because it has a low price" should be amended to say, "unless you are reasonably certain of when the price will recover and how it will do so." There are times when a stock price becomes oversold due to the impact of bad news. The oversold condition can provide an excellent buying opportunity for those who know the stock. It might be time to add new shares to an existing portfolio or obtain a new investment at bargain prices.

CHAPTER 16

Beware the "Penny Stock"

Penny stocks have certain characteristics:

1. The price per share is low.
2. The price will often go lower than one can imagine.
3. The low price makes these stocks targets for manipulation.
4. They tend to trade "thinly," sometimes going for weeks without a buy or sell.
5. At times it's nearly impossible to find buyers for those wanting to sell.
6. 10-for-1 reverse splits happen occasionally, to boost the price.
7. The risk is exceptionally high.

Although there is no set definition of *penny stocks*, many investors and brokers consider any stock selling for less than $10 a share to fit the category. Some prices on these stocks have dropped so low that they indeed sell for pennies. If shares are originally issued as penny stock, in many cases, the company itself did the underwriting. Several million shares were probably issued and are not *blue sky* (approved for trading) in every state. Such conditions can make trading the stock difficult or impossible. It's not unusual for them to be fairly easy to buy and very difficult to sell at any price.

LURE OF MYTHS

Some investors believe (erroneously) that big, successful companies started out as penny stock. Myths abound about once being able to buy IBM at 50 cents a share or 3-M at 19 cents a share. They talk about Mr. Hewlett and Mr. Packard building computers in their garage and using shares in the company as wages. Such beliefs are seldom based entirely on fact; rather, most are partial truths at best. For the very few companies that started out small and made it big, thousands of others had reverse splits until they finally disappeared.

The amount of risk in the low-price situation increases dramatically as the price of the stock drops even lower. It can be true that reward potential increases as risk increases, but this is not necessarily the case with penny stocks.

If a company whose stock is selling for about 50 cents has two or three employees left (who are looking for work) and they are unable to manufacture product or even ship product, that company will most likely go out of business and the stock price will drop to zero.

I CAN LOSE A THOUSAND

Despite the risk, some investors are attracted to stocks like these. The usual statement made is, "I thought I'd invest a thousand dollars. If I lose it, OK, but I might get lucky." In the vast majority of cases, they don't get lucky, and the thousand dollars is gone. Typically, the odds are better in horse racing or in a trip to Las Vegas where they can at least get some entertainment for their money.

SEE WHAT MISSOURI SAYS

Although every state has some problems with penny stocks, the secretary of state of Missouri put this caution on the Internet:

Watch for the following warning signs to alert you to a possible penny stock fraud:

High-Pressure Sales Techniques
Investment in a legitimate emerging company is long-term. A good little company is not going to skyrocket in a couple of weeks. Building a sound company takes years; you have a few days or weeks to decide whether the investment is right for you.

Blind Pools and Blank Checks
Do not invest in any security without being told exactly how your money will be spent. Be sure you know which properties the company plans to buy with the offering proceeds and how much money is to be spent on management and promoters.

Mismarked Trade Confirmations or New Account Cards
Be very wary if your trade confirmation is marked "unsolicited" if your broker did, in fact, solicit the trade. While it may be a simple mistake, unscrupulous

penny stock brokers often mark the confirmation as unsolicited to avoid the registration laws and the "fair, just and equitable" standard. Watch for misstatements about your net worth, income and account objectives as well. Investing in penny stocks is speculative business and involves a high degree of risk. Often, brokers will enhance the new account card to make it seem that you are suitable for a penny stock investment when you are not.

Unauthorized Transactions

Be alert to placement in your account of securities you did not agree to purchase. In some instances, a broker may try to pressure you into purchasing the stock, claiming that since you have the stock, you must pay for it. In some cases, the broker is temporarily "parking" the securities in your account, perhaps to meet the minimum distribution of an IPO, or for any number of reasons. In some cases, an unauthorized trade is simply a mistake, but in any case, complain immediately, both verbally and in writing to your broker, your broker's manager and to the Securities Division.[1]

BUY DIRECT—SELL TO WHOM?

Sometimes penny stock can be purchased directly from the company, but the company might not be willing to buy the shares back when the investor is ready to sell. Unless the investor wants to own a controlling interest and manage the company, the super-low-priced penny stocks are usually best avoided.

Taking a Flyer

If you feel an overwhelming urge to "take a flyer" on a penny stock, one way to lower the risk is to buy only those shares on which you can obtain reliable research information about the company. Use the same fundamental analysis approach as you would use to buy blue-chip stocks for a long-term investment. This will at least give you some idea as to the company's prospects for recovery.

Internet Sources

Doug Gerlach's Invest-o-rama has a small capitalization site at http://investorama.com/smallcap.shtml.

---

1. Office of Secretary of State Rebecca McDowell Cook, *Penny Stocks, A Guide for Beginning Investors*, 600 West Main and 208 State Capitol, Post Office Box 778, Jefferson City, MO 65102, or http://mosl.sos.state.mo.us/sos-sec/penstk.html.

CHAPTER 17

Give Stop Orders Wiggle Room

A *stop order* is an order to buy or sell stock when it reaches or passes through a predetermined price. *Buy stop orders* are placed above the current trading price, and *sell stop orders* are placed below the current price. Once activated, the stop order becomes a *market order* that says the investor will make the trade at the best available price.

Wiggle room is important when placing stop orders—whether buying or selling stock. Essentially, it allows the stock price to move in "normal" market swings without activating the stop. Allowing for *wiggle room* means placing the stop close enough to the current price to prevent a loss on a sell or activate a buy on an upward move but far enough from the current price that it will be triggered only by a larger-than-normal move.

When buying, the investor wants the buy stop to be activated only if the stock price is making a strong move upward. On the other side, no one really wants the sell stop order to be filled unless the price is declining at a disturbing rate. Consequently, the buy stop is usually placed closer to the current trading range than is the sell stop. It is good to give the sell stop enough room for the price to fall during a small correction without activating the stop.

SELL STOP: NOT 2 BUCKS, NOT 10 PERCENT

Some say place a sell stop $2 away from the current price; others say take losses at 10 percent. The problem with these solutions is the probability of the orders' being executed. The $2 sell stop is so close to the current price that the exchange specialist can easily be tempted to tick the price down and execute the order. The

FIGURE 17–1

Sell stop, Liz Claiborne (NYSE: LIZ), 1997–1998.

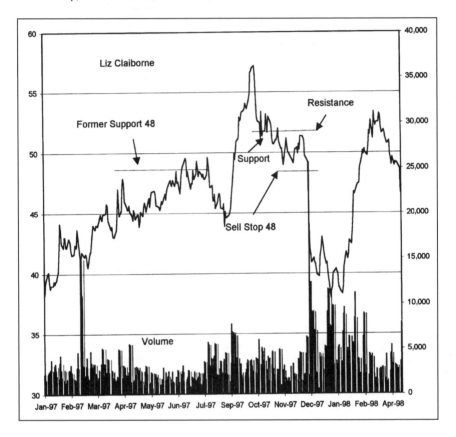

specialist is allowed to do just that. To lock all stops into a 10 percent loss is also not a good idea. Some stock prices will swing 10 percent every week, others every day. What does make sense is to look at a price chart such as the one shown in Figure 17–1, to see the price trading range.

During a good part of July, through early August 1997, Liz Claiborne's stock price established strong support at the $48 level. Eventually the price broke through that support level and dropped to $44, then turned and rallied above the $57 level. Notice, that this rally was not accompanied by much of a volume increase and therefore did not have great strength.

An investor who knows, owns, and likes Liz Claiborne notices that the price corrected and established support in the low 50s. The investor believes, if this support has a breakout, that the price could fall significantly lower. This is October, just before the 554-point one-day correction in the Dow Industrial Average on October 27. The investor looks back to find an earlier area of strong support. Remember that July through August strong support level at $48?

Breaking through 48 could bring the stock much lower. The sell stop is entered at 48 giving $4½ of wiggle room. Obviously, the stop is triggered and the stock is sold at a market price (best available price).

BUY STOP

Placing the buy stop order also requires some study of the current trading range. The distance to establish between the buy stop price and the current trading price of the stock is a matter of personal decision, and it should be based on the trading range analysis. A price chart can be of great assistance in selecting a good buy stop price. Just remember that the ideal situation is to catch the stock as the price moves and continues upward.

Look again at the price chart of Liz Claiborne as shown in Figure 17–2. The stock price fell rather slowly after the October 1997 correction. In mid-December,

F I G U R E 17–2

Buy stop, Liz Claiborne (NYSE: LIZ), 1997–1998.

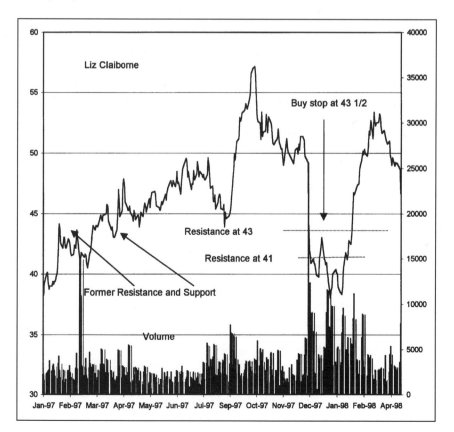

as investors lost confidence, the price fell out of bed. It dropped from the high 40s to the high 30s. From the middle of December to nearly the end of January 1998, the price of LIZ looked as though it could go lower. The investor still believes in the value of Liz Claiborne, thinks it could go lower but it might not. When it recovers, it will do so quickly. The investor places a buy stop at $43½ a share. Although the placement is somewhat arbitrary, the investor believes that if the price rises above the resistance at $41 and $43 a share, it will likely continue higher and rise to former levels in the mid-$50 area. The buy stop in this situation has $4½ of wiggle room, same as the sell stop. Often on the buy side it's better to be closer to the current trading price ($39) than on the sell side, but it depends on the specific situation, which is why it helps to look at a chart.

If the company is in trouble and the price continues to fall, the stop will probably not be triggered. The buy stop is triggered in early February, and recovery continues. By mid-March of 1998, the investor has a $10 profit, a 24 percent gain in less than a month.

LIKE MEDICINE, USE ONLY WHEN NECESSARY

An important point to remember about the use of buy or sell stop orders: If you believe a price will go up or will weaken and fall, forget using a stop and place a market order to buy or sell. It doesn't make sense to give the money away. Stops should be used only if there is considerable uncertainty.

Once the buy stop is triggered, a short-term stock trader might place a limit sell order at $51 or $51.50 a share, due to the resistance at these same levels back in November and December. The sell limit would have been activated in early March, giving a better than $7, or 17 percent gain.

Full Perspective

To put these short-term trades in full perspective, let's say the investor bought 500 shares of Liz Claiborne stock back in January 1997 and paid $38½ a share

Bought: 500 shares   LIZ   at $38.50 = $19,250

The sell stop was triggered at $48 in a rapidly falling market for LIZ. Let's say it filled at $45½ (remember, it became a market order, meaning that it was to be sold at the best available price):

Sold: 500 shares   LIZ   at $45.50 = $22,750
Buy: 19,250
Profit: $3,500

The $3,500 gain represents better than 18 percent. But we're not done. The investor bought the stock back at $43½, and it rose to $52½. If it were sold at this price, the investor would have an additional $9 a share.

Results

Sold:	500 shares	LIZ	at $52.50 = $26,250
Buy:	500 shares	LIZ	at $43.50 = 21,750
Profit:			$4,500

When we put this all together, there is a significant gain for the year 1997:

First sell:	$3,500	
Second sell:	$4,500	
Total gain:	$8,000	42 percent based on original purchase price

Most investors would consider this a great year with Liz Claiborne. Rather than selling at the $52½ level, the investor could hold and place another sell stop. It's the losing stock or the losing situation that should be sold. Although this is short-term trading and is considered speculative, it's on the lower end of risk. The biggest risk is that the investor won't get the buy or sell orders in fast enough to catch the price move.

It's important to keep in mind that the Liz Claiborne stock was selected for this example of buy and sell stops because it worked so well. It's always easier to find places to enter buys and sells while looking at the full picture. The decisions are not as easy in a real moving market where we don't know what will happen next.

GTC

Stop orders should be entered *GTC* ("good 'till canceled"), but that term has different meanings among brokerage firms. Find out how long a GTC order will remain open. Some stay in until the end of the month; others are canceled in a month. Ask the broker how long a GTC order remains in effect. Stop orders can also be changed. They can be raised on the sell side if the price keeps rising or lowered on the buy side. A recent price chart should be consulted before an order is changed.

The sell stop can provide protection for profits, and it can also limit loss in a severe decline. But remember that it should be far enough away from the current price to avoid having it triggered by a minor move. It needs more wiggle room.

The buy stop can be placed closer to the current price because it is an order the investor wants triggered. Limit prices can also be placed on stops, but the limits might prevent the order from being filled. However, with a buy stop, a limit order can prevent the order's being filled on a sudden price move due to a takeover announcement.

IF THE PRICE IS GOING TO MOVE, DO THE TRADE

Again, the most important point about stop orders is this: If you truly believe a stock price is going to move significantly, place a market order and forget the stop. If you think the price will drop, sell the stock at the market (best available price). If you believe the price will soon see a significant rise, buy the stock at the market. Placing stop orders in these situations is just giving money away.

CHAPTER 18

Buy the Stock
That Splits

"This stock split 2 for 1 at $40 a share and ran up to 40 again, all within six months. It's just incredible how fast this company is growing. The stock is now at $42 a share, and there's talk of another 2-for-1 split. It'd be great to have more stocks like this one."

This is obviously the sound of a happy investor. Stock splits are looked upon as being good news because the price will often continue to increase, given time. However, even though many stock splits are positive, sadly that is not always the case. Many times the price will soar for the split, only to fall back to previous price levels, adjusted to the split.

MECHANICS OF A SPLIT

Stock dividends and splits have basically three occurrences: announcement date, record date, and payment date.[1] To qualify for the split, the investor must be the owner on the record date (similar to the ex-date for dividends). Therefore, the stock must be purchased at the appropriate time before the record date to qualify.

Announcement Date

The announcement date can be considered the most important date because it tends to have the greatest positive impact on a stock's price. Even companies that

---

1. Actually there are four important dates: the date the board of directors approves the split, the date the shareholders approve the split, the record date, and the payment date.

do not react well to a split tend to move initially higher on the announcement. Rumors of a split sometimes leak out ahead of the announcement date, which also tends to push the price higher. Although it is not illegal according to insider trading laws to buy stock based on rumor, it is a highly speculative practice as some rumors are incorrect.

Stock split and stock dividend announcements are given to the media (including the Internet) on the announcement date. The company provides all the important details of the split and many times a brief history of the company's previous stock splits, which it sends out in the form of a press release. The company considers a forward stock split a positive event and wants to get as much free media publicity as possible.

Positive Split Story

Every so often the positive stock story appears. It might be overheard at a cocktail party or a business lunch. The story will invariably hold the attention of the listeners. Many sincerely wish they had bought the stock a year ago, when the price was still reasonable. A stock split comes along, happens and the price keeps climbing. Look at the trend for Colgate Palmolive for 1997 as shown in Figure 18–1.

The 2-for-1 split was announced in March 1997. It was payable the following May. Surprisingly the stock showed weakness shortly after the announcement, but after the payable date the stock went into a $19 uptrend. The price then fluctuated until the end of the year when it entered another strong rally, this time to more than $25. An increase of more than $44 in just over a year is a stock virtually everyone would like to own. Obviously, not all the price increase was due to the stock split; a strong up market certainly helped, but in this case, the split called attention to the stock.

Price Weakness

It is not unusual to see some price weakness either after a split announcement or shortly after a payment date. Any number of things can cause a price to drop. For example, speculators could be exiting and taking profits, especially if the price has been flat for a time. Some investors might fear that the price action is over and expect a drop, and they would rather sell too soon than too late. Obviously, others see this price weakness as a buying opportunity, and they are the investors who drive the price upward.

THEY DON'T ALWAYS GO UP

Boeing is a fairly well known aviation products company in the United States. The company announced a 2-for-1 stock split in February 1997. As shown in

FIGURE 18-1

Positive split, Colgate Palmolive Company (NYSE: CL), 1997–1998.

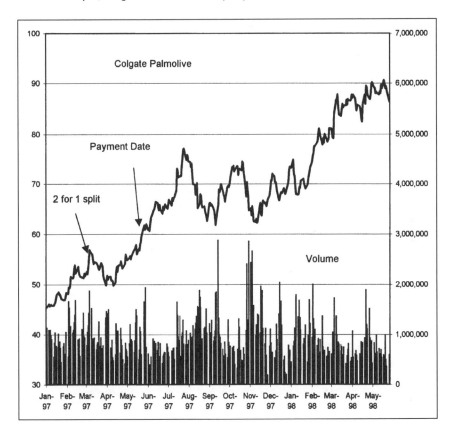

Figure 18–2, although there was a slight price increase, it didn't last long. A similar phenomenon occurred with the payment date in June. The stock ran up, peaked, and then came back down. The price then entered into a long-term downtrend with strong volatility, moving up and down as much as $5 to $10.

The Boeing speculators and contrarians pushed the price back and forth in a price tug-of-war. By May 1998, the price was down about $3 from the split announcement of February in the previous year. Although it can easily be argued that the price of Boeing might have suffered greater weakness without the stock split, the greater point is that Boeing's price did not significantly rise with the split.

WHY DO COMPANIES HAVE STOCK SPLITS?

Ordinarily, the reason a company decides to split their stock is to make it more attractive for investors to purchase. The logic here is that more people will buy the

FIGURE 18–2

Split with price weakness, Boeing Corp. (NYSE: BA), 1997–1998.

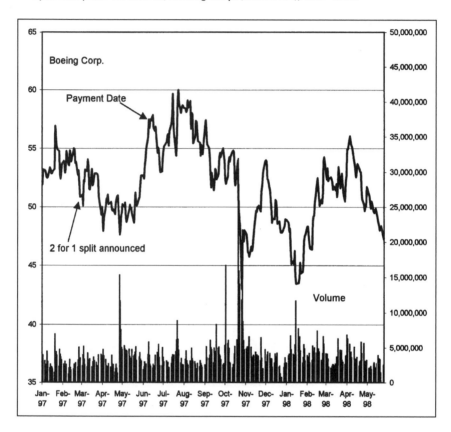

stock at $30 rather than $60. Obviously, as more people buy the stock at the lower price, the stock will rise in price. The split makes the stock more affordable to individual investors. Whereas a $120 price might be too high for many, a $60 or even $30 price will get them to buy the stock. However, there is no assurance that stock will continue to rise in price after the split. Just because the stock splits does not mean that it will rise in price after the split. Many times a stock price declines in price after a split, which can be true particularly if a stock splits more than once in a year.

Another reason for a company to have a stock split is to make more shares available, thereby broadening its stockholder base. The stock becomes somewhat more marketable and liquid. Somehow, positive publicity also fits into the stock split scenario. A company might use a stock split announcement to soften the blow of some negative news. On the other side of that coin, a company might use other good news (positive earnings) to soften the blow of a reverse stock split.

NOT ALWAYS 2 FOR 1

Not all stocks split 2 for 1. Some other frequent ratios for stock splits are 3 for 1, 3 for 2, and 5 for 4. However, regardless of the ratio used, the stock price will decline, the par value[2] will decline, and the amount of shares outstanding will increase directly in proportion to the amount of the split. Splits do not give the investor something for nothing in terms of financial gain. Splits do not make a company better or more financially sound.

WHY DOES THE PRICE RISE?

A price can rise for many reasons, due to pressure from one or several factors combined. There are still beginning investors who don't realize the price is adjusted to the split. Brokers often hear the confused and complaining phone calls asking what made the price drop so suddenly, especially on a 3-for-1 split. Whereas this group is small, it is part of the picture. Speculators buy either before or soon after an announcement because they believe the price will rise. These short-term traders pick an early exit price at which they will take profits. Their actions account for much of the price weakness that appears shortly after many splits, where they sell. Investors in general still believe the publicity that a stock split is good news for a company. Some investors believe, erroneously, that it's easier for a stock to double when the price has been lowered, even though many studies have shown this to be incorrect. Although, the stock does become more affordable for the individual investor, a forward split does nothing to add real value to a company.

Reverse Stock Split

One of the primary reasons for the forward split of a stock is to lower the market price. The opposite of a forward split, the purpose of a *reverse stock split* is to raise the market price. Companies believe that raising a price will make the stock more attractive for trading. Commonly, reverse splits are 1 for 3, 1 for 10, or 1 for 20, but they can be any quantity. In the 1-for-10 situation, 1 share of the new stock is received by the shareholder for every 10 shares owned. Instead of having the original amount of, say, 100 shares, an investor ends up with 10 shares, but the new price is 10 times higher.

Reverse splits are often considered the death knell for a company, but that is not always the case. Some companies reorganize and pull themselves together to become successful. One of the major difficulties is the selling by disappointed investors. Even though the reverse split significantly increases the market price, active selling frequently hammers it back down. To counteract this tendency,

---

2. With publicly traded stock, par value is more of an identifier than it is a financial concern.

companies will sometimes try to time a reverse split announcement to coincide with good news. A positive earnings report, followed by an "oh, by the way, we're reverse splitting 1 for 3," can stop some of the shareholders from leaving.

Reverse Splits Are Turnarounds

Sometimes reverse splits are speculative turnaround situations. Individual investors should be very careful to learn as much as possible about the company and develop some understanding as to why the chances of recovery are good. Investors may sell the stock for a tax loss or put it in the back of the portfolio. By some miracle it might recover in a few years; if not, investors may take the tax loss later.

STOCK SPLIT INVESTING

Over the past 20 years various studies have gone to great lengths to show that forward stock splits are positive events in about 50 percent of the cases. Looking ahead, about half of the companies do well for the following 6- and 12-month period. More recently studies are showing that forward stock splits are positive for good companies. Of course, a strong economy and bull market help. And that is the main problem with any study concerning the effects of a forward stock split: It is impossible to determine how much of the price growth is due to the split, how much is due to growth, and how much is due to a strong market. All of these factors work together to increase the stock's market price.

GOOD PUBLICITY

It's certain the company doesn't mind the positive free publicity. Could it be that Microsoft knew about the antitrust charges approaching and wanted the positive publicity of a 2-for-1 stock split to moderate some of the negative impact caused by the bad news? It's possible, but the company shouldn't be condemned for trying to protect their shareholders.

Splits can be traded short term, but it's difficult and high risk to do so. The price swings are usually too shallow or too fast for an individual investor to take profitable action. The investor can easily end up being whipsawed on both sides. Sometimes there aren't any price swings.

BE PRUDENT, BE NEUTRAL

The prudent approach is to treat forward splits as neutral events. If the company is a good investment and the lower price after the split makes it a viable candidate for the portfolio, buy the stock. If a price weakness appears after the stock splits, all the better to save some money.

CHAPTER 19

Institutions Show Where the Action Is Now

"Any stock in too many institutional portfolios or the subject of excess advisory bullishness should be suspect. Some day a majority will want to take profits."

Gerald M. Loeb

There are two considerations regarding institutional investing. First, can the small individual investor compete with the big money managers, and second, should individuals select or avoid stocks owned by large institutions?

DAVID AND GOLIATH

Institutional investors are the professional money managers for corporations, pension funds, mutual funds, and other investment companies. Their strategies may be long term or short term, and they implement these strategies by moving the market by buying and selling stock. Fund managers might do their own analysis or hire others to do the basic analysis for them. Every business day they deal with large amounts of money. Obviously, they have advantages not available to the individual investor. Possibly the biggest advantage to the institutional investor is the large amount of money available to them. Because of the large amount of money, institutional investors can make larger trades, thereby profiting from small price moves, and they can afford to make more mistakes.

When it comes to analysis, the only advantage held by the institutional investor is possibly experience. According to securities laws, information is made available to virtually everyone at the same time. The only exceptions are corporate insiders who must report their transactions to the Securities and Exchange Commission.[1]

Institutional stock traders aren't always right. In fact, they are frequently wrong. Peter Lynch, the former legendary fund manager for Fidelity's Magellan Fund, refers to them as "the blundering herd:"

> A sizable faction of this Thundering Herd could even be called the Blundering Herd. I can say that with confidence, having ridden with the Blundering Herd on more occasions than I care to admit.[2]

Lynch knows much about institutional investors and the things they do to make money through investing. Professional, institutional investors now dominate the investing markets. Lynch believes this fact often leads people to believe (incorrectly) that the individual has no chance in the stock market. Amateur investors now have improved chances for success in the market if they do their homework and know their companies well. As Lynch puts it:

> He or she can take an independent tack by zigging when the Herd zags and buying stocks that the Herd has overlooked, and especially the ones that the Herd has recently trampled. What holds them back is the inferiority complex they've gotten from mistaking a cattle drive for the Atlanta Braves.

This is reminiscent of Jessie Livermore's philosophy of winning big when you know you're right, as described back in Chapter 2. The thundering-herd analogy possibly refers to the earlier days of America, when cattle drives were used to deliver beef to market. Drovers would work hard to keep the herd calm and quiet. Large groups of cattle tend to excite easily and stampede mindlessly off in one direction, just as investors in their panic selling.

NOT LIKE THE BRAVES

Lynch likes the Atlanta Braves. As a professional baseball team, they know what they're doing, at least most of the time. It's the clueless cattle who represent the actions of institutional investors when the stock market goes crazy. Thanks to good public relations work, many individuals believe the professionals know what they're doing, all the time. The fact is, the professionals don't always know. They do make mistakes—big ones. The belief still exists and, according to Lynch, causes many individual investors to develop an "inferiority complex."

---

1. See also Chapter 7.
2. Peter Lynch, "Besting the Blundering Herd" 93/01, Worth OnLine, http://www.worth.com/articles/PL0.html. Peter Lynch retired in 1990 from managing the Magellan Fund, the best-performing of all mutual funds over a 15-year period.

The inferiority complex can cause investors to do three self-destructive things:

1. Imitate the professionals, buying "hot" stocks or trying to "catch the turn" in IBM
2. Become "sophisticated" and invest in futures, options, or options on futures
3. Buy what they've heard has been recommended by a magazine or by one of the popular financial programs

Information on what the pros think is so readily available that the celebrity tip has replaced the old-fashioned tip from Uncle Harry as the most compelling reason to invest in a company (as discussed in Chapter 2).

Catching the turn with IBM or any stock is coming up against stiff competition—professionals who can be profitable for an eighth or can afford to take the loss if they miss. Futures, options, and so on, can be an even faster spin with which to lose money. As for stock tips, some are good, some are bad, but most are old, and the opinion could have changed more than once by the time the investor takes action. They should never be the only reason for selecting a stock.

THE INDIVIDUAL'S EDGE

Instead of becoming self-destructive, take advantage of special investing edges that individuals have. Two kinds of investor's edges are too often overlooked by investors: first, the *on-the-job edge*, in which the investor has a working relationship with an industry and related companies with whom he or she conducts business. The other is the *consumer's edge*, with which the individual investor can capitalize on his or her experiences in, for example, restaurants, airports, and shopping malls.

Thus individuals have advantages from what he or she does for a living and what he or she does for fun, such as shopping as a consumer. Investing in the stock of an employer or a competitor makes sense. Many times, the competitor is the better selection, and there is less chance of being too forgiving if things don't turn out as expected.

As a first rough screen, going shopping can provide a whole list of possible investment opportunities. Which stores have great products and great service? Do they look as though they plan to be around for a while? Do the stores have several customers? Are the customers browsing or buying?

Make a list of the best stores, and do some background research. Select those with good-looking fundamentals, a reasonable price, and a great-looking future. Buy the stock, and watch for new developments. According to Lynch, of the 20 top-performing stocks on the New York Stock Exchange in the last decade, no fewer than six—Home Depot, Circuit City, the Gap, Wal-Mart Stores, Liz Claiborne, and Dillard Department Stores—have been under the noses of millions

FIGURE 19-1

Individual's edge, Wal-Mart Stores (NYSE: WMT), 1996–1998.

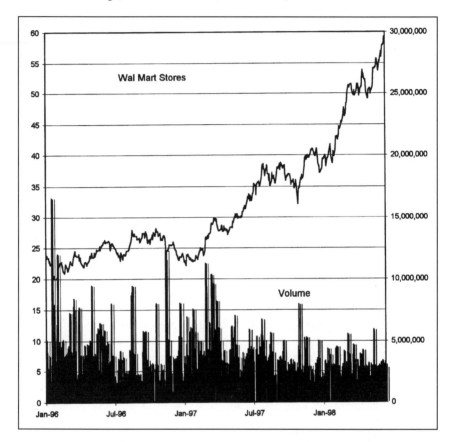

of shoppers who, if they had paid attention to the popularity of these enterprises, could have profited from their edge. Also, investors had time to choose. It regularly takes 10 or 15 years for a business to expand across the country, as more investors become aware of it, before the Wall Street professionals catch on.

Even though Lynch's comments were made in 1993, Wal-Mart Stores had a rocket behind it in 1997 through 1998, as it shot from the low 20s to more than $59 a share (Figure 19–1). By the time the stock reached that high price, institutions had grown to 1,485, or 38.2 percent, of the outstanding shares.

Whether the herd is thundering, stumbling, or just rumbling, it can be a distinct advantage to be in front of it, unlike the cattle herds of days long gone. Being ahead of the herd in the stock market can bring a lot of quick profit. Following the herd can be a different story. Pick the good-quality stocks, the companies with good value that the herd is likely to stumble across, hopefully in the next few months.

HOW MUCH INSTITUTIONAL OWNERSHIP?

It is an often-stated belief that 20 to 30 percent institutional ownership of a company's stock is an enviable situation. The institutions like it; therefore, it must be a good stock. Although a certain amount of institutional ownership of a stock can be an advantage, like the difficulties encountered by the sorcerer's apprentice, it is possible to have too much of a good thing.

The problem lies in sudden sellouts and profit taking. Stocks with large institutional ownership might have adequate shares for trading in normal, steady markets, but markets can change suddenly. If 40 or 50 percent of the stockholders are institutions and they begin selling, their quick exit can be devastating to the stock price.

How Much Is Too Much?

To begin with, it's not as easy to find stocks without institutional ownership anymore. It is estimated that institutions own at least 50 percent of the entire stock market. So how much is enough, and what constitutes too much institutional ownership? If the problem caused by institutions is price volatility, perhaps that should be the issue rather than amount of ownership. Professional fund managers have long been accused of taking money away from individual investors, in ways similar to the Disco Unlimited scenario. Does it happen? Absolutely. Is it legal? Yes, most of it is, as part of a free and open market. Is it manipulation? Yes and no. Sometimes it is clearly and easily defined price manipulation, and that is illegal. The authorities usually jump on such activities. Other times it's not as clear. In a free and open market, it is virtually impossible to stop or control all price manipulation. The individual investor has a choice of either avoiding the volatile stock or going along for the speculative ride when the price starts to move.

Selling in Up Markets

Selling of heavily institutionally owned stock could occur in a strong up market. Sometimes even a company that is fundamentally sound, that has satisfactory earnings growth, and that is 50 to 60 percent owned by institutions can experience a sell-off in a market rally. If the stock is not participating in the rally and shows light volume, with few buyers or sellers, some institutions could become nervous and start to sell. Financial markets are tightening their focus on the short term. If a stock is not matching the pace, they sell. Many believe the focus is too much on the short-term result.

> The United States economy and financial system suffer from "short-termism," an affliction caused by a lack of attention to long-term economic performance. Financial markets put pressure on corporate managers to focus too much on quarterly profits and too little on patient investment for the long haul.[3]

3. Twentieth Century Fund, "Report of the Task Force," 1995, http://epn.org/tcf /xxspec03.html.

The market continues to rally, but the nonparticipant just sits in the institution's portfolio. Eventually the institutional holders decide to sell the nonparticipant and buy a stock with more action. Sellers quickly outnumber buyers, and the stock price drops, even though the overall market is still advancing.

Percentage Ownership

Some analysts claim that the percentage of institutional ownership is not as important as the number of institutions owning the stock. If 100 or 200 institutions own 60 percent of one stock, a problem will arise if they all sell at the same time. Obviously, no one can argue with that logic. However, there are three facts that somewhat offset the too-much-institutional-ownership debate:

1. Stocks with larger institutional ownership tend to be market leaders.

2. It is difficult to find a good stock that is not heavily owned by institutions.

3. If the institutions don't like a stock, significant price growth is unlikely.

Fidelity Sold Chrysler in 1996

Reuters reported that a group led by Fidelity Investments, Chrysler Corporation's second-largest shareholder and the country's biggest mutual fund manager, disclosed that it sold more than one third of its shares in Chrysler last month.[4]

So what happened to the stock? Take a look at the Chrysler chart in Figure 19–2.

With Fidelity selling, the price of Chrysler got clobbered, but not for long. The largest institutional holder sold a third of its holdings, and the stock dropped just over 40 percent. But look what happened when the announcement came out. Nothing. That's what happened—nothing. The press release was a big ho-hum on Wall Street. The price consolidated, then rallied back up to former levels and higher. It's a near-perfect illustration of what should happen in a free and open market. Even though the stock price was beaten down by institutions, it hesitated only slightly, then rallied above previous levels. By June 12, 1998, the price was up to 57¾, with a p/e ratio of 12.7. A total of 975 institutions owned 58.8 percent of the company's stock. The total return (price growth plus dividends) for 12 months stood at 68 percent. The three-year total return came in at a whopping 142.7 percent.

The institutional sell-off hurt Chrysler's price for the short term, but it did not appear to cause any harm for the long-term investor. Chrysler saw trading in the high 50s by June 1998.

---

4. Fidelity Sells Off More than One Third of Its Chrysler Holdings," *Paul Dever—The Auto Channel*, August 19, 1996.

FIGURE 19–2

Institutional selling, Chrysler (NYSE: C), 1996.

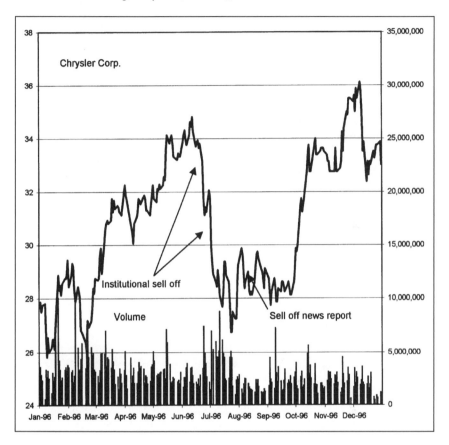

What about the Institutions?

With institutional investors accounting for half the market, avoiding them is nearly impossible. Even if it is possible to find a great stock before the herd thunders in, the price action will need the buying of the institutions to show significant movement. For the value investor, institutional ownership should be a consideration, but it should not be the sole criterion on which to decide.

Many companies have done well even though they have always had a high level of institutional ownership. Microsoft is a good example. Even now more than 35 percent of the shares are owned by institutions. AT&T has 44.4 percent institutional ownership. General Electric has an institutional ownership of 49.9 percent. General Motors has 64.2 percent institutional ownership. It's a safe bet to say that few hesitate to own shares in any of these companies just because the institutional ownership is higher than average.

What Is the Significance of Institutional Ownership?

Rather than trying to figure out whether the amount of institutional ownership is too high or too low, learn why the institutions like or dislike a stock. Why do they like General Motors and General Electric? Why don't more of them like Apple Computer? This type of analysis will give the individual investor a better idea of what gets the professionals excited. Understanding this can help with the stock selection process.

CHAPTER 20

Avoid Heavy Positions in Thinly Traded Stocks

The terms *heavy* and *thinly* can mean different things to different investors. A heavy position for one might be 5,000 to 10,000 shares; for another it could mean a few hundred shares. Thinly traded might be a stock that doesn't trade on some days, or it could mean a stock that trades less than 5,000 shares a day. The terms are not absolute; however, they should be considered together as *heavy position and thinly traded.*

YOU CAN BUY, BUT NOT SELL

A heavy position in a thinly traded stock might be easy to buy but difficult to sell. *Thinly traded* can refer to low volume or shares that do not necessarily trade every day. When they trade, they might trade several thousand shares or two hundred shares. Many stock traders consider anything less than 10,000 shares a day as thin.

Usually Low Priced

Thinly traded stocks also tend to have relatively low prices, often below $3 a share. A problem can arise in this way: Although it is relatively easy to buy 10,000 shares of a thinly trade stock, it could be difficult to sell the position. Selling might necessitate breaking the block into smaller segments of 5,000 or 3,000, or even 1,000 shares. All of those shares "hitting the bid" (pushing the price lower by selling) can be damaging to profits. The investor can also be charged additional commissions if the buys or sells cannot be executed on the same day.

Out-and-Out Fraud

Sometimes these "microcap" stocks are the subject of fraud. As the following suggests, the fraudulent activities are prosecuted, but the invested funds are not always restored to the investor:

> On Nov. 13, the U.S. Attorney in Brooklyn charged 13 people—brokers, Mob associates, and officials of two brokerage firms—with manipulating the prices of thinly traded micro-cap stocks. On the same day, in New Jersey, federal authorities announced a similar indictment. And then, on Nov. 25 [1997], came this bombshell: A federal grand jury in Manhattan handed up an indictment charging 19 people with multiple counts of racketeering and securities fraud.[1]

The stock exchanges and over-the-counter markets of the world are dedicated to creating markets that are "fair and orderly." They are serious about this because without such a policy, they will cease to exist. Prosecutions of illegal stock market activities are on the rise, but somebody always finds a new angle.

HERE'S HOW THEY DO IT

> Behind all the charges lies a simple fact that has received surprisingly little attention—even from regulators. Vast, interlocking networks of brokers are managing to obtain shares in hundreds of companies at dirt-cheap prices and are unloading them on the public. Among the people who make their living by pushing them on the public, the rogue brokers and stock promoters and mobsters, there's a name for these stocks. It is brutally simple: chop stocks.[2]

The word *chop* refers to the spread between the bid and ask prices making up a stock quotation. Normally the *bid* is what an investor will receive when selling, and the *ask* is the price an investor will pay. In a chophouse, the difference between the bid and ask is almost never anywhere near what the brokerage firm paid. Chop stocks are apparently obtained from corporate insiders, or offshore investors. The brokers pay a fraction of the prices appearing on the stock quote. The activity is fraudulent and illegal. The stocks are often worth only the pennies paid by the brokerage firm.

BE CAREFUL WHEN YOU ANSWER THE PHONE

Brokers gather business by making "cold calls," which means that they call people from a phone book, reverse directory, or other list and sell investments to peo-

---

1. "INVESTORS BEWARE: CHOP STOCKS ARE ON THE RISE: An inside look at how scamsters are taking billions from small investors," Updated December 4, 1997, by bwwebmaster, The McGraw-Hill Companies, Inc., 1997, http://www.businessweek.com/1997/50/b3557003.htm.
2. "INVESTORS BEWARE," McGraw-Hill, op. cit.

ple they have never met. This activity is not illegal in the United States, although it is illegal in some other countries. Most cold callers are reputable brokers just trying to make a living, and they are trying to meet the investor's objectives. However, the chop-stock brokers couldn't care less about objectives other than their own. They are trained for the quick, hard sell. Their philosophy is to "let the buyer beware."

Chop-stock brokers are difficult to control:

> The new promoters gain control over cheap stock, or dominate the markets for thinly traded stocks, and then push them on the public, using crews of brokers reporting to them.
>
> The NASD and Securities & Exchange Commission's highly visible campaign against small-stock abuses and the recent spate of criminal prosecutions have failed to have a significant impact on chop houses. Although regulators have shut down a handful of cold-calling powerhouses, the vast majority of questionable firms—totaling perhaps 200 nationwide, according to state securities regulators—remain untouched.[3]

USE CAUTION IN TAKING SPECULATIVE POSITIONS

Although thinly traded stocks might be worth a light speculative position of a few hundred shares, held for a long-term investment, they should probably not make up a significant position for short-term trading. Also, investors should learn about the company (make a visit) and not buy stock on the basis of some cold-calling "cowboy" who will sell anything to anybody. Brokers are required to know their client's investment objectives. Thinly traded stocks will not fit well into a non-speculative portfolio.

---

3 "INVESTORS BEWARE," McGraw-Hill, op. cit.

CHAPTER 21

There Are at Least Two Sides to a Story

Like a monster with two formidable heads, the news presents two sides of a story: one with prosperity and riches, the other with doom and gloom. The news media appear to have considered the stock market unpredictable for some time. Rather than take sides, the news media often take a more political route, in the middle. When a news story tells both sides of a story, it is not uncommon for the reader to agree with the part that best relates to the reader's background. As human beings, we tend to believe what we want to believe. An individual might claim that beliefs are based on logic and reasoning, but the fact is, beliefs tend to be founded more in emotion.

If one carefully approaches the investing message in the media, whether on television, in the newspapers, or on the Internet, one will notice that there are usually two opposing views presented. At least one of these views will be correct, in relation to future events.

Although at times the news media assume the stance of "you heard it here first," they usually try to avoid being on one side of anything that might be perceived as a prediction. They do not want to be on the wrong side of a prediction, which is why both possibilities are usually given.

One of the noble reasons this is done is to present both possibilities, to let the investor decide which "truth" works best. The important information is found in the basic facts of economic or technical indicators, political policies, and interest rates. Business trends, stock market data, and other factual pieces of information add to the picture.

Understanding and interpreting the facts and events can easily lead to differences of opinion. Although the news media enjoy pointing out opinion differences, their preference is to remain neutral.

FRESH NEWS

The most usable news is the most recently reported information. With the development of the Internet, information is available rapidly, nearly as soon as it is created. The market reacts swiftly to this instantly available news; however, the difference from former days is that the information is now available also to the general public. News reported at the end of the day may be of interest, but its investment value is questionable.

DEVELOPING NEWS

Stock traders, whether professionals or individual investors, watch as stories develop. Many of their transactions are based on the fresh news. Their actions make short-term trading very difficult for the individual who cannot watch the news. However, the longer-term investor has the advantage of observing the market results of the information.

Any Internet search engine will provide numerous stock market news sites just by typing in the words "Stock Market News." In addition, news and information can be located at the following Internet sites:

http://www.abcnews.com/sections/business/index.html

http://www.usatoday.com/money/mphotof.htm

http://cnnfn.com/

http://internetstockmarket.com/news/index.html

http://www.mfinance.com

http://quote.yahoo.com/

http://stocks.miningco.com/

Investment firm sites:

http://www.gs.com/

http://www.smithbarney.com/inv_up/

http://www.ms.com/

The following site contains a list of U.S. stock market connections:

http://www-users.cs.umn.edu/~cli/fn.html

CHAPTER 22

Follow a Few
Stocks Well

"It is easier to follow a few stocks well than it is to follow a well full of stocks."

S. A. Nelson

Following stocks can be interesting and exciting, or it can be tedious and frustrating. To many investors it is the information that starts their day. They thrill to poring over *The Wall Street Journal* or *Barron's* or *Investor's Business Daily* and other financial journals. Others spend a great deal of time "surfing the net" to find out what happened in the stock market and then learn everyone's opinion of why it happened. Some of these fastidious readers seldom invest in the stock market; they just enjoy the changes like watching a baseball World Series or perhaps the Super Bowl. They are the armchair investors who get enjoyment from seeing how the game plays out. For others, real investors, watching the market is not nearly as exciting as participating in its gains.

LEARNING THE BASIC SKILLS

To become skilled in stock watching or tracking, one must have firsthand experience. An investor will learn more by owning a stock for two weeks than he or she will by watching a stock for two years. The reason is simple: Ownership places money at risk. Risk of losing money greatly heightens one's attention. Losses that occur when the price drops are real losses. More importantly, gains that occur when the price rises are potential profits; thus the company and its price progress become a magnet to the investor's attention.

During the first few days of ownership, an investor is likely to learn more about the company than he or she will for the rest of the holding period. Keeping some of this enthusiasm can prove useful in making sound investment decisions.

Three Main Influences on Stock Prices

The price of a stock has essentially three main influences:

- Direction and strength of the overall stock market
- The current "play," or investing theme
- Earnings

At times, the direction and strength of the stock market are difficult to determine. However, reading opinions from newspapers, magazines, and other periodicals can provide considerable information on strength and direction.

Where's the Play?

The "play," or theme, is usually found in the industry group or sector such as technology, computers, the Internet, oil, health care, or waste management. In some industrires, the play can be illusive such as in fiber optics, drug rehabilitation, or lasers. The potential of lasers has excited people for more than 30 years, and yet few companies have accomplished much as "laser companies." Play can be further complicated by a company's diversification into other industries, such as tobacco companies' moving into food products.

Classifying stocks by theme, or play, helps to focus the attention on what happens with the group. When the news headline says "Stocks were up today on Wall Street, fueled by strength in the computer technology group," the computer investor's attention is drawn to the information. If OPEC members are fighting among themselves and producing too much oil, the prices of oil stocks drop. However, if oil-producing countries are in a cooperative mood, prices remain stable (or increase), oil company earnings increase, and the stock prices usually rise accordingly.

ANTICIPATE EARNINGS

The trick is to trade on the anticipation of earnings rather than on the specific earnings increase. Once the earnings increase (sometimes an earnings surprise) is announced, the price moves up immediately. Many investors buying at this point are actually buying the stock at inflated prices. When the reality of this becomes apparent, the price retreats. A small profit can quickly become a disappointing temporary loss.

Positive Earnings for Intel Corp.

Intel Corp. had an earnings surprise in April 1998 (see Figure 22–1):

> Corporate earnings season got under way in earnest Tuesday when Intel (NAS-DAQ: INTC) reported its first quarter results just after the close. And what a way to begin, by reporting profits well above expectations—81 cents a share compared with 72 cents estimated by analysts—Intel promises to add some more tone to an already solid market. Indeed, in after-hours trading, the stock was up $3 above its Tuesday close of $76. (Money.com 4/15/98)

F I G U R E 22–1

Positive earnings surprise, Intel Corporation (NASDAQ: INTC), 1997–1998.

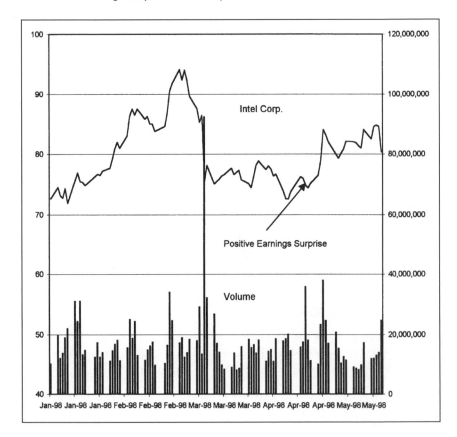

Trend Resumed

Not only did the price of Intel respond favorably to the earnings surprise, it also appeared to resume its former uptrend after wandering aimlessly for a month and a half. There appears to have been some selling during this period, and the volume increased on price declines. The selling stopped after the positive news, but the volume could be a point of concern as it is lower than expected. Notice how the volume was higher during the January through February uptrend. However, the volume in the April through May price move is higher on price advances and lighter on price declines, and that's positive.

Where the price of Intel goes from this point depends on the anticipation of whether the company can sustain earnings performance. The impact of earnings tends to be a long-term influence unless something very negative occurs.

Negative Surprise: 3-M

Just as a positive earnings surprise can push a price higher, a negative earnings surprise, coming in below expectations, can force a price lower. The financial crises in Asia, developing in the late 1990s, impacted U.S. companies that were dependent on foreign sales. In December 1997, Minnesota Mining & Manufacturing (3-M) announced that earnings would not meet expectations.

> NEW YORK (CNNfn)—When research and manufacturing giant 3-M announced Wednesday that quarterly earnings would be unexpectedly low, it blamed sustained weakness in Asian markets for the slump.[1]

Price Took a Hit

The stock price of 3-M took a quick $10 hit, followed by an additional $4 down (Figure 22–2). Even though the price had this decline, notice the quick recovery. The price hit support just above $80 a share and began a new uptrend. It will likely find price resistance between $95 and $104 a share, just because it found resistance at those levels previously. The volume is similar to former levels, but since the price is moving upward, there are more buyers here than sellers.

Even with the lowered earnings report, it's obvious that many investors anticipate improvement and found the price weakness a buying opportunity. The anticipation and a strong market started 3-M on a price recovery road in less than two months.

PRICE-EARNINGS RATIO

Price-to-earnings ratios are frequently discussed as a shorthand analysis of a company's current value. Although the concept has some validity, the analysis

---

1. Cable News Network, Inc., 1997.

F I G U R E   22–2

Negative earnings surprise, 3-M (NYSE: MMM), 1998.

should go further. By comparing a p/e ratio to previous levels or an average, as shown in Table 22–1, one can determine if it is currently high or low.

The most recent Intel p/e ratio of 23 is obviously on the higher side as shown by previous history. In the past five years, the lowest p/e ratio was 7.29 and the highest was in 1997, at 24.01. A p/e of 23 makes it the second highest in five years. Since a recent positive earnings surprise caused the stock price to rise, it is fair to say that buyers are anticipating further earnings growth with Intel's stock.

A p/e ratio of 23 for 3-M, as shown in Table 22–2, is also on the high side; in fact, it is the second highest, and only 23.69 back in 1996 was higher. The lowest p/e for the five years was 15.57 in 1997. The negative earnings surprise had some impact, but the stock price began to recover soon after the correction caused by the news.

Most investors think of a p/e ratio as the current per share market price divided by current annual earnings per share. If XYZ Company earns 25, 30, 45, 50 cents per share for each of four consecutive quarters, the earnings per share (eps) for the year is $1.50 per share. If the current market price for XYZ Company is $34.00, the p/e ratio would be 23. That's a result of the price being divided by the annual earnings. These are the p/e ratios that appear in the daily and weekly newspapers, known as the "trailing earnings per share." Investors use the figure as one of the factors for a quick analysis of value.

Several Wall Street analysts make an estimate of earnings-per-share growth, projecting it out a couple of years. They will look ahead at potential sales growth, profit margins, and tax rates to project the future earnings per share. They then consult with the company to check and refine the estimates.

T A B L E 22–1

Intel Corp. (INTC)

Recent p/e ratio: 23 (5/15/98)

Relative p/e ratio:
    Industry: Semiconductors   24.46
    Sector: Technology   38.41
    S&P 500 p/e ratio   29.23

Year	1997	1996	1995	1994	1993
High p/e	24.01	22.57	18.13	14.04	14.27
Low p/e	14.80	7.94	7.29	10.70	8.21
Year-end p/e	16.54	20.88	13.13	12.20	11.91

T A B L E 22–2

Minnesota Mining and Manufacturing (3-M) Company

Current p/e ratio: 23 (5/15/98)

Relative p/e ratio:
    Industry: Conglomerate   28.27
    Sector: Conglomerate   28.27
    S&P 500 p/e ratio   29.23

Year	1997	1996	1995	1994	1993
High p/e	20.53	23.69	22.46	20.02	22.43
Low p/e	15.57	16.90	16.31	16.17	18.64
Year-end p/e	15.97	22.90	21.34	18.71	20.85

Estimated earnings per share are also available to the individual investor:

Estimated earnings per share, Seger says, is the preferred method for calculating a company's P/E ratio. Publications such as Zack's, Standard & Poor's, Nelson's and First Call compile projections from a dozen or more analysts, publishing the lowest, highest and average P/E ratio estimates and even the standard deviation.[2]

ANTICIPATION

Reading this information from the *Detroit News* gives one a clear idea of how important anticipation is for the professional analyst and investor. Basing price-earnings ratios on estimated earnings makes a kind of built-in anticipation. Analysts combine this information with financial strength analysis, and some analysts look at where the earnings growth will come from to arrive at price projections. Oftentimes these projected figures are quite accurate. Other times earnings surprises come along, and the figures must be recalculated.

A FEW GOOD STOCKS

It was 1902 when S. A. Nelson made the statement, "It is better to follow a few stocks well than to follow a well full of stocks." Nelson was an investor, a friend of Charles Dow, the founder of Dow, Jones, and Company; he was a publisher and an author of *The A.B.C. of Stock Speculation.* For many years he had watched investors knocking themselves out trying to analyze and track too many different stocks. When an investor analyzes too many stocks, it can lead to information overload.

Keeping up with daily changing events quickly becomes impossible, and many are whipsawed on both sides of a price move. They buy at the top of a frenzied move and become disillusioned as the price turns and falls. Finally, they sell out at the bottom, only to see the price rise again.

The solution to information overload is to learn a great deal about a small number of stocks, the potential winners. Whether following 3, 5, or 10 companies doesn't really matter; what matters is that the investor learns a lot about these companies. Understanding the information that will improve the price performance of these companies will enable the investor to select better winners.

---

2. "P-E Ratios Can Be Figured Differently," detnews.com, Monday, December 29, 1997.

CHAPTER 23

Be Wary of Stock Ideas from a Neighbor

S. A. Nelson, author of the first book on the Dow theory (first published in the early 1900s), mentions the attraction of speculators to the stock market.[1] Charles Dow in 1900, also commented on the tendency of individuals to invest in a wildly speculative stock, taking more risk than they would with their own businesses.[2] Even today, it is probable that every stockbroker has heard many investors admit interest in a speculative issue of stock because "a neighbor told them." These stock recommendations can come with the best intentions, but they should be viewed with considerable reservations.

STOCK TIPS

The idea might be a good tip or it might have been a good tip. Truly good stock ideas usually don't wait around for the investors to make their move. By the time the friend or neighbor has spread the word, it could be too late to take any action. Learning more about the tip is a better strategy. Even though timing is often of the essence, answering a few questions can help to prevent a costly mistake. Where did the idea originate? Could it be a rumor? Did a broker recommend the stock? Did the idea appear in a financial journal?

Sometimes a tip can quickly be traced to a reliable source; other times the source is illusive. The frustrating fact is that the greater the reliability of the

---

1. S. A. Nelson, *The ABC of Stock Speculation*, New York: Fraser Publishing.
2. Founding father of Dow Jones & Company, publisher of *The Wall Street Journal*.

source, the less time there is to take action. If the tip was discussed in *The Wall Street Journal*, *Investor's Business Daily*, or *The New York Times*, the action has probably occurred.

Although there are times when the action just gets going as a rumor is discussed, it is the exception. If the source of the idea is a fellow worker or indeed a neighbor, some friendly conversation might shed valuable light on the insight. Was the source a vision, a dream, wishful thinking, or something else? Spending time to ask can save money.

It is also important to find out the nature of the tip. How speculative is the tip? Is it short term (a buyout rumor, by whom?)? Is it more long term (a merger, new contracts, new revenue growth)? Is the stock price less than $10 a share? Is the stock marginable? If the stock cannot be bought on margin, then the number of other investors who will be interested is limited.

Buyout rumors have a way of suddenly appearing and disappearing. Sometimes they are based on sound information, and other times they are pure fabrication. The truth sounds as good as the falsehood. The stock price can rise just the same. There are also rumors that turn into announcements, only to run into a stone wall. One of the most damaging in recent years was a takeover of UAL Corp. The rumor became an announcement in 1989, and the buyers were unable to obtain financing in October. The stock price fell, taking the rest of the market down also.

The old Wall Street saying "Buy on the rumor, sell on the news" appears again. To which, one might add, "But leave some money on the table" (see Chapter 7). Tip investing is highly speculative and subject to great risk. Sometimes positive rumors actually cause a decline in the stock price.

PAN AM IN THE 1990s

In 1990, Pan Am became the subject of a rumor. A $2 to $3 stock for a year, it handily ran above $4 when delighted sellers pounded it back down. After about the third such rumor, the price began to lose ground as each new "buyout" entered the rumor mill. This was probably because of an abundance of sellers' having limit sell orders just above the trading range. As the stock price rose, these limit sells were activated, which drove the price back down.

After assessing the source and nature of the tip, the investor should also assess the company by itself. Is it worth buying without a tip? Is research available on company fundamentals? What is likely to happen if the rumor doesn't materialize? If the stock is considerably more speculative than the investor would normally buy, it should probably be avoided. There are enough good rumors in higher-quality stocks to keep an investor busy.

DECISION MAKING

Some questions to ask in reaching a decision are the following:

How does the purchase fit into the investment strategy?
How much risk currently exists with other investments?
What proportion of the portfolio is in the risk category?

When assessing a stock tip, consider how the stock fits into the broader investment strategy and goals. If some funds have been established as speculative money, by all means make use of them. However, limiting and controlling risk whenever possible are always prudent.

RISK AND REWARD

Investing in the stock market always has an element of risk. Some risk is low and often is lessened over time. Other risk is high and is strictly short term. Greater risk does not always bring greater rewards. Before investing in high-risk, speculative situations, it is worthwhile to ask a few extra questions and do some research on the initial source of information. This will not eliminate risk, but it can allow you to enter an investment being aware of the risk—an awareness that may prompt you to go in another direction.

CHAPTER 24

Get Information before You Invest, Not After

$\mathbf{M}$any complicated aspects of our lives could be clarified by searching for related information before taking action. Asking why and digging deeper is often viewed as an inconvenience because it calls for analysis, thought, and the formation of a conclusion. These activities take time and energy, and they can lead to confusion and frustration. To avoid these problems, many depend on the wisdom of others or adopt a shoot-from-the-hip approach when dealing with frustrating situations in the stock market.

Depending entirely on the wisdom of others or shooting from the hip can lead to misunderstandings. Misunderstanding can cause bad timing or poor strategies. Investment advice can be helpful, but it can be even more useful as a point of reference rather than being accepted as a total approach.

In the stock market, the odds of doing well are improved for the investor who becomes familiar with the current action of the market and the particular stock of interest. Becoming familiar with the action can be accomplished by asking why: Why is the market making this move? Why is the stock an attractive purchase now?

MARKET MOVES

The stock market is a continuous auction, with the same product being bought and sold every business day. If there are more buyers than sellers, the market and prices of individual stocks rise. If there are more sellers than buyers, prices fall. It's that simple.

If it's so simple, why does it seem so complicated? Why are all these investors buying and selling stock? If they're investors, shouldn't they all be buying and holding stock for its investment value? Why are people surprised when the stock market drops a few hundred points? Does a severe market correction mean the economy will take a nose-dive? The newscasters always say the stock market forecasts the economic situation six months to a year away. So what gives?

ANTICIPATION

The most important fact to remember is that the stock market always trades in anticipation of future events. Often investors are looking ahead 6 to 12 months, but not always. If the Dow Industrial Average is down 150 points or more, the major, professional investors couldn't care less about what might happen in 6 to 12 months. They are concerned only with what might happen in the more immediate future, that being the next 10 minutes. The faster the market drops, the shorter their focus becomes. The believers of doom and gloom busily pat themselves on the back for being correct, and those who know better take a more moderate stance. Thankfully, it usually takes more than an overreaction in the market to cause an economic recession.

REAL, IMAGINED, AND FABRICATED FACTORS

A real factor motivating stock market buyers or sellers is money—specifically, the availability of money. Money availability, as it changes with a movement of the interest rates or the earnings of corporations, is one of the strongest factors of stock market movement.

An imagined factor can be the respected opinion of an economist or market analyst as to the current strength or weakness of the stock market.

A fabricated factor is the merciless hammering of computerized sell programs. The sells are often implemented with the intent of testing market strength by pushing the market down as far as possible. That point is reached when buyers enter the scene and stop the decline.

OCTOBER 1989

On Friday, October 13, 1989, these market factors came into play simultaneously when a buyout of UAL Corp. failed to obtain the necessary loan approvals (money availability). Some market analysts said this was a sign of further tightening of money (imagined), and the computer sell programs were activated (fabricated).

F I G U R E 24–1

Dow Industrial and Transportation Averages, 1989.

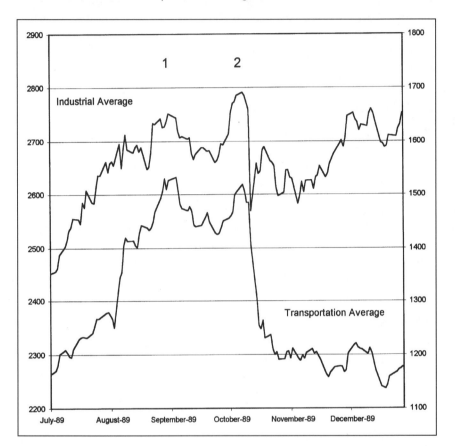

The effect was to drop the Dow Industrial Average by more than 190 points. Fortunately, the Federal Reserve announced that it stood ready with an influx of cash if it was needed by the stock market. Confidence returned, and the market's retreat was halted. By the end of the year, the market had regained most of the loss, and the events of October 13 were referred to as "a sharp correction."

Was this "correction" predictable? Not totally. However, there were signs of weakness developing in the market, as seen in the market trends and other indicators shown in Figure 24–1.

During this time the Dow Transportation Average moved up due to several takeover rumors. The effect on the market is easy to see. Only one of the rumors concerned UAL Corp., but it was the key to what was happening in both the transportation and industrial averages. The increase in the industrial average did not have the fuel of takeover rumors; therefore its increase was less pronounced than that of the transports. The industrials were also vulnerable to a sell-off in the transportation average.

As shown by the chart, both the industrials and the transports peaked on Tuesday, October 10, and began to fall. They continued to fall lower during the remainder of the week. To the technical analyst, the chartist, the falling off throughout the week meant that the Dow Industrial Average had formed a "double top," which was confirmed by the transportation average. They were likely the ones selling off before the breakout.

The announcement stating that financing for the UAL acquisition was rejected came as an important economic signal. Many analysts said this was the beginning of tighter money. It was also stated that this rejection could lead to higher interest rates in the near future.

Until this signal, money was easily attainable in almost any quantity. An earlier leveraged buyout of another airline, NWA Corp., went through without a hitch. Resistance to borrowing easy money sent a shiver through Wall Street. It meant tighter money and higher interest rates. Higher interest rates means lower earnings for companies. Lower earnings expectations means the stock market could have a sell-off. Lower corporate earnings usually means lower stock prices. Many investors decided to pull out of the market, and the Dow Industrial Average fell.

The investor who noticed the turn in the stock market by observing the daily decline in the Dow Industrial and Transportation Averages and listened to the market opinions given by many analysts before October 13, would likely have taken some protective action earlier in the week. Market anticipation had been fueled by takeover plays, starting shortly after the first quarter of 1989. Once the takeover theme came to a sudden halt, so did the market rally. The market correction was more severe than expected due to strong selling effects of programmed trading. Some would say the market became oversold, as shown by a quick recovery.

The Dow Industrial and Transportation Averages are just two of many market indicators that can help the investor understand more about the strength and direction of market moves.

STOCK MOVES: DOWN

Buying a car, a computer, or a new television, only to see it on sale the following week can be a big source of irritation. Of course, the same holds true for stocks. To pay $52 a share one day, then to hear some negative news and see a price of 42 the next week, is not a pleasant experience. If the investor's research and selection are valid, the price will probably recover and move to new highs. But the price damage on the way down can be difficult to endure. An interesting phenomenon can occur with a stock price that appears to keep on dropping

As the price declines, investors will appear to buy up shares at perceived bargain prices. If enough of these bargain hunters appear, they can stop the price halt, but often they are overpowered by sellers until the price hits bottom. *Bottom* is where the price stops declining and goes flat or begins to retrace its upward trend.

The reason for a price decline can be serious; lower earnings or estimates are predicted, the credit rating is lowered, or a possible lawsuit or tax problem has developed. The reason for a price decline might not be as serious—market correction, profit taking, employee stock distribution, or no news-related reason at all. Whatever the reason for a stock price move, it can be worthwhile to find out why it is moving before investing in it.

Information about a stock in question can be obtained from the news media, the Internet, or by calling the company directly. Calling the company might be difficult if hundreds of other investors are trying to do the same thing. Oftentimes calling the stockbroker or checking a news service on a computer will provide the answer. Learning why a stock is declining in price can enable the investor to form a strategy of buy, hold, or sell.

STOCK MOVES: SIDEWAYS

Why isn't the stock price moving? If other similar stocks and the market are doing well, there is a reason for a lack of movement in a given stock. Has there been bad news recently that has created a lack of investor interest, or is the stock currently a gem, waiting to be discovered?

Although rare, undiscovered gems can experience dramatic price surges with even a small amount of publicity. Some investors follow a strategy of seeking out these gems, but often they end up with well-run companies that the market doesn't like. Usually they are basically good companies with limited growth potential. Major investors search for companies with virtually unlimited growth potential.

STOCK MOVES: UPWARD

Why a stock price is moving upward is often important to investors only if they currently don't own it, but they would like to be in on the action. "Why" becomes extra important to these investors. The increasing price makes these investors nervous. No one wants to buy at the top price and watch the stock fall back to previous levels. Many times they will hesitate, waiting to see if the price drops and becomes more attractive.

When these nervous investors investigate the reason behind a price move, they are better able to make a decision and not waste time wondering. Owners of a rising stock price will do well to pick a selling point based on price and earnings. As the price continues to escalate, it is also prudent to plan a protective strategy.

Take the time to ask why. Make an inquiry into a stock move or market move. The information should be gathered before the investment decision is made and the action implemented. Then the information can be used for making better decisions and setting effective strategies. Asking "why is this happening" and finding an answer increases the odds of making a sound, profitable decision.

CHAPTER 25

Never Fight the Tape

Technical analyst Marty Zweig is an author and newsletter publisher and the creator of one of the early "basket funds" (Zweig Fund in 1986; and The Zweig Total Return Fund in 1988, followed by others).[1]

Three statements are credited to Zweig concerning the stock market—statements that contain general strategic wisdom. The concepts behind the statements have been with investors for many years, but Zweig has kept them in focus:

- "Never fight the tape."
- "The trend is your friend."
- "Never fight the Fed."

"The tape" is a term that goes back to earlier days, when the progress of the market and individual stocks was tracked by means of the Edison Ticker. It used the famous ticker tape. A series of symbols was communicated electronically to the tickers, which then perforated a paper tape in coded numbers and symbols. Business executives and interested investors had these stock tickers in their offices, where they could keep a close eye on the stock market.

The term "the tape" now refers to the current trend of the stock market or the price trend of an individual stock. "Fighting the tape" refers to investing contrary to the current trend.

---

1. Martin E. Zweig, *Winning on Wall Street,* revised and updated, New York: Warner Books, June 1997.

Price Trend

A price trend, once established, represents the current buying and selling sentiment of investors. If the sentiment is favorable and the stock price is rising, it will continue to rise until the sentiment and actions change. Even though a stock can rise above someone's perception of its current value, buyer sentiment can push the price even higher. No law or principle exists that says the stock must trade within a certain price range. Buying sentiment is caused by investor anticipation of improved earnings and price growth.

As a stock price runs unusually high, some skeptics say it is "overbought" and sell short the stock at the highest possible level. Yes, a stock price can rise high above its value based on income and earnings, but that does not necessarily mean the price will correct and fall back. Selling short near the top can be like stepping in front of a moving train. Momentum and increased attention can bring new buyers to the scene, pushing up the price even further.

THE TRAIN

When Microsoft Corp. began its steeper acceleration curve back in 1996, there weren't many opportunities for short selling. It was a train that few would step in front of, as the price kept moving up. A few weak areas appeared in mid-1996, and the following year (1997) also had a couple of weak areas. Recovery from price weakness was normally swift. It was a price trend that few would be willing to fight, in a stock market (the tape) that was going the same direction (see Figure 25–1).

MARTY ZWEIG

Here are Zweig's words: "I can't overemphasize the importance of staying with the trend in the market, being in gear with the tape, and not fighting major movements. Fighting the tape is an open invitation to disaster."[2]

Fighting the trend of a stock price is gambling, especially in a rising market. Strong rising markets in which the prices of some stocks double will often see the same prices double again. Investing counter to such strong markets could become costly. Usually, the more effective strategy is to observe the primary trend and invest in its direction (see Figure 25–2).

Although there is a highly specialized strategy used by the contrarian to invest against the trend, the approach requires considerable analysis and is extremely risky. Even contrarians look for signals of a turn in the trend before they take action. Again, the words of Zweig: "I absolutely and utterly refuse to fight a

---

2. Martin E. Zweig, op. cit.

FIGURE 25-1

Price trend, Microsoft Corp. (NASDAQ: MSFT), 1995–1998.

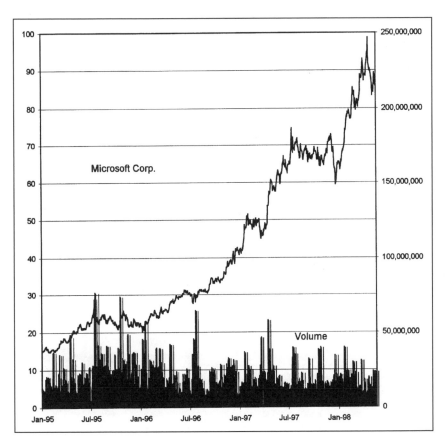

major trend in the market. I'll simply move with the tape even if it means being whipsawed every now and then."

"The Trend Is Your Friend"

The conclusions drawn from the preceding segment on "never fight the trend" are similar to those of "the trend is your friend." Momentum builds as stock prices move, especially on the upside. Investors continue to buy a stock as long as they believe the economy, the stock market, and corporate earnings will continue to grow at the present rate or improve. In a strong, stable economy, stock prices will continue to grow, even though the market experiences occasional corrections. Although the price of any stock will sometimes run ahead of earnings, the mar-

FIGURE 25–2

Price trend, Dow Industrial Average, 1994–1998.

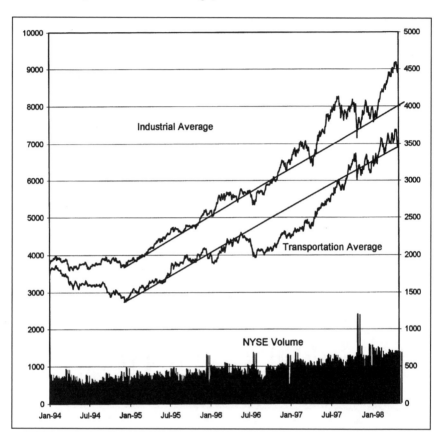

ket, and the economy, a stock should not necessarily be sold or sold short. In fact, with a strong stock situation, a price drop can be an excellent buying opportunity.

Zweig engages in complicated technical analysis to determine the momentum and strength of a trend. While his analysis enjoys the respect of the financial community, few investors have the time or patience to follow a complicated analysis system. However, investors can benefit by just understanding the basics of "never fight the tape" and thinking of the trend "as a friend."

Although we don't want to fight our friend the trend, trends can change. Signals can be seen in technical aspects, such as prices failing to reach new highs or declines in trading volume, and in fundamental aspects, such as slower earnings growth of a stock or a weakening of the market. Such financial information is readily available in newspapers, on television, and on the Internet. Following the daily financial news can help the investor understand the impact of changes on individual stock prices.

"Never Fight the Fed"

When interest rates rise enough, stock prices usually drop—that's a fact. On the other side, as interest rates drop, stock prices rise. Most stock prices move the opposite direction of interest rates. Corporations borrow money. When they borrow, they have to pay interest. The interest they pay comes from the earnings they hope will increase by borrowing money. When companies pay out more dollars in interest on loans, they obviously have less money in the form of earnings. Consequently, earnings have a direct relationship to the price of a company's stock. Essentially, when a company has higher earnings, the price rises. When the earnings are lower, the stock price declines. However, one must always remember that the stock market trades in anticipation of higher or lower earnings. The uncertainty of anticipation can cause periods of unexpected volatility.

INTEREST RATES

Many economic factors and philosophies influence interest rates. The primary source of influence is the action of the Federal Reserve Board (the Fed), which can influence the interest rates charged between banks borrowing funds from each other to meet their reserve requirements. The rate one bank charges another is called the *Federal funds rate,* or, more simply, *Fed funds* (Figure 25–3).

Notice how the Fed funds move with some fluidity. The daily change of interest rates in influenced by the buying and selling in the bond market, to some extent the action of the stock market, and also the current position of the Federal Reserve Board on the availability of money. Compare the daily movement of Fed funds to the more rigid moves of the Federal discount rate.

From a high of more than 19 percent to a low of just over 3 percent, the Federal discount rate has moved around in the last two decades. Back in the early 1980s, inflation was believed to be spiraling out of control. It's obvious now that was not the case. Inflation was brought under control and interest rates were forced down.

The Fed directly controls two important factors affecting interest rates: the Federal Reserve requirements and the Federal discount rate. The *reserve require-ments* are the dollar amounts required to be maintained in the individual banks (Figure 25–4). They do not change often. The *Federal discount rate* is the inter-est rate charged by the Fed to banks that borrow money directly from them. It is a direct link in the chain of interest rates and a main factor in determining the *prime rate,* the interest that commercial banks charge their largest borrowers. The Federal discount rate can be changed at any time, for any reason. It generally is changed an average of twice a year; however, the Fed is not limited as to the num-ber of times it can change rates.

The prime rate, being the interest rate charged by commercial banks to their larger borrowers, is frequently used as the base for calculating other consumer-

FIGURE 25–3

Fed funds, 1988–1998.

oriented interest rates. As the chart in Figure 25–5 shows, the prime rate bottomed out at 6 percent in 1992. It started up in 1994, which was part of the reason the stock market had a weak year. It peaked again at 9 percent, then dropped to 8½ percent.

The three rates—Federal discount rate, Fed funds, and prime rate—are set individually but influenced by changes in the other rates. Fed funds change daily; the others are realigned periodically. Small changes tend to have little effect on the stock market. Large changes upward can make the market decline, and large changes downward can cause the market to rise.

Interest rates appear to have inertia. Once in motion, they continue in motion for the next few months. When they settle back down, they tend to stay calm for a few months. The stock market can whip back and forth from day to day, but the basic interest rates move more slowly; this is especially true of the Federal discount rate and the prime rate.

Raised Interest Rates

When interest rates rise slowly and are being used to slow an overheating economy, it is a positive sign. Overproduction leads to a surplus of goods or a lack of customers to buy goods. Prices have to be reduced, thereby leading to deflation and economic stagnation. When interest rates can be raised gradually, they can help to prevent the economy from overheating. This is why it is possible to have stock prices rising while interest rates are moving up. Investors recognize the need to slow the economy, and they continue to buy stocks.

Lowered Interest Rates

If the economy is moving slowly and needs a boost, it seems as though nothing works better than to lower the interest rates (Figure 25–6). This action makes

F I G U R E 25–4

Federal discount rate, 1988–1998.

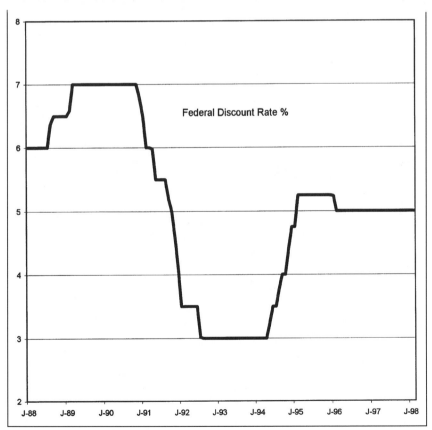

money available, thereby enabling companies to borrow and produce more goods. The stock market rallies at the news of lower interest rates. Investors believe it's a sign of a healthy, growing economy with a bright future.

Obviously there are times when the stock market rises, even as interest rates are rising, partly due to anticipation of the future. But virtually nothing stimulates the market like dropping interest rates. As interest rates were forced down from just under 10 percent in 1989 to the 3 percent level in 1993, the market moved ahead. Fears of an overheating economy in 1994 made the market uncertain, but rates peaked in 1995 at just over 6 percent and fell back slightly. Rates appeared to be under control. The stock market advanced as never before, rising more than 4,000 points in four years. It more than doubled. That's the kind of tape investors shouldn't try to fight.

F I G U R E 25–5

Prime rate, 1988–1998.

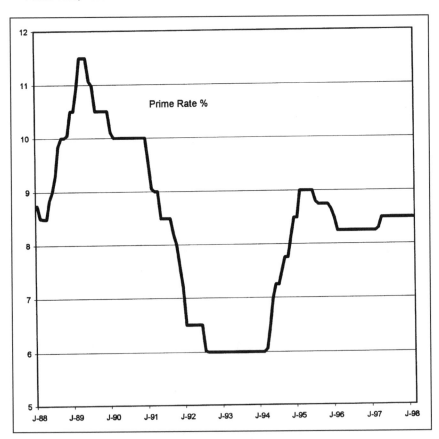

F I G U R E 25–6

Dow Industrial Average (monthly) and Fed funds rates.

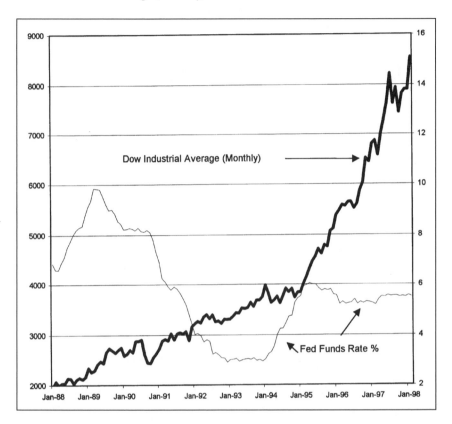

CHAPTER 26

Heavy Volume, the Price Rises—Light Volume, the Price Falls

On the surface, this seems to make sense. When more investors become interested in a stock, they buy. The volume increases. Less interest means lower volume. Although this is true in some situations, it is not always the case. Whether or not this is true depends on several factors including the current market strength and direction, as well as the strength and direction of an individual stock price.

To understand how volume may increase before prices increase, it is important to remember the existence of limit sell orders. Many times volume will suddenly increase; the price starts to increase and then falls slightly. Part of the reason for the decline is the presence of limit sell orders. Another possible reason is nervous stock traders who buy on the volume increase but don't see the quick price advance, and so bail out.

EXXON

Exxon, a well-known oil company, has had the industry's share of difficulties with low oil prices. Because it is a commodity, the supply of oil needs to be controlled in order to keep prices high. If too much is produced, the market becomes competitive and prices fall, which has a negative impact on prices.

Looking at the price and volume chart for Exxon in Figure 26–1, you can pinpoint occasions when increased volume precedes an increase in the share

F I G U R E 26–1

Price and volume, Exxon Corp. (NYSE: XON), 1997–1998.

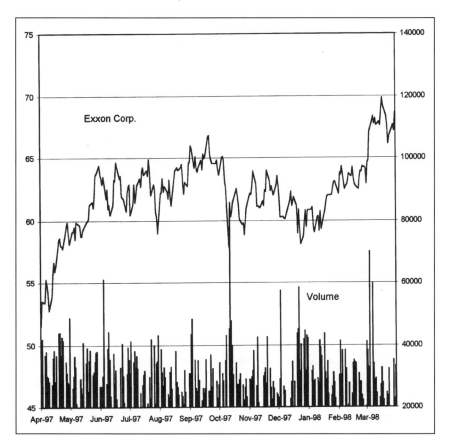

price. The volume increase in March through April 1997 is especially pronounced when compared to February. It increased from about 4 million shares a day to more than 6 million. The price did a quick $4 rally and fell back; then in mid-April it took off. The price climbed $13.75 by early June, then consolidated back and forth until February 1998. What did the volume do? It suffered a slow decline through December and then shot up in January. The price consolidation continued through January, but the high-to-low range kept narrowing, suggesting an approaching breakout. Here, the price rose more than $16 between February and May 1998. Those are significant price gains for a short time.

ON-BALANCE VOLUME

Individual one-day spikes can also be significant signals, but notice that many of them are increased volume on a dropping price. Because of this, the signals can become confusing. Some investors counteract the confusion by using *on-balance volume* by which they compare the volume to the price.

On-balance volume (OBV), developed by Joseph Granville, can be a helpful indicator. OBV creates a volume line along the bottom of a price chart and is easily constructed. Start with a number that is relatively high, such as 50,000. On the first day, if the close is positive, that day's volume is added to the 50,000 beginning number. If the day's close ends lower, subtract the volume. On up days, add the volume, and on down days, subtract the volume. The result creates a fluctuating line.

On-balance volume can show an approaching trend change. The belief is that "smart money" sells a security when it's near a top; and smart money buys near a low. When the other investors catch on to a stock's rise in price, volume will increase and the OBV line will increase rapidly and faster. On the other side, on-balance volume will start to decrease while the price is still rising, indicating that the smart money is leaving the stock.

The on-balance volume is also informative when it is decreasing while the price is increasing (diverging). A signal is generated that the rally may not be strong. When the price is declining and the OBV is increasing, the investor shouldn't become too bearish, because a reversal could be coming.

General Motors

Take a look at Figure 26–2 to see General Motors with its on-balance volume. In June 1997, there was a clear divergence as the OBV started a distinct uptrend while the price was declining. The price bottomed out at about $54.50 and headed upward to $71.50, which was reached in September. Notice that during August and the first part of September, the OBV was rather flat, with the price moving upward. Many would see this divergence as a weakness or even a sell signal. A false buy signal followed the divergence. The OBV began an uptrend in the last half of September, but although there was a brief price rally, the price kept dropping.

A clear buy signal appears in December when the stock price is still dropping, while the OBV is rising. The year 1998 is mostly flat for the on-balance volume, even though the stock price shows some advance. The divergence again suggests technical weakness in the 1998 rallies.

Although on-balance volume provides signals of approaching advances or declines in stock prices, it should not be the only indicator followed. As shown by the General Motors chart, false signals can appear; also, it doesn't necessarily signal every approaching price move.

FIGURE 26–2

On-balance volume, General Motors (NYSE: GM), 1997–1998.

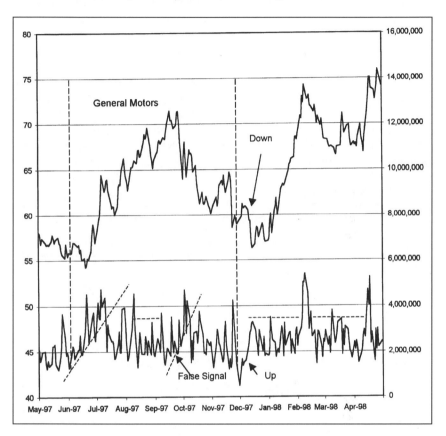

MARKET VOLUME

Volume as an indicator for individual stocks can be informative or misleading. However, volume as an indicator of the overall market can be significant. In general, the higher the volume, the greater the strength of the market move.

When there is a 100-point move on the Dow Industrial Average, the NYSE volume will normally spike to a higher-than-normal level. But it's not usually a spike that sends the signal; rather, it is a broader change. If the New York Stock Exchange volume has been averaging 500 million shares a day but then steadily increases to 600 or 700 million shares a day, the market moves. When the Dow Industrials move 100 points on the average or below the average volume, it is a sign of weakness. A market move on weaker volume indicates that many large investors are skeptical, which means that the likelihood of a reversal is high.

Take a look at the New York Stock Exchange volume chart in Figure 26–3 for September 1997 through January 1998. Although it's interesting to see the weakness before the October 1997 correction (the Dow Industrials dropped more than 554 points), much of the rest of the volume indicates strength. Volume surges are unlikely when they are already near record levels. There is a weakness during the last half of December 1997, but that is not unusual for December, when many traders are on vacation.

Volume in 1998 jumped above the 600 million share mark and stayed there during January. It's interesting to note that this time period contains several record volume days for the New York Stock Exchange, as shown in Table 26–1.

The tallest single spike on the chart shows the day after (October 28) the big correction in the Dow Industrial Average. October 29 had the second-largest volume, with the following day having the third-largest volume for that time pe-

FIGURE 26–3

Total daily volume, New York Stock Exchange, 1997–1998.

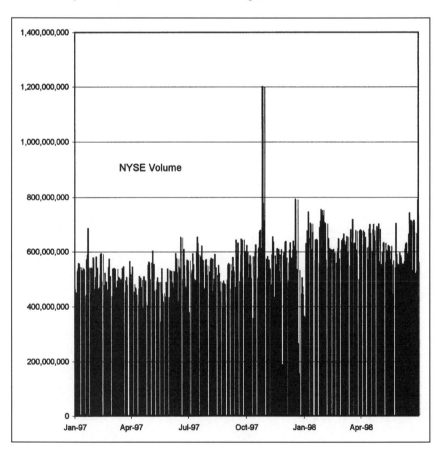

TABLE 26-1

New York Stock Exchange
Volume from October 28, 1997,
through January 28, 1998

Daily Volume	Date
1,201,347,000	10/28/97
792,946,000	12/19/97
776,331,000	10/29/97
754,111,000	1/29/98
745,003,000	1/9/98
711,969,000	10/30/97
710,903,000	1/28/98

Source: NYSE Data Library, nyse.com.

riod. These one-day volume records were accurate for the time of the chart. The strength coming back to the market after the October 1997 correction makes one wonder why the market corrected so sharply.

CHANGES IN VOLUME

Always look for changes in volume for clues to strength. Short-term and long-term changes both indicate strength, but the longer-term change is normally the most meaningful. In the short term, if the market rallies on weaker volume, the rally will not likely be sustained. If the market falls on light volume, it usually turns up fairly soon. Over the longer term, if the volume goes flat and then trends downward, it will often lead to a weaker market. The greatest strength is shown by an uptrend in a market index (Dow Industrial Average or Standard & Poor's 500 Index) and an uptrend in the volume. When these diverge, it often signals a change in direction.

CHAPTER 27

Buy on Weakness, Sell on Strength

$B_{uying\ on\ weakness}$—that is, when a stock price is declining—should take place prudently and after it has been determined that the company is still fundamentally sound. Many investors have had the unpleasant experience of buying a stock, that has dropped in price, only to see it fall further. How is weakness determined?

The price of a good stock in a relatively stable market will tend to move up in surges and then hesitate, sometimes even falling back slightly. It will often drift lower, looking for support from new buyers. When it finds support, the price where buyers enter the market, it will rise again. Investors' taking early profits often causes the hesitation and drifting.

Sometimes this weakness is found in a company that has announced stock buyback programs (and actually does buy back the stock) or has recently increased the amount of its dividend, as seen in Figure 27–1. It is usually the stock that had good earnings growth for the same period the previous year. In fact, the earnings probably look good for the preceding three to five years. It is a company that can handle its debt servicing and has a strong balance sheet. It is well managed and is one of the growing leaders in its market. The company sticks to the knitting of what it does well, rather than diversifying into unknown areas. It is a company that either is now or will likely become a dominant force within its own industry.

Note the climb of AT&T during the 1997–1998 time period. Nicknamed "Telephone" by the stock market, it has historically been considered a large, slow-growth company. During the time shown, the price grew at a nice even pace, more than doubling in less than a year. It also provided a few areas of price weakness in which investors could buy. Notice that the areas of weakness follow a period of sideways price consolidation.

FIGURE 27–1

AT&T (NYSE: T), 1997–1998.

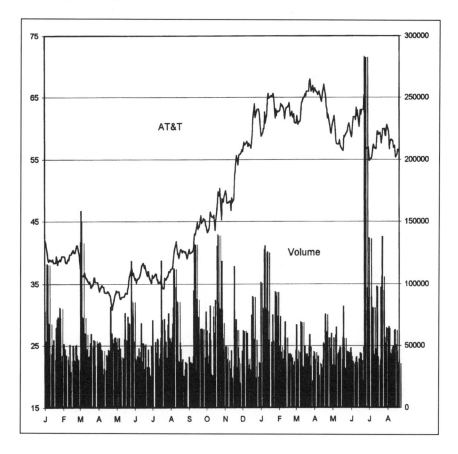

When comparing the 1997 through 1998 areas of weakness to a larger picture as shown in Figure 27–2, we see how important this price movement became. In the year from April 24, 1997, to April 24, 1998, the price of AT&T more than doubled. It went from $30.75 a share to $62.312. Such growth is no small achievement, especially for Telephone with its former record of slow but steady price growth. The only other recent and significant upward price movement was in 1996, when the price moved from the mid-30s to the mid-40s. If there was ever a time to buy stock on any price weakness, AT&T would have been an excellent target. Even buying as late as October 1997 would have produced substantial gains.

F I G U R E 27–2

AT&T (NYSE: T), 1994–1998.

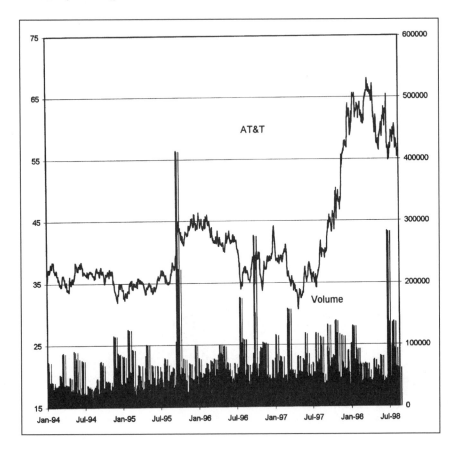

A GOOD STRATEGY FOR ANY TARGET

Buying on weakness can be looked at as an alternative to using a limit buy order. It's a way to avoid changing the limit order and chasing a price. First analyze and select stock targets. When the market has an off day (not a suspected turn in the trend), check the price quotes on the targets and place an order to buy.

SELLING ON STRENGTH

Although the investor wants to sell a loser as soon as possible, selling into a rally will produce better results than selling into a price weakness. It can be difficult for many investors to wait for strength. They just want out, immediately, even though a little patience and careful watching could enable them to finesse the sale as the price is rising. Also, there will be times when waiting for strength to sell would have been about the same as selling on weakness.

A MATTER OF FINESSE

Buying on weakness and selling on strength should be a matter of finesse rather than a total strategy. The finesse enables the investor to be more in control of the situation. It is taking action rather than reacting to a market situation.

At times a strong market will not allow the investor to use finesse. Then it is time to take action and buy or sell at the earliest possible moment. But during those times when the investor is in control, finesse can add a few extra dollars to each transaction and make the experience of investing more enjoyable as well as profitable.

CHAPTER 28

It Is Best to Trade "At the Market"

Market orders have priority. It's important to remember that fact. A market order says that the investor is willing to buy or sell shares immediately at the "best available price." The order takes precedence over any other kind of order. It must be presented to the "trading crowd" by the specialist on the stock exchange at the earliest possible moment. In reality, a computer matches the vast majority of market orders. The result is a nearly immediate execution and report.

IMPLICATIONS OF A MARKET ORDER

A market order implies that the investor desires a fast execution. It says that the investor wants to buy or sell the stock immediately. The only time delay that occurs is when a broker is entering the order.

It also implies that any price is acceptable. The fact is often forgotten until an investor pays more than expected for a stock purchase or receives less than anticipated on a sell. In a steady, evenly paced market, a buy order will be filled at or near the current offer on the stock quote (at or near the bid on a sell).

In a fast-market situation, an investor could pay a few or even several dollars more per share when his or her order is actually executed. This can be of real concern in a takeover situation, where $20 or $60 or more extra per share might be paid with a market order. It is the main reason takeover offers are normally not announced during trading hours. The uncertainty of price necessitates that buyers check the current trading price when placing an order to buy or sell stock.

Although the vast majority of trades are filled at one price, a market order is quoted in terms of a *round lot*, normally 100 shares (there are exceptions). This practice can create a problem with thinly traded stocks. If necessary, multiple round lots can be broken into smaller lots, with different prices.

The main reason it's best to trade at the market is simply that the market moves quickly. Order qualifiers such as price limits or *all or none* (AON) do not have the same priority as market orders and might not be filled. Direction can quickly and unexpectedly change, leaving the investor twisting in the wind with a limit order. Also, when a decision has been reached, why take an action directly contradicting the strategy? I want to buy some stock because I believe the price will rise, but I might be able to get it cheaper. So I place an order below the current price. Why do such a thing? Why buy a stock believing the price will go lower? On the other hand, why sell a stock believing it will rise higher in price? The actions don't match the strategies.

The idea of placing a buy or sell of securities as a market order is to obtain an immediate execution at the best available price. If the investor nit picks over a few cents per share, opportunity is lost, and the ensuing cost of frustration and time lost is high. Such costs can easily be higher than any movement in the stock price while the market order is being placed. Do the analysis, make the decision, set the strategy, and stick with it when placing the order.

The only time to avoid using a market order is when a price is rising rapidly. If an investor is interested in a company whose stock price is rapidly moving up, but the investor desires to have some control over the buying price, a limit order or better can be entered. The term *or better* is normally assumed, but in this situation its intent is to confirm that a limit order is being placed above the current trading price.

Let's say that XYZ Corp. is currently trading at $50 a share, up $5 for the day. An investor wants to buy the stock but wants some control over price. An order to buy 100 shares is placed with a limit of 50¼ or better for the day. Since the limit is above the market price, it might be considered an error if the or-better qualifier is not added. At this point either the order will be filled between 50 to 50¼ or it will not be executed.

Whereas this can be a good strategy on the buy side, on the sell side it is different. Although a similar order can be placed on the sell side, it might not be prudent. If the price is dropping rapidly and a decision has been made to sell, it should be sold as quickly as possible. There is a risk that placing a limit on the sell order will result in the order's not being executed.

BEST AVAILABLE PRICE

Market order means to buy or sell stock at the "best available price." If an order is filled at a price considerably away from the quote given to the investor, the time of sales can be checked with the broker to see why the order was executed at the price reported. Although errors are possible, they are usually the exception.

Another instance in which it might not be advisable to use a market order is with low-priced, usually thinly traded stock—for example, speculative stock that sells for less than $10 a share. In these situations a limit order is usually best, but again, there is still the risk that it won't be executed.

A FAIR AND ORDERLY MARKET

Exchanges and over-the-counter market makers strive to fill orders quickly and as close to the current price as possible. It's part of the integrity essential to maintaining a fair and orderly market. If a public market for securities does not operate with this integrity, it will cease to exist as a continuous public auction. Stock exchanges around the world, whether in emerging markets or developed markets, are striving to make their markets fair, orderly, and stable. Many have adopted rules to stop trading if a stock's price or the market fluctuates beyond a certain percentage in a trading session. Calling a halt to the trading won't stop declines, but it will allow everyone an opportunity to learn about the situation.

Market orders work best in the majority of situations because they can be executed rapidly at a reasonable fill price. Most of the time these advantages outweigh the benefits of placing a limit order, which often cannot be executed. If bad fills are being received, they should be checked for possible errors and the strategy should be reexamined.

CHAPTER 29

Understand the Types of Orders

There are many different types of stock orders an investor can place. Some of the different types are of debatable value and seldom used. Below are simplified descriptions of some of the basic types of orders.

Market Order Best available price; it should be filled as soon as possible. For example, an investor calls a broker and learns that shares for XYZ Corp. are trading at 55¼ to 55⅜ and the last trade was at 55⅜. The investor says: "I want to place a market order to buy 200 shares of XYZ at the market." Computers make this order easy to enter and easy to fill. In all likelihood the investor can get a verbal confirmation of the order execution while still on the phone. The broker comes back to the phone and says: "Confirming a buy of 200 shares of XYZ at the market. The order was filled at 55⅜. The settlement is regular way, in three business days."

Limit Order Specific acceptable price; it should be filled when the trade can be completed at the order price or better. If the order cannot be filled it remains as a limit order until canceled. It can be entered as a one-day only order or as a *good-till-canceled* (GTC) *order.*[1] For example, "Buy 200 XYZ at a limit price of 55 good for today only." The order is entered by the broker. If 200 XYZ can be purchased at $55 a share or better, the order is executed. If the limit is not activated, the order is automatically canceled at the end of the trading session.

---

1. Good-till-canceled orders (on stop and limit orders) can run to the end of the month, end of the next month, or some other time set by the brokerage firm. At the end of the time period, they are automatically canceled.

Stop Order Best available price once the stop price is traded on or through.[2] "Buy 200 XYZ with a buy stop at 59. Put the order in, Good Till Canceled." The buy stop is placed above the current trading price. The investor wants to buy the stock only if the price is moving up.[3] The order to buy 200 shares will become a market order if XYZ stock trades at $59 a share or higher. If the order is not executed within a time specified by the brokerage firm (usually end of the month, 30 days, or the end of the following month), it is canceled.

Stop Limit Order Specific acceptable price, once the stop price is traded on or through. The limit price can be placed at the same price as the stop or at an entirely different price from the stop price. If the order cannot be filled, it remains as a limit order until canceled.

"Sell 200 shares of XYZ at a stop of 48, with a limit of 46, Good Till Canceled." The stop will be triggered if the price of XYZ Corp. trades at or through $48 and will sell immediately if and only if the order can be executed at $46 a share or better. Again, the unexecuted order will remain in the system for a length of time designated by the brokerage firm unless the order is canceled.

Market if Touched (MIT) An order qualifier for buy orders placed below the current trading price and sell orders placed above the current price. They are executed if the security trades at or through the current price. Effectively, they are the opposite of stop orders in terms of dynamics. Such orders are used extensively with futures trading.

Market on Open (On the Open) An order that specifies the market opening as an activator. It is a market order and does not guarantee the opening price. Obviously, this type of order must be placed before the market opens.

Market on Close (On the Close) An instruction to a stock exchange floor broker to execute the trade at the best available price during the last 30 seconds of the trading session. There are no guarantees that the order will be filled or that it will be filled at the final trading price.

---

2. The most used and most important types of orders for the individual investor are the market, limit, and stop orders.
3. A sell stop (stop-loss order) would be placed under the current market price, far enough that it will be triggered only by a major move.

CHAPTER 30

Order Modifications Might Cause Delay

Careful consideration should be given to any modification placed on an order because an order with any qualifiers other than *market order* can take more time to be executed.

Good till Canceled (GTC) The order stays "open" until it is executed, canceled, or changed by the investor, or it is canceled by the brokerage firm. Brokerage firms have different policies as to how long they will carry an open order on their books. Many cancel at the end of 30 days, or the end of the following month, whereupon the order must be reentered to remain open. Automatic cancellation helps the investor remember the open order and prevents duplications.

Open orders can be changed or canceled by the investor at any time; however, the investor should question the value of making several changes, usually referred to as *chasing*. It's usually better to make the trade than it is to chase a price. Changes are costly to the brokerage firms, and those costs end up being passed on to investors. Also, too many changes can lead to confusion and costly errors.

Do Not Reduce (DNR) Buy and stop GTC orders are generally modified by the instruction *DNR*. *DNR* means simply "do not reduce." Most investors want an order filled even if it has become ex-dividend. *Ex-dividend* means the investor is buying the stock without the current dividend attached. The stock's price is reduced by the amount of the dividend at the beginning of trading. Many firms require the DNR designation on all GTC orders.

When an investor decides to change an open order, it is necessary to notify the broker of the existing, previously placed order. Otherwise, two orders could be executed, with the investor's bearing responsibility for any liabilities. A new or changed GTC order does not automatically cancel a previously entered order.

The advantage of the good-'till-canceled order is its automatic feature. The order stays in effect, day after day, and it does not need to be reentered until it is changed or canceled. The investor's transaction will be executed when it is possible to do so, and it does not need constant attention. The disadvantage of using an open order is that doing so could cause delay. Situations can arise where other limit orders have been placed at the same price. The investor's order execution is delayed by "stock ahead." Also, keep in mind that market orders always take precedence.

Market orders are automatically "day orders," but they may be entered GTC on thinly traded stocks. Some preferred stock and issues from small companies do not trade every day.

Day Order   The *day order* is just what it says. It's an order placed for the day only. If the order cannot be executed by the end of the trading session, it is canceled. A notice of the cancellation is sent to the broker "firm nothing done." The broker notifies the investor. A day order can be changed or canceled by the investor at any time during the trading session.

The frequent trader or day trader is likely to use day orders. Their strategy is normally based on momentum that is building during the day, so they have no reason to keep an order open longer than the current trading session. The main disadvantage of using the day order is that the investor must wait for a status report at the end of the trading session. Obviously, the report can take longer after an exciting day in the stock market.

Or Better (OB)   The term *or better* refers to the price most advantageous to the investor. "Or better" is always assumed with limit buy orders placed below or sell orders placed above the current trading price. Usually the OB designation is added to a buy limit placed at or above the current price and on sell orders at or below the current price. The OB designation clarifies the investor's intent to buy or sell.

For example, let's say that the stock of ABX is trading at 21¼ and is up 1¼ from the previous day's closing price of $20 a share. The full quote looks like this:

Symbol	Last	Change	Bid	ASK
ABX	21¼	+1¼	21	21¼

The investor wishes to buy ABX and take advantage of a continuing uptrend; however, a market order could fill higher than the current ask price. This could present an extra problem in an IRA account that is limited to the funds available. The investor is willing to pay as much as $21½, but only if necessary. The OB also confirms that the investor is serious and that the order is not an error. Since limit buy orders are usually placed below the current price, a limit placed above might be considered an error and be returned for clarification.

The order is entered as a limit, or better: "Buy 500 shares ABX at a limit of 21½ or better, day order." If the order can be executed, the investor will buy the 500 shares for $21½ a share or less. If the price is higher than the limit by the time the order is entered and stays higher, the order will be canceled at the end of the day.

The advantage of using or better with a limit is price control. The obvious disadvantage is that the order might not be executed.

All or None (AON) The qualifier *all or none* can be used with multiple round lot or block orders. Block orders normally receive special handling through a brokerage firm's block order desk. The purpose of the modifier is to avoid a partial fill of an order. If a person desires to buy 1,000 shares of BBB Corporation at $20 a share, with the stock currently at 19⅞ to 21⅛, a limit order can be entered at $20 or better for the day. It might be possible to buy only 500 or 600 shares at that price. The order can be filled for 500 shares at $20 a share, leaving the investor 500 shares short. If the modifier *all or none* is added, there are only two possibilities at the end of the trading session: Either the investor will have bought 1,000 shares of BBB at $20 a share or the order will have been canceled because it could not be filled.

Even though a partial fill might be desirable in some stock situations, in most cases the investor would rather have the total amount of shares. If limit orders are entered "good till canceled," a separate, full commission could be charged for each day a partial fill occurs, thereby increasing the investor's cost.

The main advantage to the all-or-none modifier is that it enables the investor to control the filled quantity. It must all be executed at the same time and price. The main disadvantage is that in some situations, the order will be difficult to fill.

Immediate or Cancel (IOC) This order modifier is added to a limit that is at or close to an executable price. It specifies a maximum quantity, but it can be less. It says to buy (sell) 2,000 shares right now if you can. If you cannot, buy (sell) 1,500 or 1,000 shares and cancel the remainder of the order.

Fill or Kill (FOK) Although similar to the IOC, the FOK says to make the transaction for the full amount immediately or cancel the order. This differs from the AON, which allows some time to fill the order at the limit price.

Not Held (NH) Used primarily with large orders, this modification allows the floor broker to use time or price discretion for the effective execution of an order.

Not held indicates that the investor will accept what the floor broker can accomplish with the execution of the trade.

Note: During unusually fast markets, brokerage firms may accept only "market orders not held," meaning they are not held to a price based on the current price quotation. When the system becomes overloaded, orders ahead can change the price showing on the computer by the time an investor's order is cleared.

Odd Lot on Sale   Occasions can arise when an investor is selling a combination of a round lot (usually 100 shares) and an odd lot (less than the round lot) of stock. An amount such as 125 shares of XYZ Company is a combination of the round lot of 100 and the odd lot of 25 shares.

If a limit order is placed to sell the stock, the investor might want to add the modification *odd lot on sale* to indicate that the round lot is available at the limit price, but the odd lot may be sold at the market price. This modifier simplifies the transaction and makes it easier to have the order executed. The odd lot portion of 25 shares could be charged an extra ⅛ of a dollar (12½ cents). The extra fee is known as the *odd lot differential*, and it is assessed for the extra costs involved with trading an odd lot of stock.

Placing a combination round lot–odd lot sell order with the odd-lot-on-sale modifier can make execution of the trade easier and faster. The only disadvantage is that the investor must accept a lower price for the odd lot shares.

Modifiers such as price limits, AON, or IOK can have an impact on the speed at which an order is executed. Although there can be sound reasons for placing limits and other modifiers on buy and sell orders, in most cases the time saved by placing a market order is worth more than the time lost waiting for another 12½ cents per share. Placing market orders will usually save the investor time and money.

CHAPTER 31

Remember That Others Might Have the Same Idea

Sometimes investors spend a great deal of time arriving at the decision to make a stock trade. No matter what the conclusion—buy, hold, set a limit, or stop—the chances are good that several other investors have the same or a similar idea. More importantly, these competitors could have placed their orders earlier.

One example of this same-idea phenomenon is illustrated by the fact that most limit orders are placed on whole numbers, halves, and quarters. Seldom are such orders entered at eighths or smaller. The competition can create problems. If there are other orders ahead, the individual investor's limit order might not be filled. Market orders might keep the stock price away from the desired limit.

Another example of the same-idea problem can be seen when a buyout offer appears overnight. The stock might have closed at $56, and the buyout is at $75 a share. Although many investors might want to buy the stock on the open near $56 a share, executing this type of order is usually not possible. In most situations the stock price will quickly run up near the buyout price.

DIGITAL EQUIPMENT

For example, look at what happened to the price of Digital Equipment when Compaq announced their takeover. The price had been trading in the high 30s when it suddenly rose to the high 50s. There was some play for the next few days, and it rose to $62 a share.

FIGURE 31–1

Buyout, Digital Equipment (NYSE: DEC), 1998.

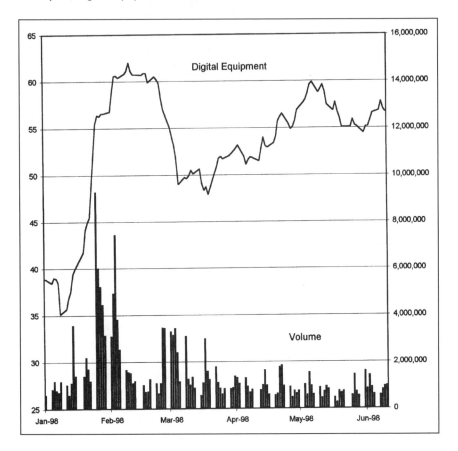

The price collapse of Digital back to the low 50s came because of an announcement by Compaq that earnings would not meet expectations. Compaq's price also dropped (see Figure 31–1). Anyone who shorted DEC between $60 and $62 did all right when the weaker earnings report emerged. There was a potential gain of 10 or more dollars a share.

COMPETITION AMONG INVESTORS

When implementing a strategy it is important to keep in mind that other investors might have the same idea. This can be helpful for the leaders of the pack, but frustrating to the followers who miss the move. The ideal is to anticipate what might happen. With Digital, there were probably a few investors who sold short once the price leveled out around $61 a share. Although they couldn't have known about the upcoming weak earnings announcement by Compaq, they might have been aware of a general weakness in the computer industry.

THE WORTH OF THE UNDISCOVERED IDEA

Some investors try to formulate an idea no one else has discovered. However, in most situations the investor would have been better off if he or she had focused on what others had started to find or will soon discover. It takes a crowd of buyers to make the market rise. The same is true for individual stock prices. To correctly anticipate what will happen tends to bring the solid gains. The idea is to be in front or at least in the middle and have the crowd bringing up the rear.

CHAPTER 32

Use Limit Orders as Insurance

Limit orders, a minimum sell price or a maximum price on a buy, can be used as a type of insurance. On the buy side, limits can protect investors from paying too high a price, or they can be used for a bottom-fishing strategy. *Bottom fishing* is an attempt to buy a declining stock at the lowest possible price.

When an investor places an order with a broker without specifying a desired price, it is a *market order*, which means that the investor will buy the stock at the price that it is trading at that day (the best available price). When an investor sets a price at which he or she is willing to buy or sell a particular stock, the investor has placed a *limit*, or restriction, on his or her order.

ADVANTAGES AND DISADVANTAGES TO LIMITS

There are both advantages and drawbacks to using a limit order. The market for any security is the price someone is willing to pay for it (the *bid*) or the price at which someone is willing to sell (the *offer*).

For example, the market for the stock ABC is 40 bid, 40¼ offer. If an investor places a market order for ABC, the order will likely fill at 40¼, the lowest price that a seller is willing to accept. Another option available to the investor is to place a limit order to buy the stock at 40⅛. However, if no one wants to sell at this price, the investor may have to wait until the offer price falls to the limit order price or until another customer submits a market order to sell ABC stock, in which case the two may be matched up.

STOCK EXCHANGE LIMITS

How the limit order is handled depends on whether the stock is traded on the NASDAQ market or on an exchange such as the New York Stock Exchange. Limit orders for securities traded on an exchange are normally sent to a specialist assigned to handle all orders in that stock. The specialist matches up buy orders with sell orders and sometimes buys for his or her own account when there is not enough interest on both sides to match. Exchange rules do not allow a specialist to trade for his or her own account at prices at or better than the limit order price without filling the customer's limit order. When the limit order to buy ABC at 40⅛ is placed, the specialist cannot trade for his or her own account at that price or better until he or she has executed the investor's order.

OVER-THE-COUNTER

The NASDAQ (over-the-counter) market is made up of *market makers* who compete with each other to buy and sell securities for their own accounts at their bid and ask prices. If a brokerage firm is also a market maker in the security being bought or sold, the investor's order will be executed by that market maker at the firm. Market orders to sell are executed against the highest bid from among competing market makers and against the highest offer in the case of market buy orders. Limit orders are typically not executed until the highest bid price (in the case of sell orders) or the lowest ask price (in the case of buy orders) are equal to an investor's limit price.

MARKET MAKER

Like the specialists on stock exchanges, market makers at firms that accept limit orders are not allowed to trade for their own account at the limit order price or better without first executing the customer's limit order. Since September 6, 1995, all customer limit orders, whether they come from the firm's own customers or from another member firm's customers, must be handled in the same way by the firm accepting the limit order. That is, the member firm must not trade ahead of any customer limit order it holds without protecting that order. It is important to note that firms are under no obligation to accept limit orders in NASDAQ issues, and some may accept orders only in those securities in which they make a market. So it is important to find out your broker's policy for handling limit orders before placing that type of order.

RISK ON A BUY LIMIT

The main risk with all limit buy orders is that the order will not be executed. In other words, the buy or sell does not take place because the price did not trigger the order. If a buy order is not filled, it can mean a lost opportunity, but not a loss of money. There are always other stocks to buy.

RISK ON A SELL LIMIT

The risk on a sell limit is also that the order will not be executed, but it can mean real losses if the stock price continues to drop. If used, limit sells should be carefully placed. Normally, investors desire to have their orders executed and their stock sold.

If an investor believes that a stock price will decline after a short rise, it may be appropriate for him or her to place a limit order. However, if the limit is not triggered by the stock price and the stock price begins to decline, profits begin to evaporate. The investor can then lower the limit price and "chase" the price or change the limit order to a market order. A market order is executed as soon as possible at the "best available price."

Limit orders are best used as insurance against an unexpected market move or for an attempt at price control in a fast market. When a stock price quotation appears on a computer screen, it's already history. No rule says a market order must be filled at the current price quotation. Rather, a market order is always filled at the "best available price" when the order is received. A little protection could be in order for an unusually volatile stock.

For example, ABC stock is showing a bid price of $25 a share. The offer (buy price) is 25⅛. Some investors will be tempted to place an order to buy 100 shares at 25. The strategy is intended to save the investor 12½ cents per share, but the order might never fill.

If the investor wants to buy the stock and stay in control of the situation, he or she places the order on the offer 25⅛ or higher (with an or-better modifier). Placing the buy order with a limit price on the offer would look like the example in Table 32–1. It illustrates buying into a moderate market.

This order has a high likelihood of being executed. The stock is up a small amount on moderate volume. If the order were placed as a market order, the fill

T A B L E 32–1

Price Quote

Stock	Last	Change	Bid	Ask	Volume
ABC	25	+⅛	25	25⅛	30,000
Buy: 100 shares ABC 25⅛ limit Day					

T A B L E 32–2

Faster Market

Stock	Last	Change	Bid	Ask	Volume
ABC	25	+2⅛	25	25¼	130,000
Buy: 500 shares ABC 25¼ limit Day					

T A B L E 32–3

Slower Market (declining)

Stock	Last	Change	Bid	Ask	Volume
ABC	25	–⅛	25	25⅛	30,000
Sell: 100 shares ABC 25 limit Day					

could be identical to the limit. However, look at the situation in Table 32–2, which illustrates buying in a faster market, where the limit is truly protective.

This order has a chance of being filled, but at the pace the price is moving, backed by heavy volume, it could be difficult to fill. The limit will prevent the order from causing an up tick to 25⅜ or 25½, although it might not be possible to obtain a fill of the order.

The investor can increase the chances of an execution by setting the limit price higher than the current offer and adding the modifier *or better* (such as "25½ or better"). This order would greatly increase the probability of an execution and ensure a price of no more than $25½ a share.

Table 32–3 is an example of selling in a slow to moderate declining market. Placing the limit on the current bid showing helps to ensure an execution and does prevent the stock from selling on a down tick. If it is time to sell the stock, it should be sold on the bid or at the market. This is not the time to try and squeeze another 12½ cents a share out of this security.

Compare this to selling stock in a declining fast market, as shown in Table 32–4. A market sell order of 500 shares could hit a down tick and execution of 24¾ or even 24½ (depending on orders ahead). Normally it would down tick ⅛ per trade, but only three orders ahead of this sell could push the price that low. Also, a fast market like this can down tick the price at a greater rate. The limit price of 25 will ensure the price, but it will not ensure an execution of the order. If the order is not quickly executed and the price continues to drop, the investor might wish to change this sell to a market order.

TABLE 32–4

Faster Market (declining)

Stock	Last	Change	Bid	Ask	Volume
ABC	25	–2⅛	25	25¼	130,000
Sell: 500 shares ABC 25 limit Day					

IMPLICATIONS OF A MARKET ORDER

Time

A limit order (good 'till canceled) implies that the investor is willing to wait as long as necessary for the order to be filled. It might take an hour, a day, or a week, or it might never be filled.

Partial Fill

A limit order of multiple round lots implies that the investor will accept part of the order being filled. The investor can avoid this partial filling by placing the modifier *all or none* (AON) on the order, although this could make the order even more difficult to fill.

Price Direction

A limit order often implies that the investor believes the stock price will move opposite to its current direction and then resume. This is the way many limit orders are placed, even though the strategy and the action are not in line. It might be used when a stock price has risen $1½, but the investor wants to save an eighth or a quarter and places that limit buy below the current offer. The largest risk is that the order will not be filled and the investor will not participate.

OR BETTER

A limit order implies that the investor will accept the order being filled at the limit price or a better price. The term *or better* should be applied only when the investor is placing a limit above the current offer on a buy or below the current bid on a sell.

CHAPTER 33

Values Can Be Found Bottom Fishing

B*ottom fishing* is a technique of using a limit buy order to purchase a stock that has been going through difficult times and has shown a significant price decline. The company might be currently out of favor, or the industry could be having its own recession. Cyclical stocks, such as car companies, oils, heavy equipment, and to some extent food, all lend themselves to bottom fishing. Other industries such as airlines, computers, and defense equipment manufacturers tend to go out of favor periodically. When they do, the bottom fishers come out in force. They grab their long-term price charts to see how low the price fell during the last down cycle. Then they assess the current market situation, pick a price target, and place their limit orders. The objective is to pay a price as close to the bottom as possible.

FORMER BOTTOM FISHERS

It once was said on Wall Street that a market bottom was near when one could see well-dressed aged men and women walking quickly to the brokerage offices to buy their favorite stocks at bargain prices. These were the experienced bottom fishers, and it was believed that a market rally would soon be seen. Apparently, this analogous indicator disappeared with the advent of the telephone.

Bottom for Amgen?

A look at Amgen in Figure 33–1 shows one of the difficulties of trying to fish at the bottom. There is no way to know if that $46 level back in October 1997 was

FIGURE 33-1

Bottom fishing, Amgen (NASDAQ: AMGN), 1997–1998.

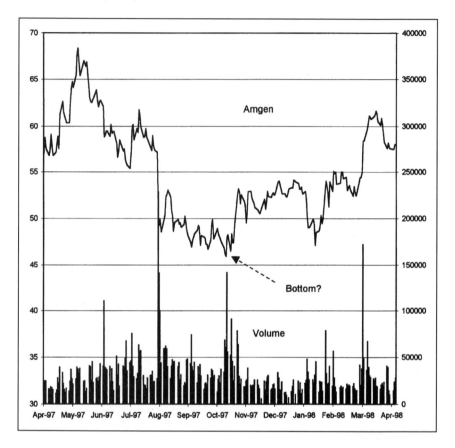

the bottom. Although there is evidence of strong support between the $45 and $50 range, the support is even stronger between $50 and $55. The strong support is important. It shows the level where buyers have entered the market and have stopped the price from falling further. When the volume increases in early January 1998, it suggests that a number of buyers believe the bottom has passed. Another significance of the support between $50 and $55 is that if the price falls through and drops below 50, it will likely fall even further.

Infoseek

Infoseek, an Internet search engine company, shows some interesting support at the $5 level (Figure 33–2). During April through August 1997, the stock price rallied on increased volume, after it dropped down to that $5 level. By April 15, 1998, the price had risen to $34½ a share. The stock provided investors with several months of support, suggesting that $5 was indeed the bottom.

Infoseek made a swift recovery, providing $30 a share or more to investors who were fortunate to pick the bottom. Some investors exited near this point; others hung on until the uptrend appeared to be subsiding. Although the trading volume does surge on price advances, it seems to have trouble maintaining strength. This can be seen in the November through January period, as well as in March 1998. Weakness in volume isn't preceding the price much but is rather keeping in step. It will be difficult to watch volume for a possible sell signal if the trend continues.

FIGURE 33–2

Bottom fishing, Infoseek (NASDAQ: SEEK), 1997–1998.

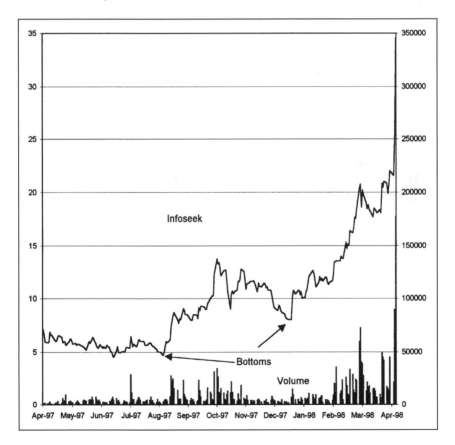

HIGHLY SPECULATIVE

Bottom fishing can be highly speculative, as there is no way to know how low the price of a stock will fall. Although it is helpful to look at a long-term price chart for past support levels, those supports may not hold. The strategy is most effective in an overall market decline, where value remains in individual companies. It can be quite risky in individual stock situations, especially where stock price trends are moving counter to the stock market. If a stock were about $80 a share last year and is now at 45, will it go to 40, or keep dropping to $25? Even if the investor sees a low price of 39 during the last down cycle, there is no assurance that the same level will be repeated. That the price will not find support after an investor buys it is the main risk a bottom fisher assumes. If the investor is correct, the strategy can bring great profits as the price recovers to former levels. If incorrect, he or she may lose profits if the price drops and stays at the bottom for a long time.

CHAPTER 34

Heavily Margined, Heavily Watched

To *margin* is to borrow money using stocks or other securities that have been fully paid for as collateral. These borrowed funds can be used for any purpose (the cash can be withdrawn), although the money is most commonly used to buy more stock or other securities. A margin can be a useful tool to leverage investments for greater profits. In essence, an investor puts up one-half the value of the stock that he or she purchases on margin.

MARGIN RULES, REGULATIONS, AND REQUIREMENTS

The rules, regulations, and requirements regarding margin accounts come from three sources:

1. The Federal Reserve Board sets margin requirements as part of monetary policy. These are referred to as *Fed requirements.*
2. Stock exchanges also set margin requirements that their member firms are required to observe, and when the exchange setting the requirement is the New York Stock Exchange (NYSE), most or all firms observe the requirement whether or not they are NYSE member firms. These are known as *exchange requirements.*
3. Brokerage firms set their own, more rigorous margin requirements, and their margin allowances are more restrictive than the Federal Reserve's. They are allowed to do this in order to limit their risk. These rules and regulations are known as *house requirements.*

INTEREST CHARGES

Brokerage firms make money on margin accounts from the interest they charge on the loans and also from commissions on the larger transaction sizes that buying on margin allows. However, lending money carries risks for the brokerage firms similar to the risks that banks face when lending; the borrower may not want to or may not be able to pay back the money borrowed.

REGULATION T

Current Regulation T requires that investors pay for 50 percent of the value at the time of the transaction. A minimum of $2,000 equity is also required to be in the account. The $2,000 can be in the form of cash or fully paid marginable securities. For example, to buy 200 shares of POW Corporation at $106 per share could be financed as follows:

Total cost: $21,200
Investor puts in: 10,600
Amount borrowed: $10,600 (margin debit)

STOCK PRICE RISES

If the price of POW Corp. rises to $150 per share, its total market value will be $30,000. The investor owes only the margin debit and whatever interest has accumulated (the debit is a loan, and interest is charged only for the days the debt is outstanding). In the POW Corp. example, the investor still owes the debit of $10,600, plus interest:

Current market value: $150 per share
Total market value: $30,000
Debit owed: 10,600
Investor's equity: $19,400

If the investor sells the position and takes profits, the picture would look like this:

Investor's equity: $19,400*
Original investment: 10,600
Profit: $8,800

* After the margin debit is repaid.
Note: There will also be interest charges and commissions for the trades.

Essentially, the investor has doubled the gain through leverage by buying twice as many shares, with half of the total amount purchased by means of a loan. Although the maximum of 50 percent loan value is used in this example, it is allowable to borrow less than that amount.

STOCK PRICE DROPS

Using a margin is fine as long as the price of the stock rises. The problems with margins occur when the price begins to drop. What if, instead of rising in price, POW Corp. were to fall to $50 a share?

200 POW Corporation
$50 per share market value: $10,000
Margin debit owed: 10,600*
Investor's equity: ($600)
* The debit remains constant. It is unaffected by market price changes.

If the investor sold out at $50 a share, not only would the original investment of $10,600 be lost but the investor would also owe an additional $600. This is reason enough to watch margined positions carefully.

MAINTENANCE CALL

In reality, the investor would usually receive a *margin maintenance call* before this low level were reached. However, in a rapidly declining market, there might not be enough time to deliver the additional funds or fully paid marginable securities necessary to cover the maintenance call. Maintenance requirements can be anywhere from 25 to 50 percent equity (a 30 percent equity requirement is common for many stocks) of the current market value or $2,000 (whichever is greater). Although the calculations can become complicated with variations in a margin portfolio, they are based on the following simple formula:

$$\text{Equity} = \text{market value} - \text{debit}$$

In other words, an investor can expect a margin maintenance call for the deposit of additional funds or fully paid, marginable securities if the market price of the stock falls below the borrowed amount (debit) plus 25 to 30 percent (the actual amount depends on the brokerage firm's requirements).

UNMET CALLS MET

If the required margin is not maintained, the brokerage firm has every right to sell securities in the account to cover the amount or prevent further loss without notifying the investor beforehand. This was a common occurrence during the 1987 crash. Investors, some of whom were on vacation, returned to find their stock portfolios, once worth hundreds of thousands of dollars, totally gone. In fact, many still owed substantial amounts of money to the brokerage firm.

"Heavily margined, heavily watched" is a market axiom well worth remembering and following. It is also prudent to protect margin positions. Total protection is not possible, but a few precautions can lessen the blow of a severe decline.

PROTECTION

Protect the margin position with careful and deliberate attention. Brokers are often amazed at the number of investors who make stock purchases just before leaving on vacation. It's as if there were some special list of things to do: Stop the mail, load the car, get the kids, and buy some stock. It is usually not the best time to buy any stock, and in fact it can be exactly the wrong time to increase a margin position. A lot can happen to the stock market in a week or two. Most people leaving for vacation have enough to do without keeping an eye on the market.

MARGIN STRATEGIES

Margin can be used with minimal risk and maximum impact, but doing so requires care and attention. Margin positions can be well maintained by implementing a few simple strategies, as follows.

Daily Observation

Keep an eye on the developing market situation by computer, communication with the broker, or checking the newspapers.

EXTRA PRECAUTIONS

Take extra precautions when leaving town on a vacation or business trip. Consider making special arrangements with the broker to have someone bring money or fully paid securities to cover any possible maintenance calls. Keep in touch. It can be a good idea to reduce or totally pay off a margin debt if your trip is planned for an extended period.

Place Protective Orders

This could be a good situation for stop-loss orders wherever possible.

Sell Margined Positions

Keep only the fully paid securities, and reduce the debit to zero. This would eliminate the possibility of margin calls.

Be Extra Cautious with a Short Position

A short position has a potentially unlimited risk, since there is no limit to how high the price of a stock can rise. Carefully placed buy stop orders can help control this risk.

USE MARGIN FOR LEVERAGE

Margin can be a useful tool for leverage when buying securities. It should be used carefully and deliberately. Like all investment strategies, an investor must have a basic understanding of the workings of a margin before using this leverage. It is possible to learn more about using a margin by asking the broker for information, finding books on the subject, or searching the Internet.

INTERNET SITES

http://www.savoystocks.com/educate/m_basic.htm

http://www.hedleyfinance.com/trading.htm

http://www.e-analytics.com/glossary/glossar8.htm

CHAPTER 35

Winners Keep on Winning

Winners usually keep on winning. They keep on winning as long as the factors that make them a winner remain in effect. Others tend to run till they drop.

From the individual's viewpoint, the concept "running with a stock until it drops" means hanging onto a stock that should be sold. There is always a balance between waiting patiently for expected results and taking the action to close out a position. Differences in individuals and the lack of similarity of market situations make identifying the optimal selling point difficult. It is a technique developed through experience and observation. It is timing. Timing is the key to earning consistent profits in the stock market.

PROFIT AND LOSS PLAN

A profit and loss plan should be developed, as it would be for any business venture. It need not be complicated, but it should be well defined, and it should have the flexibility to take advantage of exceptions. Here is a simple profit and loss plan for short-term trading:

Take profits at 20 to 30 percent if weakness appears in growth.

Take losses at 10 to 12 percent when weakness appears in growth.

Solid, continuing growth is a reason for raising the profit-taking price, but before doing so, the situation should be examined carefully and the investor should consider protection such as a stop-loss order. The idea is to win big, not to ride a stock up and back down again. Here is a simple profit and loss plan for long-term trading:

Take profits when earnings weaken.

Take losses when earnings growth is hampered.

Select replacements before selling.

TEN BAGGERS

Most investors would like to find what Peter Lynch fondly refers to as "ten baggers." These are the superstocks with prices that seem to have no stopping point. In the past they were stocks like the following:

- 3-M, when it was at a dollar a share
- Microsoft, when it was at $19 a share
- Alaza, when it was at $4 a share

These are the kinds of winners investors are trying to buy—companies that have steady growth year after year. They are the kind of stocks many stockbrokers like to recommend but frequently have trouble selling. Too many people are trying to triple or quadruple their money in the next year or so. Either they don't buy any stock and the money sits in a low-paying money market fund, or they invest in a high-risk, speculative stock that goes tubular. At least part of the problem here is the belief that greater risk leads to greater reward. It doesn't—at least it doesn't in the stock market. All too often, greater risk means no reward.

To become a ten bagger usually takes time. Such companies are often good companies at the beginning. They have a good line of products, and they work to become the leader in their industry. Even though they become a ten bagger in time, they also usually remain as good long-term investments. Some, like GE or IBM, eventually become hundred baggers and still continue to grow.[1]

CONVERSATION TOPICS

Ten baggers are wonderful. The buyers have a conversation topic for the next several years. Every investor would like to tie into one of the "hotter" issues of stock.

---

1. General Electric is the only company from the original Dow Industrial Average (1896) to be still in the Dow and retain its original name.

Although some investors seem to have a knack for picking hot stocks, in many cases, those who buy a marvelous stock do so by accident. They might buy on a tip or after careful analysis, but they didn't know at the time they bought the stock how well the stock would do.

If an investor has time, data access, and analytical skills to search for the next superstocks, that's great. But the problem is usually with time. Analytical skills improve with practice, and data access has greatly improved via the Internet. However, most people do not have the luxury of being able to devote a considerable amount of time to stock analysis. Thus, for most people, stalking the ten bagger is a difficult task.

When an investor is fortunate enough to be holding a ten bagger, he or she should hang on and watch the earnings, revenues, and competition. The investor should be hesitant to sell, unless problems develop that could permanently hamper the company's growth.

CHAPTER 36

Indicators Can Meet Overriding Factors

"No matter what the current indicators are saying, they can be overridden by other, unexpected factors."

S. A. Nelson

On Friday, May 11, 1990, the Dow Industrial Average rallied more than 63 points. Considering what has happened since, in 1998, 63 points is nice but small. However, the 1990 rally surprised many investors because several stock market indicators had been signaling weakness.

The Dow Industrial Average, Transportation Average, and Utility Average had been drifting apart (see the first arrow in Figure 36–1) and showing weakness. Earlier, the Transportation Average did not participate in the January 2 rally, which brought the Industrial Average up to a record 2,810. The Utility Average had been drifting since the preceding December. Trading volume on the New York Stock Exchange had been dropping lower. Interest rates were creeping up, and the market continued to weaken.

THE PRODUCER PRICE INDEX

It was also the Friday when the new Producer Price Index (PPI) information was released. The PPI information came out, showing a 0.3 decline. The PPI is frequently used by professional investors as the actual measure of inflation. It had been creeping higher since the latter part of 1989.

F I G U R E 36–1

Indicators overridden, Dow Averages and NYSE volume, 1990.

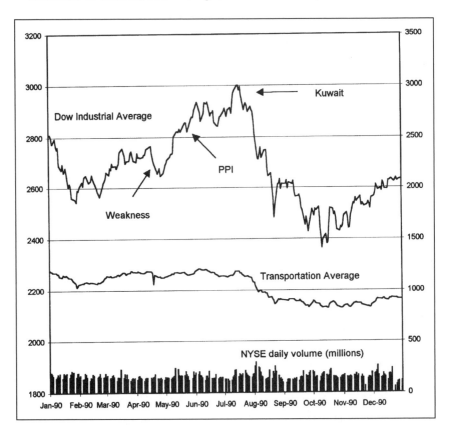

The decline in the Producer Price Index was a good-news shot in the arm for the stock market. What had been a slow and drifting market became a raging bull market. The upward move existed not only in the Dow Averages but also spread to the broad market. Advancing stocks led decliners nearly four to one. The volume on the NYSE climbed to more than 250 million shares, when the average had been about 90 million shares a day.

The positive Producer Price Index overrode all of the negative indicators and brought anticipation of improved growth. Many times it's the other way around: The positive indicators are overridden by a negative indicator or event. In fact, that's why the example from 1990 was selected. Just as the stock market roared to new highs in July, Iraq accused Kuwait of overproducing oil and of stealing oil from Iraq territory.

The news made the stock market nervous. Wars and threats of wars tend to be inflationary, especially if they are relatively short in duration. Because of its dependence on foreign oil, the United States stood ready to protect and defend its oil sources. A large portion of the rest of the world was ready to do the same. Also, Kuwait is a large oil producer; if anything interrupted the flow, it could cause the price of oil to climb much higher.

POSITIVE INDICATORS OVERRIDDEN

The positive indicator from the Producer Price Index, as well as those from other sources, that had strengthened the stock market were overridden by the Iraq-Kuwait situation. The Dow Industrial Average became a bear and dropped from the 3,000-point level to 2,365, just over 365 points. The oil crisis created by the Iraq-Kuwait situation was enough to turn the stock market from a bull to a bear.

Here are some other examples of events that can override positive indicators:

- Funding for a large project (such as a corporate takeover) can fail to materialize at the last minute, sending the entire market into a spin.
- A U.S. Treasury bond auction might not go as well as expected, thereby causing interest rates to rise.
- An earthquake, flood, fire, hurricane, or other natural calamity can unexpectedly send the market down.
- War can break out and have global economic implications.
- A national scandal can appear in the news.
- The U.S. dollar can weaken and fall too low or strengthen and become too high.
- Interest rates might be raised with the intention of slowing the economy.
- Economic distress in places other than the United States (such as the Asian crises in 1998) can have a negative impact on the stock market.

Any of these events, as well as many others, can appear suddenly and cause the stock market to change direction. It can happen even when all of the stock market indicators are showing a strong and stable market.

CURRENT EVENTS AND THE MARKET

It has been said that "information makes the market." More accurately, it is the reaction to the information that makes the market. The reaction is part of anticipation. The stock market will often rise on good news and fall on bad news. When the bad news is expected, the market often ignores the information because it had already been discounted by the market. The market made its adjustment before the news appeared.

Understanding the economic implications of the news can help the investor know what to expect in the stock market. It's important to know what scares investors and what gets them excited with anticipation. The knowledge can help the investor understand the sudden market corrections or rallies.

Indicators, whether technical or fundamental, are important, but they can be and often are overridden by other events or situations.

CHAPTER 37

Take a Loss Quickly

Taking a loss is not pleasant. No one likes to do it. Yet, if one is to be an active investor, it will become necessary to take a loss from time to time. Many of Wall Street's "Big Players" from past years believed they only had to be right about half of the time to make a profit. Sometimes the best analysis encounters unanticipated problems; therefore, it is inevitable that losses will occur at times.

WHEN TO SELL

If the decision has been made to sell and take a loss, it is inappropriate and risky to delay in hopes of getting a little extra. Sometimes a novice investor will decide to take a loss, but at the last minute he or she places a limit order just above the current trading range. Just squeeze an extra quarter or eighth of a dollar out of that loser. But the order doesn't fill, and the price drops lower.

THE CHASE

The investor still firmly believes it will fill just above the current price; after all, it was just there a few moments ago. The investor lowers the limit sell order in an effort to chase the price down. Even if the price does up tick close to the investor's limit, the chances are several other limit sell orders will hammer the price right back down again. Other investors with yet higher limit orders will change them to market orders and continue to pound the price down.

Near the end of the day the frustrated investor finally converts the limit sell order to a market sell (best available price) order, and it is executed, but at a loss significantly lower than the investor initially anticipated. This sequence of events

F I G U R E   37–1

Intraday price, Western Digital Comp. (NYSE: WDC), June 10, 1998.

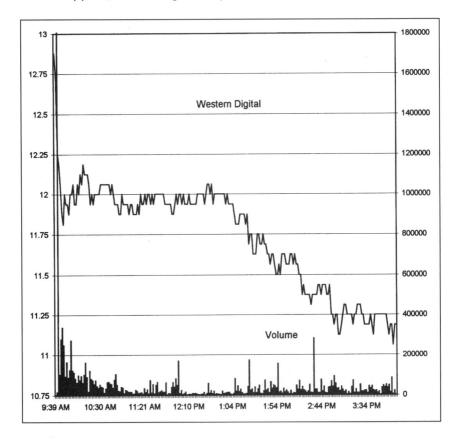

can happen with high-priced stocks or low-priced stocks. Take a look in Figure 37–1 at Western Digital's price for June 10, 1998, a day when the Dow Industrials dropped 78 points.

Western Digital, a maker of computer equipment, hit a peak of $54 a share back in August 1997. The entire computer industry developed an oversupply problem in 1997 and 1998 and began to show price weakness from company to company. A combination of weakness in the market, industry, and company caused some significant selling on June 10, 1998.

THE VOLUME SURGE

The open was slow; then more than 2 million shares were sold, initiating a price collapse of more than a dollar a share, more than 10 percent of the market value.

From just under $12, the price showed a small rally. The buyers could have been bargain hunters or short sellers closing out their positions. The price went flat until just after midday when it entered a steady decline. Notice how the volume also went low and flat.

A DECISION TO SELL AT 2:00 P.M.

An investor placing a sell order in the afternoon decline would have done best to sell as a market order. Granted, it looks as though some were using limit orders for an extra eighth or quarter. From the chart it's also clear how an investor could chase the price down, without obtaining an executed order.

MOVING ON

Sell, be done with it, and move on to a winner. Once you have made a decision to sell and take the loss, you should complete the action as soon as possible. There is no good reason to take the risk of placing a limit sell order. Why risk losing another 10 percent on the price? The market sell order will accomplish the sell with the greatest speed.

CHAPTER 38

Beware the Triple Witching Hour

'T'is now the very witching time of night,
When churchyards yawn and hell itself breathes out
Contagion to this world.

—William Shakespeare, *Hamlet*

The third Friday of every month is the last day to trade stock options. Options actually expire on Saturday, but it is the expiration of trading that can cause concern. Unusual volatility can occur in this third week, due to the unwinding of options positions. At times this volatility seems unrelated to any of the usual market indicators, as though it exists for itself.

THE TRIPLE WITCHES

March

June

September

December

These are the months when options, futures, and index options all expire on the same third Friday of the month. In recent years new regulations and stricter controls have helped to moderate the situation, but the potential for a hyperactive market during these times is still with us. By spreading out the due dates over Thursday and Friday in recent years, the options exchanges have diluted the impact. Additionally, trading circuit breakers limit huge gains or losses in the stock markets, thereby making it more difficult for institutions and short sellers to drive the market down.

EXPECTING THE WORST

Stock exchange volume still increases, but the point moves are not nearly as severe as back in the 1980s. In June 1996, some were expecting a wild ride in the third week of the month:

> Investors are hanging on for a wild ride this week as the market heads toward Friday's "triple-witching hour"—when heavily traded stock options and futures contracts expire.

For all the worry, not much happened. The New York Stock Exchange trading volume ran higher than average, but not much higher. The Dow Industrial Average closed up more than 45 points, and it was business as usual (Figure 38–1).

F I G U R E 38–1

Triple witching months, Dow Industrials and NYSE volume, 1995–1998.

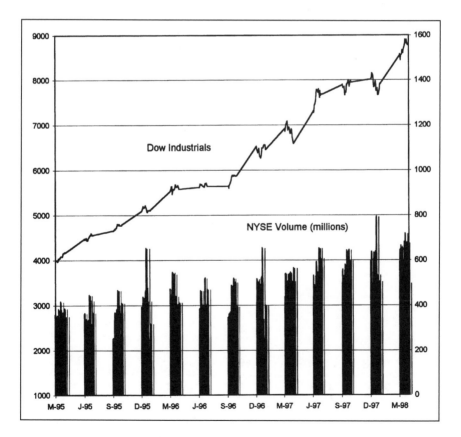

   If significant economic news comes out at the same time as the expirations occur, the volatility can be magnified, but that can confuse the issue, and it's difficult to tell if it was news that made the market volatile or if the triple witching was more to blame.

   The moves involve large traders changing positions from index options and futures to other positions or the actual stocks. An individual investor should be aware of the event as the days still have some teeth. Notice in Figure 38–2 the amount of change in the Dow Industrial Average on the third Fridays.

   December 1997, saw the Dow Industrials down more than 90 points, while March 1998 saw the average roar upward by more than 100 points. Situations like this can help the investor prevent a loss, take profits, or look for new buying opportunities.

F I G U R E 38–2

Friday's expiration changes in the Dow Industrial Average, 1993–1998.

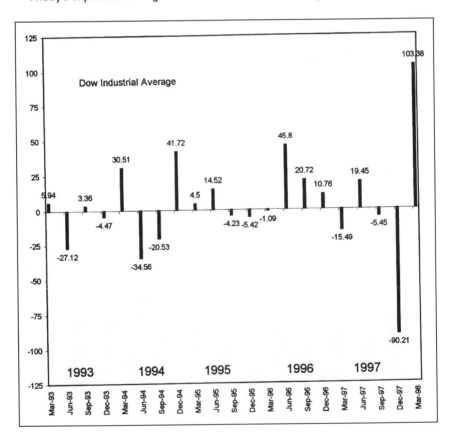

AN OPPORTUNITY

Since the specific direction of the volatility is unpredictable, this situation is usually not ideal for short-term trading. Investors trying to outguess volatile markets can easily get whipsawed and have profits cut in both directions. Nevertheless, taking advantage of the infamous witches can be a part of a long-term strategy if one is careful. It can hammer stock prices low enough to provide some real bargains.

Buy on Monday, Sell on Friday

Publisher and author Yale Hirsch has studied stock market patterns all the way back to 1953.[1] His book *Don't Sell Stocks on Monday* and annual almanac *The Stock Trader's Almanac* have been quite popular with traders and investors. Although Hirsch's statistics are indeed interesting, investors should always keep two points in mind:

- Former performance does not necessarily predict future performance.
- The only certainty is change; if a consistent pattern appears and traders take advantage of it, the pattern changes.

For the 37 years from 1953 to 1989, the market had a tendency to drop on Mondays and rally on Fridays. The saying "Buy on Monday, sell on Friday" became well known to those who traded stock. Apparently it became well known enough for investors to follow the advice. Starting with 1990, the market stopped its pattern of correcting on Mondays. In fact, Monday became one of the best days of the week. Obviously, if a majority of investors start buying on Monday, the market will rally. Table 39–1 lists Hirsch's data from 1953 through 1989; Table 39–2 shows the changes beginning in 1990.

---

1. Yale Hirsch, *Don't Sell Stocks On Monday* (Penguin Books, New York, 1987).

TABLE 39-1

Annual Dow Point Changes for Each Day of the Week, 1953–1997

Year	Monday	Tuesday	Wednesday	Thursday	Friday	Closing DJIA	Point Change
1953	-37.39	-6.7	19.63	7.25	6.21	280.90	-11.00
1954	9.80	9.15	24.31	36.05	44.18	404.39	123.49
1955	-56.09	34.31	45.83	0.78	59.18	488.40	84.01
1956	-30.15	-16.36	-15.30	9.86	63.02	499.47	11.07
1957	-111.28	-5.93	64.12	4.26	-14.95	435.69	-63.78
1958	14.36	26.73	29.10	24.25	53.52	583.65	147.96
1959	-35.69	20.25	4.11	20.49	86.55	679.89	95.71
1960	-104.89	-9.90	-5.62	10.35	46.59	615.89	-63.47
1961	-17.66	4.29	87.61	-5.74	46.85	731.14	115.25
1962	-88.44	13.03	9.97	-4.46	-9.14	652.10	-79.04
1963	-43.61	81.85	16.23	26.07	30.31	762.95	110.85
1964	3.89	14.34	39.84	21.96	67.61	874.13	111.18
1965	-70.23	36.65	57.03	2.75	68.93	969.29	95.13
1966	-126.73	-54.24	56.13	-45.69	-13.04	785.69	-183.57
1967	-73.17	35.94	25.50	98.37	32.78	905.11	119.42
1968*	3.28	37.97	25.16	-59.00	31.23	943.75	38.64
1969	-152.05	-48.82	18.33	17.79	21.36	800.36	-143.39
1970	-99.00	-47.14	116.07	1.81	66.82	838.92	38.56
1971	-15.89	22.44	13.70	6.23	24.80	890.20	51.28
1972	-85.08	-3.55	65.24	6.14	147.07	1,020.02	129.82
1973	-192.68	29.09	-5.94	41.56	-41.19	850.86	-169.16
1974	-130.99	29.13	-20.31	-12.60	-99.95	616.24	-234.62
1975	59.80	-129.96	56.93	129.48	119.92	852.41	236.17
1976	81.16	61.32	50.88	-26.79	-14.33	1,004.85	152.24
1977	-66.38	-43.66	-79.61	8.53	7.64	831.17	-173.48
1978	-31.79	-70.34	71.33	-65.71	70.35	805.01	-26.16
1979	-27.72	4.72	-18.84	73.97	1.60	838.74	33.73
1980	-89.40	137.92	137.77	-112.78	51.74	963.99	125.25
1981	-55.47	-39.72	-13.95	-13.66	33.81	875.00	-88.99
1982	21.69	70.22	28.37	14.65	36.61	1,046.54	171.54
1983	39.34	-39.75	149.28	48.30	17.93	1,258.64	212.10
1984	-40.48	44.70	-129.24	84.36	-64.1	1,211.57	-47.07
1985	86.96	43.97	56.19	49.45	98.53	1,546.67	335.10
1986	-56.03	113.72	178.65	32.17	80.77	1,895.95	349.28
1987	-651.77	338.45	382.03	142.47	-168.30	1,938.83	42.88
1988	139.28	295.28	-60.48	-220.90	76.56	2,168.57	229.74
1989	-3.23	93.25	233.25	70.08	191.28	2,753.20	584.63

* Most Wednesdays were closed the last seven months of 1968.

Source: Data from *The 1999 Stock Trader's Almanac,* http://www.hirschorganizaiton.com//default.html.

T A B L E 39–2

Annual Dow Point Changes, 1990–1997

Year	Monday	Tuesday	Wednesday	Thursday	Friday	Closing DJIA	Point Change
1990	153.11	41.57	47.96	–330.48	–31.70	2,633.66	–119.54
1991	174.58	64.52	174.53	251.08	–129.54	3,168.83	535.17
1992	302.94	–114.81	3.12	90.38	–149.35	3,301.11	132.28
1993	441.72	–155.93	243.87	–0.04	–76.64	3,754.09	452.98
1994	133.77	–22.69	29.98	–159.66	98.95	3,834.44	80.35
1995	203.99	269.04	357.02	150.44	302.19	5,117.12	1,282.68
1996	631.88	150.08	–34.24	261.66	321.77	6,448.27	1,331.15
1997	762.68	2,362.53	–590.17	–989.48	–85.58	7,908.25	1,459.98
Totals	763.16	3,648.28	1,945.27	–304.00	1,563.64		7,616.35

Source: Data from *The 1999 Stock Trader's Almanac,* http://www.hirschorganizaiton.com//default.html.

It is easy to see how the down Monday pattern changed in 1990. Some argument could be made for buying on Thursday and selling on Monday (best since 1990) or Tuesday. It is not possible to calculate if the pattern changed because investors followed the old "Buy on Monday, sell on Friday," axiom or some other rationale. But whenever a pattern is discovered in the stock market, investors tend to trade accordingly. Trading either reinforces the pattern, such as with some technical analysis, or it changes the pattern.

The patterns shown in the preceding tables are generally created from the closing levels of the Dow Industrial Average. Each day was added to or subtracted from the rest, for each year. For the 37 years, the buy-on-Monday concept appeared to be correct, although it didn't work as expected every time. Obviously, several of the Mondays were up. The resulting tendency was probably best used as an indicator rather than an absolute for every stock. As with all indicators, the investor should prudently rely on more than one for planning and implementing a trading strategy.

CHAPTER 40

Never Get Married to the Stock

Investors tend to get married to just a few types of stock. It might be the stock of a company they once worked at or the stock of a company that has a new miracle product—"This company has a product that will automatically cool a can of soda pop." It is often the stock they end up being frustrated with and stay with until death, usually the death of the company. But they are willing to stay with it, through thick and thin, sickness and health, etc.

The ideas behind new businesses are often exciting—one might even say irresistible. Sometimes the management has a celebrity working for them in some capacity. Frequently it is an individual with a background in something other than business. A heart surgeon can be the best in the country but make a terrible corporate president.

A lot of money goes into these start-up companies. When the stock is issued, its price might run up for a short while. Before long, the stock has dropped back to the original price and below. Many times the stock languishes for several years with very little movement. The stock doesn't perform well for many reasons, some of which are listed in the paragraphs that follow.

WHY COMPANIES SOMETIMES UNDERPERFORM

No Earnings

New start-up companies are frequently struggling on a small amount of money left over from paying off the venture capital group who brought the stock public. They may have been publicly traded for a year or more, but it could be three to five years before they show any real earnings. No earnings means cash flow problems, debt problems, supply problems, and a host of other difficulties requiring cash. Not enough money is often the main reason new companies fail.

Poor Management

New companies often fail for lack of management either in amount or in experience. The world's greatest physician might not make a good CEO. A former astronaut or famous athlete does not necessarily have the ability to guide a company through its difficult early years. Ideally, upper management should come from a similar business or at least have a solid background in business. Often times, high-profile professionals are too accustomed to having details handled for them without their having to fight for results. In a new company, it is usually a battle for results from the top to the bottom of the organization.

Investors sometimes get married to the stocks of larger well-established companies as well. Usually this is a case in which they have been employed by the company at one time or another. They buy the stock with its price dropping and hang on to it because they know how "well run" the company has been in the past. It might have been well run when the investor worked for the company, but times have changed. Why else would it be having difficulties? The company is no longer well run, or it has been unable to adapt to changes in the marketplace.

Limited Product Line

New companies may be ahead of their time and may not yet have a realistic market. Sometimes a product gets stuck in the development phase—forever. In some cases there might not even be any intent to actually bring the current finished product to market. It is possible that the stock has been issued for public sale for the purpose of returning capital to the venture capitalist. A company without a working product might hope to pick one up along the way. How different is that from Microsoft's earliest days.

Insufficient Financing

New companies might have trouble getting proper financing to successfully manufacture the product and supply it in sufficient quantities to fill orders. It comes back to not enough money again, still the number 1 problem.

Lawsuits

Start-up companies are frequently engaged in lawsuits from unhappy employees, vendors, or moneylenders. Another source of lawsuits is patent infringement.

Sometimes these lawsuits get nasty and time-consuming, which can tie up assets and time. In addition, they can hamper the ability of management to keep the start-up company going, whereas the larger company has the resources to make it through these difficulties.

Companies with problems like these are often the kinds of stocks some investors buy and never want to sell. The price drops, and still investors hold on, thinking they might get lucky. Sometimes luck will prevail, and the company will recover, but this can take several years. The gain on the investment might not be worth the wait. It is usually better for the investor to take the loss and move on to other opportunities.

WESTERN UNION: AN EXAMPLE

The unfortunate decline of Western Union in the 1980s was a great disappointment to many former employees who bought the stock when it began to head down and then lost a lot of money as the price continued to drop.

Rather than, out of blind loyalty, buying the stock of a company an investor once worked for, he or she should evaluate the company and its competitors.

Actually, an individual might know even more about the competition than they do about the future of a company they used to work for, even recently. In fact, many times it could be better to invest in the stock of a competitor.

Although a case can be made for holding onto a stock when the price has declined severely, getting married to a stock, then staying with it through thick and thin, can be a dangerous strategy. Buy and sell decisions in the stock market need to be made with logic and reason, without emotion.

CHAPTER 41

Diversification Is the Key to Portfolio Management

If the title of this chapter were totally correct, virtually any diversified mutual fund of stocks would be the perfect investment, but that is not the case. Although diversification has value as a prudent investment strategy, it has limitations.

Diversification of investments has been bandied about like some child's favorite rag doll. Actually, it has only a few useful functions and doesn't even begin to offer the amount of protection many people think it does. Many investors place their funds in well diversified funds, thinking they will be safe from market setbacks. If they watch the price of those funds, they are usually disappointed when the market experiences a severe correction. Back in 1987, the disappointment turned to action as many sold out of their declining mutual funds. Their actions became part of the problem creating the sharp drop in the stock market. As mutual fund investors redeemed (sold) their shares, the fund managers had no choice but to sell into a falling stock market in order to pay out the cash.

WHAT IS DIVERSIFICATION AND WHAT DOES IT DO?

Portfolio diversification is the placing of financial assets into significantly different investments, for the purpose of increasing the chances for larger profits, protecting against loss, and simplifying the analysis and selection process. "Significantly different investments" does not mean buying the shares of three different computer companies. Seagate Technology, Digital Equipment, and

Apple Computer might be good companies, but investing in these stocks alone would not necessarily be good diversification. If one invests in a computer company, a food company, and a department store company, the mix is diversified. Although they are bound by general economic conditions, the diversification is into a growth industry, a defensive industry, and a consumer products industry.

Having more shots at the profit target enhances the opportunities for large profits. It is often difficult to know where the next rapid economic growth will appear. Investing in the stocks of companies in different areas of the economy should increase the chances of participating in surges when and where they occur. Also, simple logic says the odds of acquiring a winning stock are better when more than one company is selected. When given a chance, most people would rather have 100 chances to win a $1 million than 1 chance to win $100; the odds are better with more chances.

Safety is improved when investing in more than one company because the individual problems of one company probably won't affect the others. However, in a bear market or economic recession, diversification won't make much difference unless the diversification extends to companies less affected by economic weaknesses. Just as a declining market influences virtually all stock prices, most companies are impacted by economic slow periods. Companies less affected are those supplying products necessary for basic existence (e.g., food, utilities, and fuel).

CAN DIVERSIFICATION PROTECT AGAINST MARKET DROPS?

Until the market swings of recent years, many people had assumed diversification also gave them some degree of safety in a market downtrend. In the days leading up to the crash of 1987, market corrections showed mutual fund investors how much their investments could be hurt. On October 19, many of them started to bail out of their mutual funds, only to see values drop record levels. These mutual fund sellouts were one of the main reasons the Dow Industrial Average fell more than 500 points. Diversification did little to protect investors during this crisis. Later sharp corrections did not experience the mutual fund sellouts, suggesting that investors learned something from their first bad experience. A market drop is generally not the best time to sell holdings. If anything, it is a time to look for buying opportunities.

HOW MUCH DIVERSIFICATION IS ENOUGH?

How much diversification depends on the experience, time for analysis, and assets available to the investor. Investment advisors are quick to give glib answers, which don't work well. "If you have $10,000 to invest, it should be diversified in

10 companies and three different industries." Even buying round lots of 100 shares as low as $25 would enable an investor to buy the stocks of only 4 companies, and he or she would have to add extra money for fees or commissions. The 10-company rule would create several odd lots of stock. There is no depth to such investing. Remember the axiom says to "Make winners win big" (Chapter 1). It would be better to avoid the odd lot (less than 100 shares) situation and begin with diversification into 3 or 4 different stocks in three industries. Doing so will still provide safety and increase the chances of selecting a good winner. Later on either the depth or the breadth of diversification can be increased with additional money to invest.

Also, think of the time involved in analyzing and selecting 10 companies. How about the amount of time required to maintain a close watch on the performance of those 10 companies in three industries? Most people will allocate some time for stock portfolio, market, and economic analysis, but the last thing they want is for it to become a second job.

HOW MUCH MUTUAL FUND DIVERSIFICATION IS ENOUGH?

A growing number of investment articles is appearing in the late nineties about diversification with mutual funds. How many mutual funds are enough? Since mutual funds are already diversified, how much more diversification is necessary? Notice what *Fortune* had to say about mutual fund diversification in a recent Internet article:

> A recent study by Boston-based Kobren Insight Group suggests that this syndrome is even more common than many fund advisers suspected. Among investors who had more than $500,000 in fund investments (the size of the median FORTUNE subscriber's investment portfolio), some 78% had at least ten funds and a gregarious 45% had more than 15. That's probably too many. The only reason to own multiple funds is to lower your portfolio's risk by holding funds that react differently to the same market stimulus.[1]

Too much diversification can also dilute performance significantly. An investor would probably be better off in U.S. Treasury securities or insured certificates of deposit (CDs). It is possible that owning too many mutual funds may position an investor at a point of diminishing returns.

ARE THERE OTHER WAYS TO DIVERSIFY A PORTFOLIO?

A practical diversification strategy that will protect all of the original capital is to buy U.S. Treasury bonds and use the interest from them to invest in the stock

---

1. Maria Atanasov, "Why Owning More Funds Won't Make You Merrier—Having six to ten funds gives you good diversification. Having more just gives you a headache," © 1998 invest-o-rama! (Internet source).

market. If the bonds are held to maturity, the principal is never at risk.[2] Instead, it is returned as the bonds reach maturity.

Another form of easy diversification is to take half of the money available for investment and buy zero coupon U.S. Treasury securities with a maturity date out far enough to double in value.[3] If the entire stock portfolio goes to zero (unlikely, unless highly speculative companies are selected), the investor still retains the principal when the bonds mature. Obviously, there is a high opportunity cost if this unlikely event occurs. Although both of these approaches have tax implications and some risk, they are valid strategies for investing with lower risk.

Diversification is important in an investment strategy. It can be used to lower the overall risk and increase the chances for better profits. It is important to remember that risk is not eliminated with any form of diversification. All investing carries some risk; therefore, it is prudent for the investor to be aware of strategies to moderate that danger. Diversification of the investment portfolio can be an excellent risk-moderating strategy.

---

2. The only risk is *reinvestment risk*. If interest rates are lower when the bonds mature, obviously they will produce less income for the stock investment.
3. Tax implications are not considered here, but they do exist.

CHAPTER 42

Partial Liquidation Might Be the Answer

"Reduce your line down to a sleeping point!"

Robert Rhea

Uncertainty often causes the greatest frustrations in life. Uncertainty in the stock market should lead the investor to be prepared by having some sort of strategy. When downtrends come along, as they inevitably will, the investors who expect them can see them through without increasing their own risks by acting rashly. Some people have the patience to wait, anticipating a development, and others are not able to hold back. Thus, part of a sound long-term investment strategy includes the investor's appraising his or her own level of anxiety about investing money in stocks.

Most investors will usually sell an entire stock position at once, although this extreme action is not always required. A block of a 1,000 shares can certainly be sold in lots of 500 or even 100 shares. Such actions cost more in commission, but in some situations the strategy is worth the cost. This is not to say that an investor with a large quantity of shares should keep hitting the bid by selling small lots one after the other. This type of action could drive the price of a stock lower with each sell, especially if the stock is not actively traded. The better strategy is often more to lighten the load, to take some profits if there exists an extra amount of uncertainty with a specific stock position.

A takeover situation could be a time to sell part of a position, especially if it is selling into the strength of higher-price anticipation. Until the deal is done, it could fall through. The stockholder with a substantial quantity of shares should seriously consider selling at least some of the position. It is not the time to become overly concerned with the extra cost of commission. If the takeover stock has nearly doubled in price and the buyout fails, the stock will go back to its former trading level or lower, and thousands of dollars could be lost.

There seems to be a kind of mental block that develops in the minds of many investors. The belief appears to be: "I have 2,000 shares; therefore, when I sell, I must sell all 2,000 at the same time." If the shareholder believes the company will have hard times and the stock price will drop, yes, the 2,000 should all be sold. But when it is uncertain as to what will happen next, a partial sale provides an alternative strategy.

Selling the same 2,000 shares short (short against the box—see Chapter 12) would also lock in the current market price, but if the situation stabilizes and the price begins to rise again, the investor would not participate in any additional gains.

If an investor is concerned that the stock market has stalled and is acting in an unusual manner, it can be prudent to sell part of the portfolio rather than entirely liquidating every position. The strategy would especially strengthen a margin position and reduce the possibility of a margin call for additional funds. Selling part of a position protects some of the profits and can allow the investor to sleep better.

CHAPTER 43

Act Quickly, Study at Leisure

A question from a customer to a broker might go like this:

> That's right. I want to sell 500 shares of IBM at the market. By the way, how's Apple doing? And Intel—what about Intel?

When a market order is being placed is not the time to check on other information. Once the broker has read back the order, it should be placed immediately. It is just not the time to check other quotes. Market price is good only until the next transaction. It could change and go against the trade. In the time it takes to place an order, hundreds or thousands of others could be coming in ahead of it and hammer the price down.

What if the sell on IBM were being placed on May 26, 1998, just before the market closed? Take a look at the intraday chart in Figure 43–1 to see what might have happened. In just a few minutes the price dropped more than $1—that's $500 less for the shares. Certainly that's motivation enough for the investor to avoid any unnecessary delays.

The same concept can be extended to the action decision. Once a course of action has been decided, it should be acted on at the earliest opportunity. Waiting a day or even a few hours can change the situation to something entirely different.

Study and planning strategy do not mix well with implementation. They should be done as separate activities. Doing so will help prevent taking actions based on partial information and will make an analysis more effective when planning strategy.

F I G U R E 43–1

Act quickly, IBM (NYSE: IBM), May 26, 1998 (intraday).

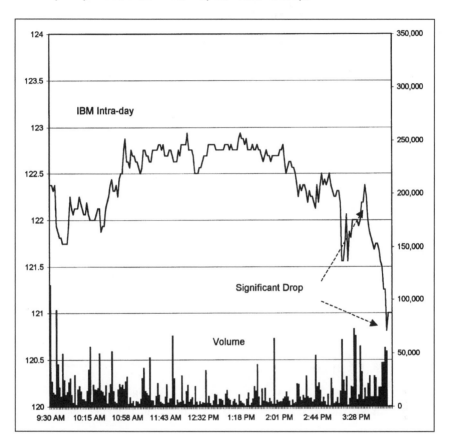

CHAPTER 44

Records Can
Make Money

Record keeping can be an important investment. Records of trades, confirmation slips, and monthly statements can provide information that will actually be worth extra dollars. Reliable record-keeping systems can be important time savers. At tax time nothing can be more frustrating than trying to find mislaid records of transactions to verify dividends and capital gains or losses.

CERTIFICATES HELD

One of the biggest mistakes investors make is placing the stock certificate in a safe deposit box with no other records of the transaction. Years later the investors will wonder what the cost of the stock was at the time of purchase. To avoid this problem, the "confirmation" notice of the buy should be clipped to the stock certificate when it is stored. Doing so will prevent endless headaches when the stock is sold and it's time to calculate the capital gains.

The IRS has an easy method of figuring the cost basis when the owner is unable to do so for a stock. They consider the entire proceeds from the sale as capital gains and tax them accordingly. Needless to say, this action could become costly.

IMPORTANT DOCUMENTS

Stock certificates that are sent out to the buyer are very important documents. They are similar to titles or property deeds. Although they can be replaced if lost, destroyed, or stolen, it takes time to do so. Significant losses can occur while the owner is waiting for the new certificates. Time is lost while a stop is placed on the old certificates and records are searched to ascertain whether or not the certificates have been previously sold.

If dividends are being reinvested, see if the company will hold the certificates in a special account and have them issued in lots of 100 shares or more. This will prevent your ending up with several hundred certificates, each worth 2 or 3 shares.

OPEN ORDERS

Save open order (good-till-canceled) notices, and match them to the open order cancellation notices when they arrive. When a limit order to buy or sell stock is placed, an open order notice is generated. (Over-the-counter securities do not necessarily generate this notice.) The note informs the customer as to the details on the GTC order. Check these notices carefully for accuracy, and keep the notice where it is accessible. It will help prevent your placing the order twice.

It can be irritating to sell the same stock twice and have to pay for the repurchase. When a buy or sell is executed, the open order notice should be placed with the confirmation of the trade. The notice should be clipped to the certificate if it is shipped out to the investor or filed in chronological order if the certificates are held at the brokerage firm in street name. The notices can be more important than old canceled checks, and they should be kept in a safe place for a reasonable length of time. Many investors keep them the same length of time as tax records.

MONTHLY STATEMENTS

Monthly brokerage account statements are also important records and should be kept for a reasonable length of time. Twelve statements a year is not a lot of paper. They can be helpful in tracking down possible errors or figuring out the details of transactions. Eventually, stock certificates will be eliminated, and all investment securities will be held in book-entry format. Many stock exchanges around the world have already taken this action. It could make confirmations and statements even more important than they are now.

RECORDS ORGANIZATION

An organized system for keeping track of transaction records and certificates can save the investor time and money. The cost can be astronomical to have an accountant or lawyer sort out the details of transactions. Investors should think of record keeping as an important part of the investment process.

CHAPTER 45

Fraud Is Unpredictable

Anything can happen in the stock market. It is possible to research and select a stock for investment purposes that is about to double or triple in value, and it is possible to buy a stock that is just about to fold the tent and head for the cellar. The most unpredictable bad news to anticipate is the news of fraud within a particular company. It can happen to anyone—individual and professional investors alike. There is usually no way to see fraud coming.

There has long been a kind of code of honor that says all financial information a company releases is composed of factual and accurate details. However, any time the integrity of information depends on codes of honor, somebody will figure out a way to get around the requirement. Audits often confirm the accuracy of only the data presented. If cleverly done, fraudulent data presented to auditors can look real. The investor—individual or institution—has no way to know whether the information available on any company is true or false. This is simply part of the risk of investing.

SOMETIMES IT'S NOT FRAUD

Companies are frequently sued when their stock price drops, as if it were somehow their fault. Although it might be their fault, what they did might not be fraudulent or illegal. It might have been poor management or something the company didn't control. Such lawsuits are filed either by angry investors or attorneys looking for big fees. Even if they reach a settlement, most of the money never reaches the shareholder.

SELL SOON

In most cases the investor is making a prudent move to sell at the first sign of true fraudulent activity. The institutional investor will quickly sell a position and the situation will not likely improve. This is why it is important to find out as soon as possible why a stock has had a sudden, severe drop in price. The investor must discover the content of the bad news and take appropriate action quickly.

USE CARE WITH INTERNET TRANSACTIONS

In recent years, the Securities and Exchange Commission has become concerned about fraudulent securities available via the Internet. Apparently some unscrupulous individuals are surfing right into people's life savings. Here are some of the approaches they use.

The Pyramid Scheme

The first people entering the pyramid sometimes get high returns, but the last to enter lose everything. The "high returns" come from new investors who pay the old investors. Eventually it all collapses.

> "How To Make Big Money From Your Home Computer!!!" One on-line promoter claimed recently that you could "turn $5 into $60,000 in just three to six weeks."[1]

According to the SEC, this was just an electronic version of the classic pyramid scheme. It's well suited to online computing where a lawbreaker can send messages to a thousand people with the touch of a mouse button.

The Risk-Free or Low-Risk Scheme

> "Exciting, Low-Risk Investment Opportunities" to participate in exotic-sounding investments, including wireless cable projects, prime bank securities and eel farms, have been offered on-line. One promoter attempted to get people to invest in a fictitious coconut plantation in Costa Rica, claiming the investment was similar to a CD, with a better interest rate."

At times scam artists misrepresent the risk by comparing the product to something an investor considers safe, such as bank certificates of deposit. The obvious intent is to make the investor comfortable. Other times, the investment product does not even exist.

The Pump-and-Dump Scam

It is common to see messages posted online urging readers to buy a stock quickly that is poised for rapid growth or telling them to sell before it goes down. Often

---

1. Examples from the Securities Exchange Commission, *SEC Investor Beware*, Office of Investor Education and Assistance, June 1996, http://www.sec.gov/consumer/seefraud.htm.

the writer claims to have "inside" information about an impending development or will claim to use an "infallible" combination of economic and stock market data to pick stocks. According to the SEC, the promoter might be an insider who will gain by selling shares after the stock price is pumped up by gullible buyers. It might also be a short seller who stands to gain if the price goes down. The ploy is often used with little-known, thinly traded stocks.

INVESTIGATE BEFORE INVESTING

Download and print a copy of any online solicitation. Make certain to copy the Internet address (URL), and note the date and time that you saw the offer. Save the printout in case you need it later.

Check with your state securities regulator or the SEC to see if they have received any complaints about the company, its managers, or the promoter. Don't assume that people online are who they claim they are. The investments that sound best could be figments of imagination and nothing more.

Check with a trusted financial advisor, your broker, or attorney about any investment you learn about online. You can also ask the promoter where the firm is incorporated. Call that state's secretary of state, and ask if the company is incorporated with them and has a current annual report on file.

Look for other information at your local public library. For example, some resources provide information about companies, such as a payment analysis, credit report, lawsuits, liens, or judgments.

Don't assume the access provider or online service has approved or even screened the investment. They don't do that sort of thing. Anyone can set up a Web site or advertise on the Internet without any check of its legitimacy or truthfulness.

Before you invest, always obtain written financial information, such as a prospectus, annual report, offering circular, and financial statements. Compare the written information to what you've read online, and watch out if you're told that no information is available.

If a company is not registered or has not filed a Form D with the SEC, call the SEC's Office of Investor Education and Assistance at (202) 942-7040 or your state securities regulator. You can also visit the SEC's Web site at www.sec.gov or contact them by e-mail. Contact the Office of Investor Education and Assistance at help@sec.gov or the Division of Enforcement at enforcement@sec.gov.

Or write to the following address:

Securities and Exchange Commission
Office of Investor Education & Assistance
450 Fifth Street, NW Mail Stop 11-2
Washington, DC 20549

To reach a state securities regulator, check the SEC state government section in a local phone book, or call the North American Securities Administrators Association (NASAA) at (202) 737-0900.

FRAUD CAN BE DIFFICULT TO SPOT

The advice "If it seems too good to be true, it probably is" can be difficult to follow. It might have kept many people away from companies like Microsoft, Apple Computer, or Winnebago back when they first started. They were not fraudulent investments in any way, and that's what the scam artist is counting on to convince the investor.

Fraud can sneak up on an investor. A personal visit to a company can be helpful, but it doesn't ensure the integrity of the information. Companies tend to be good at putting on a dog-and-pony show for investors and brokers. Even the worst of companies can usually put together a good show for an audience. Many times the best defense is to not invest if there is any doubt or sell out if fraud appears.

CHAPTER 46

Use Margin for
Leverage Only

...and I've got 500 shares of stock worth about $80 a share. I'd like to take out a
margin loan so I can buy a new car. I figure $20,000 will do it.

The statement above, or one like it, is often heard in the broker's office. Someone
has some stock that might have been sitting in a safety deposit box for many
years, or it might be stock received from an estate. After reading or hearing about
margin loans, using stock as collateral, the old stock suddenly becomes an easy
source of money.

The question many brokers would like to ask next is, "When the price drops
and you get a margin call, are you willing to sell the car to cover it?"

COULD IT COME TO THAT?

Yes, it could come to that. This investor could end up without the stock and have
to sell the car to cover the margin loan. Brokers and their firms do not like to see
these problems develop because the customer loses and sometimes ends up
wrongly blaming the brokerage firm. Also, brokerage firms make more money if
their customers make money. When the customers lose, the firms lose the customer and the money.

BE ABLE TO MEET THE CALLS

To ensure that investors will be able to meet margin calls is the reason many brokerage firms require 40 percent margin maintenance (instead of the usual 25 or 30

percent) if the investor is margined on a small number of stocks. The higher margin maintenance decreases their risk and the customer's risk. The debit (amount of money borrowed) remains constant whether the stock price rises or falls.

If an investor borrows 50 percent of the value of one stock and that stock drops a bit more than 10 percent in price, the investor will likely receive a margin call to bring in additional funds or marginable securities as soon as possible. This call could put the investor in a difficult situation. If the market and the stock are stable, there might not ever be a problem, but the risk is ever present in a margin situation. As discussed earlier (see Chapter 34), the investor can end up losing all the securities and owing additional money. Therefore, margin loans should be used with a great deal of care and understanding.

USE MARGIN AS LEVERAGE

Margin loans should be used primarily to leverage an investment position. Although the cash is available and can be used for any purpose the investor desires, it is most prudent to use the funds to buy additional marginable securities. The reason for this is liquidity. If the margined securities decline in price, part of the position can be sold to cover the entire margin maintenance call, or the position can be liquidated before any more damage occurs. Selling stock or other securities is generally easier than selling a car, a weekend cabin, or the children's college education in order to meet a maintenance call.

LEARN AND GAIN EXPERIENCE

As the investor becomes more familiar with margin loans through study and experience, the use of funds can be expanded. But until these understandings are developed, it is best to be conservative and careful. Margin loans are best suited to leveraging a securities position.

CHAPTER 47

Avoid Overtrading

For some people, the trading of stocks, options, or other securities can become an addiction similar to gambling. It can be like a nickel or dime stock machine—win a few jackpots and keep putting the coins back in until they are gone. It is like betting on one more horse to make up for the losses or extend the winnings.

As with other gambling addictions, the trading addicted person is usually not making any money. At best they tend to break even, which only adds to their compulsive activity. The day is just not complete unless they can make one or two stock or option trades.

STORIES AND COMPLIANCE

Every brokerage firm has a few stories of a stock or option trader who became addicted to trading. The stories usually involve fairly large sums of money after a few years' time. Eventually, the trading-addicted investor runs out of money, or the brokerage firm's compliance department steps in and puts a halt to the activity. Compliance departments are quite diligent in this regard, although it is difficult for them to closely watch every account.

One such story involves an investor who became addicted to trading index options on the Standard & Poor's 100 Index, often referred to as the OEX Index. During a three-year period, this investor traded an average of two to five times each day. He consistently lost an average of $10,000 every year. When compliance brought the activity to a halt, the customer's biggest disappointment was not the money lost but rather being forced to close the account due to not being able to maintain the 2,000 minimum equity in a margin account.

The investor did have a disciplined approach to trading. Sometimes the strategy worked, and other times it failed to produce anything but losses. The system was possibly too inflexible to deal with the daily changes in the stock market, although it was not helped by a compulsive need to make a trade every day.

The main failing of the compulsive system seemed to be the missed opportunities caused by closing out the option positions too soon. In several situations, the investor had the right idea but did not allow time for the strategy to do its work. If the investor had waited patiently only a couple of days, the positions would have been profitable.

OVERTRADING AND CHURNING

The securities industry regulatory organizations consider overtrading and "churning" to be nearly the same activity. Most people think of churning as a stockbroker-initiated activity, but the end result is the same. The activity generates commission charges for the stockbroker and the brokerage firm. Unsuitable trading, where recommendations are not in keeping with the customer's financial condition, investing sophistication, or investment objectives, is also a related activity.

Unsuitable Trading

The NASD suitability rule requires that the broker's recommendations be appropriate in light of the customer's financial condition, level of sophistication, investment objectives, and risk tolerance. The suitability rule and the closely related "know-your-customer" rule require that the broker use due diligence to obtain information about the customer's financial situation, needs, objectives, and understanding.

Violation of NASD and stock exchange rules, including the suitability and know-your-customer rules, may be the basis for a cause of action on its own. For example, the violation of the suitability rule and the NASD rules may itself constitute a basis for a breach-of-contract action. Unsuitable trading has also been held to constitute fraud and to constitute a violation of federal and state securities laws. A broker clearly is prohibited from recommending unsuitable investments, and there have been indications that a broker should refuse to execute unsuitable transactions even when the investment is originally the customer's idea.

Churning

Churning is trading at an excessive frequency motivated by the broker's desire for personal gain through commissions. For overtrading to constitute churning, the broker must exercise control over the trading in the account and abuse the customer's trust by engaging in transactions that are excessive in volume and frequency considering the character of the account.

Overtrading can be difficult to control, especially with increasing access to the market through the Internet. The flexibility, convenience, and accessibility of information can encourage the investor to trade more frequently. When working with a brokerage firm, carefully checking records can help the investor prevent overtrading. Taking the time to analyze the trades on a monthly statement can help the investor stay in control of the amount of trading. Other ideas are presented below.

PREVENTING OVERTRADING

Keep Organized Records

Look carefully at the monthly statement from the brokerage firm, and make a short note as to the reason for each trade. If you normally do a lot of trading in a month, you should keep these notes on the confirmation slips that arrive by mail a few days after the transaction.

Ideally, you should keep notes on your strategy in a stock trading log. This way you are making the notation at the time of the transaction, when the strategy is still fresh in your mind. The notation should briefly mention how the trade fit into the specific strategy and possibly the overall plan you have prepared.

Look for Profit in Transactions

Although an account can be profitable but still overtraded, it's worse to be losing and overtraded. If there have been several unprofitable transactions, it's time to reassess or redefine your objectives or strategy. In this situation, checking the timing of the trades can be helpful. Might the delay of a week or two have increased the profits? Perhaps you should check your analysis of the current market strength.

Look for Patterns in Trading

Are trades occurring every day or every other day? Is there a pattern such as trading every three out of five days on a consistent basis? If you notice a pattern, what is the cause of it? Finding a pattern might point out trading that is becoming an addiction.

Assess the Amount of Contact You Have with Your Broker

Is this contact on a daily basis, or is it several times a day, perhaps even hourly? Very close contact with the market can easily lead an investor to overtrade an account. The individual can develop an addiction to the market action. The information addiction can easily cause the investor to overreact to minor moves in the stock market. The first overreaction leads to another, and soon the account is in an overtraded tailspin.

Overtrading and trading addiction can be detrimental to any investment strategy. It is extremely difficult to build profits when too many transactions are being whipsawed by short-term market swings. Flexible strategies, good records, solid investment objectives, and pulling away from unprofitable market activity can help an investor avoid many of the pitfalls.

CHAPTER 48

Buy When There's Blood in the Streets

Every time the stock market takes a plunge, this axiom is taken from the shelf and dusted off. It's the kind of saying many people believe makes a lot of sense. Actually, it can be disastrous as a strategy.

THE 1929 CRASH

The 1929 crash was amazing by any standard (Figure 48–1). It followed an incredible bull market that had been rising for nearly a decade. The Dow Industrials hit a high of 386 in September 1929. After the infamous crash, the Dow did not return to that level for 25 years, until November 1954. At its worst level, the Dow dropped to 40.56 in July 1932, a drop of 89 percent. Even many of those who waited until the bottom still had trouble as companies continued to go broke and ceased doing business. If investors selected the right companies, they did better.

As the chart illustrates, 1928 was a good year with the Dow Industrial Average rising from the 200-point level to just above 312. There were a few corrections along the way, including a 36-point drop in December, but the year looked good. Volume on the New York Stock Exchange increased along with the advancing market.

Look what happened during the first half of 1929. The Dow Industrials formed strong support at the 300-point level but found fiercely tenacious resistance about 20 points higher. The resistance was finally penetrated in June, and the market chugged another 20 points higher. But look at what happened to the

FIGURE 48–1

Market crash, Dow Industrial Average and NYSE volume, 1928–1929.

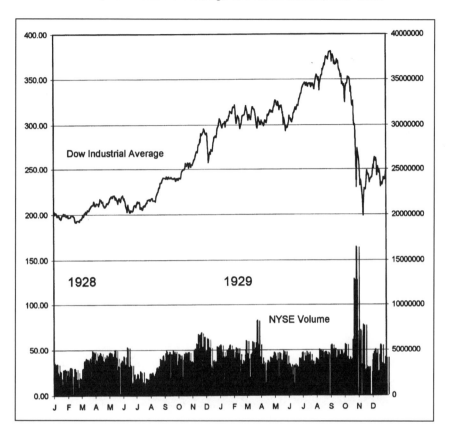

volume. The volume had been declining since January. It increased as the market resumed its advance but not enough to keep the rally going.

From mid-July to mid-October, the market made what would now be called a *head-and-shoulders* technical pattern. The pattern is a signal of weakness and says that the market is likely to correct a minimum amount, measured from the top of the head to the neckline, just under the shoulders. Obviously, the Dow fell that minimum amount and much more.

After a brief hesitation at the 300-point support level, the market fell again. It finally stopped just under the 200-point level. At this point many people probably breathed a sigh of relief, thinking the worst was over, but it wasn't, as shown in Figure 48–2.

F I G U R E 48–2

Bottom, Dow Industrials and NYSE volume, 1930–1933.

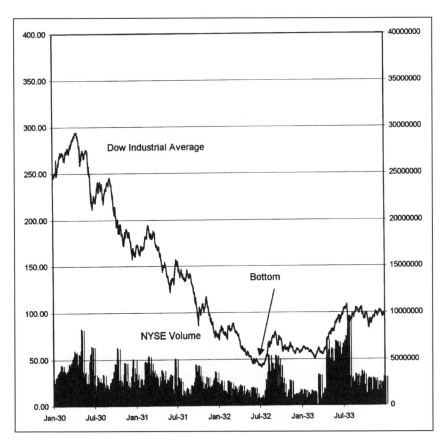

Fortunes Lost

A number of family fortunes were lost along the way, as people believed they were buying stocks at bargain prices. Each time they thought the bottom was reached and bought, the market fell again. In April 1930, the Dow retraced back up to 294, only to fall back to 158 points in December. A weak economy and not enough money for liquidity were bringing the stock market to its knees.

Bad Advice from Experts

These investors were receiving what they believed was the best expert advice. Myron E. Forbes, President, Pierce Arrow Motor Car Co., on January 12, 1928, made the following statement:

> There will be no interruption of our permanent prosperity.

An expert even more highly regarded than Forbes, E. H. H. Simmons, President of the New York Stock Exchange, said in January 1928:

> I cannot help but raise a dissenting voice to statements that we are living in a fool's paradise, and that prosperity in this country must necessarily diminish and recede in the near future.

The stock market and the economy are influenced by public attitudes. When people believe they are reasonably secure, they buy goods and they buy stock. If they are frightened, they sell stock and don't spend any money. In fact, those who were predicting doom and gloom were accused of making matters worse than they had to be. So that is a dilemma: If a disaster is coming, do you inform the public, who will then panic and make matters worse, or do you put up a positive front and hope for the best:

The Aftermath

Fortunes were lost, not just in the stock market, but in banking as well. Banks were closing all around the country, with businesses closing and life savings evaporating. There were no federally supported depositor insurance programs like the FDIC, and banks were allowed to buy stocks as investments for customer deposits. The economy and the market collapsed and stagnated.

The stock market, considerably leaner in terms of the number of companies remaining, continued to trade, gradually working its way back to new highs (Figure 48–3).

25-Year Retracement

It took more than 25 years for the Dow Industrial Average to set new highs, after the crash of 1929. It was a long and difficult road, requiring the rebuilding of an economic system, as well as financial systems for securities trading and banking. The Securities and Exchange Commission (SEC) was organized. The SEC created and strictly enforced several measures to protect and keep fairness and integrity in the trading of securities.

THAT WAS THEN

The crash of 1929 and ensuing depression in the thirties was one time when it was probably not a good strategy to "buy when there's blood in the streets." It was a time when serious economic problems came to the front to push and keep the stock market down. These were problems that couldn't be easily corrected because the knowledge and resources to make the adjustments were missing.

FIGURE 48-3

New highs, Dow Industrial Average and NYSE volume, 1934–1954.

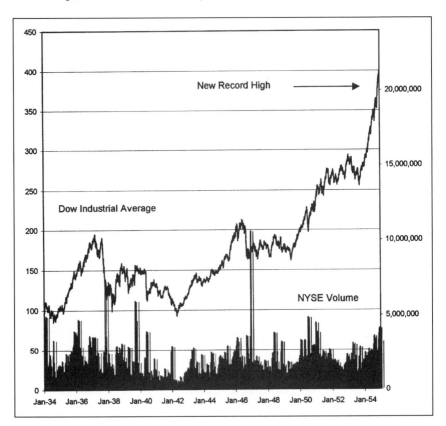

THIS IS NOW

However, in the 1990s, usually once or twice a year, the Dow Industrial Average falls a few hundred points. These corrections have been excellent buying opportunities. The stock market can still have down secondary trends and bear markets, but it is less likely to have weakness problems like those of the Great Depression. That is not to say that a depression is no longer possible but rather that many of the system flaws that caused the 1930s depression have been dealt with effectively. If the U.S. economy is ever hit by another severe depression, it will have been caused by other factors.

Recessions

Economic setbacks are now called *recessions*, not *depressions*, but the effects can be similar. The economic structure of the nation is now based on global considerations. This helps to create a moderating buffer when the economy and the market slip. Professionals and individuals now regard severe stock market declines as buying opportunities. But overall recessions, or *rolling recessions*, which go from industry to industry, can still create tough economic times. It is always difficult to know how severe a market drop will be. Individual stocks can be an even larger problem.

Individual Companies

If a stock takes a sudden and severe decline that is not market driven, the company is having serious problems from which it might never recover. At the very least, the company will have to resolve the fundamental problems that caused the price decline. If a stock buyer chooses such a stock for investment, it is important to either be well acquainted with the industry sector involved and the company's ability to recover or to buy the stock on total speculation. Frequently, speculative investors will buy junk and hope for a dollar or two in recovery. At times the prices of these stocks fall quite low. Some may drop below a dollar a share.

Doubling, Not Likely

If an investor is tempted to "buy when there is blood in the streets," first make certain that the patient is being well cared for and will soon be on the road to recovery.

CHAPTER 49

Look for Divergence in Trends

The stock market seldom has "a normal day." Upon close analysis, each day is unique with its own special pattern of change. One day technology stocks will be hot and oil stocks will be out of favor. The next session might see oil stocks as the biggest gainers. One day the Dow Industrial Average will be up 60 points and the outlook for business development will appear favorable. The following session has the market correcting 100 points on the Dow, with growing inflation becoming a real threat.

MARKET PREDICTIONS

As J. Pierpont Morgan so succinctly put it, the market will indeed "fluctuate"; it tends to do that during every trading session. When stockbrokers are asked the question "What will the market do?" they will either attempt to be positive or neutral on the subject. Many analysts will give a lengthy explanation of what the market should do and why. It's a simple fact that no one knows precisely what the overall stock market will do. The best one can hope for is to find a few signals of strength or weakness. One way to look for these signals is to look at trends.

Stock Market Trends

The concept of looking at stock market trends began in the late 1800s with Charles Henry Dow, one of the founding fathers of Dow Jones & Company and *The Wall Street Journal*. Dow followed market trends based on the Dow Industrial

Average and the Dow Railroad Average (now the Transportation Average). He followed what he called "primary, secondary, and tertiary" trends. The creation of the Dow Averages and definition of trends formed the basis of the technical analysis used today. The study done by Dow and later editor William Hamilton eventually became known as "the Dow theory." Here we will look at trends in relationship to divergence, support, and resistance.

Three Trends

The daily movements of the stock market (*tertiary trend*) are important in the way they affect the secondary and long-term trends. The long-term trend (primary trend) shows the overall direction of the stock market for an extended period of time (usually six months or more). The term *current trend* can refer either to the long-term trend or secondary trend. The *secondary trend* is a short-term trend showing a reaction or move that is in the opposite direction to the primary trend.

THE TENDENCY OF STOCK PRICES TO MOVE AS A GROUP

One concept that all analysts agree on is the fact that stock prices tend to move as a group. Dow Average stocks, Standard & Poor's stocks, and NASDAQ (over-the-counter) stocks tend to move as a group. If they diverge from moving as a group, it is a signal of weakness in the stock market.

The tendency of stock prices moving as a group is what makes up a trend. *Divergences* are changes in trend that show stocks not moving as a group. It is difficult to know whether the signal means a change in trend or the appearance of a secondary trend. However, the divergence is a technical signal of market weakness. There can also be times when divergence occurs and the stock market ignores a divergence signal and continues to move upward. The investor who is aware of trends has the advantage of knowing whether or not the market is strong and what direction it is going. First comes the divergence signal, then the reaction, followed by a turn in direction.

The sequence can be illustrated by the events surrounding the 1987 crash:

- An all-time high for the Dow Industrials was reached in August.
- The Dow Utility Average had been declining since April.
- The Federal discount rate was raised, signaling a rise in interest rates.
- The reaction: The Dow Industrials drifted lower, down 200 points by October 19.
- Finally came the turn in the trend, as the Dow Industrial Average fell more than 500 points.

SIGNALS

Signals can be confusing; a market trend can ignore what is supposed to happen and continue on its merry way. It is able to do this because it is a market of individuals all making judgment calls.

Many times active investors are all waiting for someone else to make a move. Groups form, believing the market will fall. Other groups form and take actions to prove the first group wrong. As the struggle ensues, buying or selling groups will gather and lose supporters until finally a majority of buyers or sellers emerges. The participants in this struggle will search out news and information to support their belief. If the news suggests their stand is incorrect, they will switch sides and the market moves accordingly.

All the individual investor has to do is look for signals of a struggle or weakness. Such signals will often appear in trend divergence. It can be a divergence between the Dow Industrial Average and the Transportation Average, or it might be a divergence between the Dow and an individual stock.

The October 1997 Divergence

On Monday, October 27, the Dow Industrial Average fell 554.26 points—a new record one-day drop for the prestigious Dow. Although some analysts believed it was doomsday, others believed the drop to be a short-term correction. There was divergence between the Dow Industrial and Transportation Averages during the few weeks before the record correction.

When the Dow Industrial Average is compared to the Transportation Average, it's usually the transports that show weakness in relation to the industrials. In Figure 49–1, we see a strong uptrend in the transports, while the Industrial Average is declining. Also, the increased volatility, with the market surging back and forth, was a signal of weakness (Figure 49–2).

The NYSE Volume

A look at total NYSE volume for 1997 shows a cycling pattern, but not much in the way of a weakness signal. Although volume weakness appears near the end of August and again near the end of September, it seems to be similar to earlier weakness events that did not cause such significant corrections.

The highest volume spike appearing in Figure 49–2 is actually the day after the big crash. 1,201,346,607 shares changed hands on October 28, 1997, another new record for one day of trading. The Dow Industrials regained more than 337 points, with the Transportation Average moving up better than 95 points. The strength was there; it was just time to test the market.

FIGURE 49–1

Divergence, Dow Averages August through December 1997.

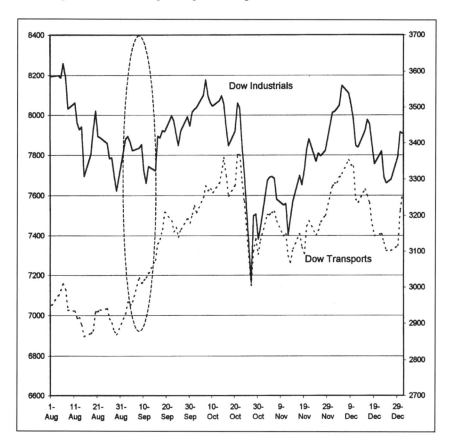

What to Look for

Look at the relationship between the Dow Industrials, Dow Transportation Average, and to some extent the Dow Utility Average. If they are closely matching each other in direction and the volume is steady or growing, the market is strong. If the averages do not match direction or the volume is showing signs of weakness, the market is weak and could correct.

Secondary Opportunities

When corrections are short-term secondary trends, they present buying opportunities to the investor. If the Dow Industrials drops more than 20 percent or is

F I G U R E 49–2

Volume weakness, New York Stock Exchange, 1997.

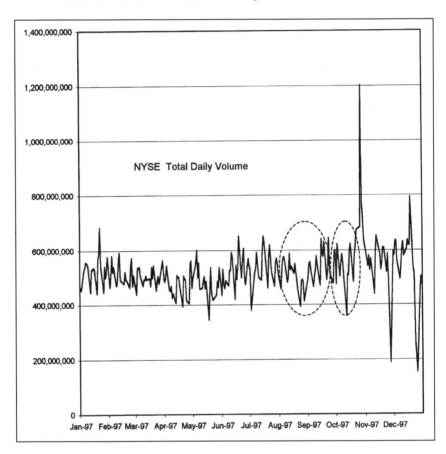

down for more than two consecutive months, it most likely is the formation of a
bear market. The investor might want to wait for signs of stabilization as shown
by less volatility and trend confirmation.

CHAPTER 50

Invest in What You Know Best

Diversification in an investment portfolio is always advisable; however, investing in an industry or a company where the investor has been employed can be profitable also. If an investor works in the auto industry, it is logical for hime or her to do some investing in automobile stocks. A person who has worked for Ford Motor Company for several years will undoubtedly have special insight into how the company works. An investor with that background could also have a unique understanding of vendors used by Ford. Working directly with a supplier gives one a strong understanding of that company's ability to supply products and services. The understanding could be worth more than spending numerous hours analyzing that vendor's balance sheet.

A pharmacist should have insight into the potential growth of pharmaceutical companies, and the electrical engineer could do well investing in high-tech companies. Investing in companies related to the investor's background is logical, but it is often not done. Doctors often invest in Aerospace stocks. Aerospace engineers invest in drug companies, and drug company employees invest in high-tech computer companies.

IS IT ALL PUBLIC RELATIONS?

The main problem with this strategy is the investor's vulnerability to public relations. Because the investors are unfamiliar with what is real and what is so much window dressing, it is more difficult for them to discern which information is significant. However, the same people often have a tremendous amount of first-hand knowledge about the workings of their own industry. They might have 10 or 20 years experience—experience that can be used as a basis for analysis. Their work experience gives them advantages not available to the stock analyst. Most good analysts would love the opportunity to work for 30 days in the companies they follow and do the work incognito. The knowledge gained would be priceless. However, analysts do not have the time for such an activity, much less the opportunity.

When an investor already has the work experience, it only makes sense to make good use of the knowledge. If the stocks selected do well, consider the profits a work-related bonus for using job-related information.

KEEP AN EYE ON THE COMPETITION

Competitive companies might even be better targets. Sometimes a person knows more about the competition than they do about their own company. A person working for IBM might actually know more about Compaq or the other way around. The Compaq employee knows that IBM's most recent development will generate strong sales. Investing in the stock of a competitor can be an excellent strategy including the following advantages:

- No emotional involvement
- Early observation of developments
- Easily followed financial growth
- Insight into problems

Investing in the stock of companies with which one has practical working knowledge will not guarantee success, but it can help to make the analysis more meaningful and improve the chances of success. It can have the additional advantage of helping the investor keep an eye on the competition's successes and failures. Information like this can serve as a valuable resource for the investor's regular employment.

LOOK FIRST TO WHAT YOU KNOW

The learning curve regarding investing is steep, and mistakes can be costly. Investing in companies an investor knows and understands significantly reduces the amount of information to learn. This can lead to quick understanding and fast decisions when it comes to buy or sell the stock.

Buy Stock Cheaper with Dollar Cost Averaging

What is *dollar cost averaging*? It means to buy stocks with the average cost per share being less than the average share price. How can this be done? By purchasing a larger number of shares when the price of the shares is lower and fewer shares when prices are higher.

IT'S A DISCIPLINE

Dollar cost averaging is the discipline of setting a regular, long-term investment program for a portfolio, in terms of a set dollar amount that the investor can afford (e.g., $100, $1,000, $5,000 invested monthly or quarterly). The periodic investing takes the place of attempting to predict when a stock is at its low or at its high.

By investing the same amount regularly, say, $1,000 every month, the investor will buy more units when prices are low and fewer units when prices are high. The strategy results in a portfolio with an average of costs. Obviously, units purchased at a lower price will outperform those bought at the higher price. Since dollar cost averaging is being used, more of the "high-performance units" are bought when prices are low.

AT&T

AT&T, or "Telephone," has long been an accumulation stock for individual investors. It has had that slow, steady growth, with some dividend payout. One of

FIGURE 51-1

Dollar cost averaging, AT&T (NYSE: T), 1994–1998.

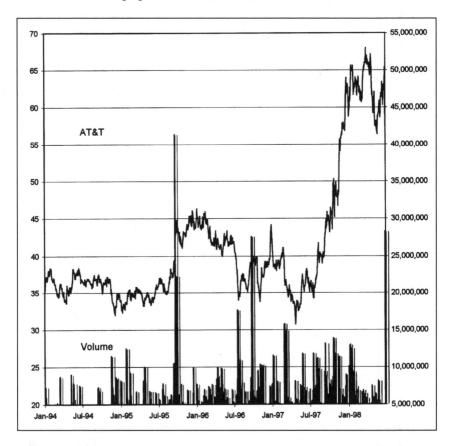

the old broker pitches on this kind of stock was, "Get paid the dividend while you wait for the growth." Well, the growth finally arrived in a big spurt during 1997. The stock had settled back in the comfortable low 30s, when it suddenly took off and didn't really stop until it reached $68 a share in March 1998. Maybe the old brokers were right or at least as surprised as many investors. Take a look at Figure 51–1.

Whoever "bottom ticked" the AT&T stock at $30.75 on April 24, 1997, bought it at one of the lowest prices it had been at in years. From then on, it was an uphill ride and a rather fast one, doubling the investment right before Christmas of that same year, in less than eight months.

But What about Dollar Cost Averaging?

Ahh . . . yes, dollar cost averaging, a system that effectively and automatically cuts back on purchases when the price is high and automatically increases the buys when the price is low. It is a system designed to be used by a long-term investor but just doesn't work well for the short-term trader.

Table 51–1 shows what would have happened to an investment in $1,000 worth of AT&T stock, bought on a quarterly basis, from the beginning of 1994 through April 1998. Obviously when a dollar cost averaging system is used over several years, the savings can be considerable.

TABLE 51–1

Dollar Cost Averaging ($1,000 per quarter), AT&T

Date	Price	Invested	Shares
1/3/94	35.57	1,000	28
4/29/94	34.64	1,000	29
7/29/94	36.922	1,000	27
10/31/94	37.175	1,000	27
1/31/95	33.711	1,000	30
4/28/95	34.302	1,000	29
7/31/95	35.654	1,000	28
10/31/95	43.258	1,000	23
1/31/96	45.202	1,000	22
4/30/96	41.4	1,000	24
7/31/96	35.316	1,000	28
10/31/96	34.875	1,000	29
1/31/97	39.375	1,000	25
4/30/97	33.5	1,000	30
7/31/97	36.812	1,000	27
10/31/97	48.875	1,000	20
1/30/98	62.625	1,000	16
4/30/98	60.125	1,000	17
		18,000	460

The average price per share	$40.52
The average cost per share ($18,000/460)	$39.16
Total shares purchased	460
Total dollar amount invested	$18,000
Total dollars saved	$625.94

IT'S VERSATILE

Dollar cost averaging can be used with virtually any investment portfolio, although it tends to work better with mutual funds. Funds are advantageous because their units can be split up, allowing an investor to buy a specific dollar amount instead of a specific number of shares. Dollar cost averaging also allows one to follow a primary rule of investing—pay yourself first. Many people don't invest because they believe they don't have enough money to do so. Here again, mutual funds are advantageous because with some funds, investors can put away as little as $50 per month!

DON'T WORRY ABOUT THE MARKET

The message is that an investor can make good returns even though the market may be unstable. Every investor would like to "buy low and sell high," but that's not an easy thing to do. Markets fluctuate up and down. An investment strategy of dollar cost averaging takes advantage of this variability by consistently investing a fixed amount of money at predetermined intervals (monthly or quarterly). By doing this consistently, the fluctuations in the market value of the investment are smoothed out. The investor using this strategy purchases more shares of stock or a mutual fund when the prices are low and fewer when prices are higher.

Periodic investment plans such as dollar cost averaging do not assure a profit or protect against loss in declining markets. The investor using this strategy continues to make purchases through periods of low and declining prices. In this way, he or she gains from purchasing more shares at lower prices. The investor still must carefully select the specific investment, whether stocks, bonds, or mutual funds.

CHAPTER 52

There's Always a Santa Claus Rally

Santa Claus is comin' to town . . . and to the stock market. To the purist, any rally between the Thanksgiving holiday and Christmas day is a Santa Claus Rally. Actually, virtually any rally in the months of November or December is credited to the "jolly old elf." It's the buying season, a time when some retailers make their year profitable. Consumers go shopping with a frenzy, not just for presents to place under a tree. Many excited shoppers also buy themselves presents. The Friday after Thanksgiving remains the busiest day of the year for retailers. Consumers have been saving their money and curbing their buying impulses just for this day. It's only natural that the buying frenzy would extend itself into the stock market (Figure 52–1).

WE'RE SORRY . . .

At the end of 1990, it was as if the traders were apologizing for stomping on the Dow Industrial Average for much of the second half of the year. The Dow had been driven from 3,000 down to 2,365 points, qualifying it as a bear market.[1] Then in mid-October, it made a minor double bottom and rallied for the rest of the year, closing at 2,633.66, still down 119.54 points for the year. However, the visit from Santa saved the Dow 268.66 points. It was as if the hard-nosed traders were apologizing and buying back shares to show how sorry they were.

---

1. *Bear market* is defined as a market that is down for two or more consecutive months or down more than 20 percent.

F I G U R E 52–1

Santa Claus Rally, Dow Industrials, 1990–1997.

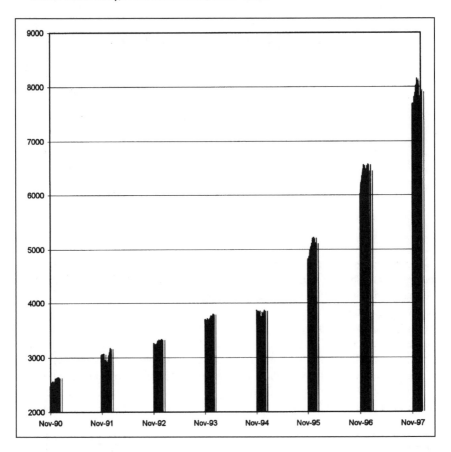

The market was up 247 points at the July 3,000 level, and then it got clobbered. Kuwait was becoming a serious problem for the world, and many professional investors became obviously nervous. The market needed a jolly red-cheeked symbol with a big smile, and Santa rode in early.

A STRANGE, INDECISIVE YEAR

In 1991, the Dow Industrials started with a correction, then rose about 300 points and bounced back and forth until the December rally. Conflict in the Middle East between Kuwait and Iraq made the economic situation uncertain. The 1991 December rally rose 303.45 points before it was over. The Dow Industrial Average finished the year with a total gain of 535.17 points, certainly a respectable showing.

It's interesting to see that the year 1991 closed the way it began. A gain of 300 points early in the year, a 100- to 150-point cycle for most of the year, and then another gain of 300 points (after a 100+ point correction) all made an unusual year. Santa wasn't early this year.

1992: SANTA IN OCTOBER

The year needed some kind of rally by the time October came around. After breaking ever so slightly above the 3,400 level on the Dow Industrials, the market went into a bear market lasting just over six months. The bear hit bottom (3,136.58, down, just over 260 points from the high and down 32 points from the beginning of the year) on October 9, 1992, and the Santa Claus Rally started. Although the rally wasn't straight up, it was a strong uptrend through the end of the year. There were a few areas of price consolidation and at least five significant corrections. The market was gaining strength, but some of the players were obviously nervous.

The 1992 rally was significant because it had enough momentum to end the year with a 132-point gain and carry on into 1993. Whether the entire October through December time period is considered part of the Santa Claus Rally or just the December portion doesn't matter much, unless one is specifically analyzing such phenomena. It's a rally with strength and direction.

1993

It was a nice year for the stock market, 1993, with the Dow closing up more than 450 points for the year. It had good strength and direction, with enough volatility to keep things interesting for the speculators.

The Santa Claus Rally started on November 29 and ran until December 13, moving the Dow Industrials up 86.68 points to 3,764.48. Just to see how serious everyone was, the Dow gave up half the rally, correcting more than 47 points. In a show of firm resolve, the Industrials staged the final rally of the year, rising 77.41 points to a new high of 3,794.33 points. Many would call this a second Santa Rally.

A year-end sell-off brought the Dow Industrials down to 3,754.09 with an excellent gain of 452.98 points for the year.

1994

The average moved around, but at the end of the year hadn't really gone anywhere. The Dow Industrials' high for the year came early on January 31, at 3,978.36, reaching for that 4,000 level. The low for 1994 came on April 4— 3,593.35, a total of 385.01 points down from the high. The rest of the year fluctuated between those two points. It was a year of consolidation for the Dow

Industrials. The year did end on the upside, thanks to a nice Santa Rally starting on December 9. At the end of 1994, the Dow Industrial Average had risen 80.35 points. The modest increase was a certainly better performance than the Dow Transportation Average closing out the year with a 307.29 loss.

The near 176-point rally was a nice end to the year, even with a small sell-off at the end. However, the importance of this rally was the fact that it became a launching pad for the next few years, pushing the Dow Industrials above 9,000 by 1998. That's an increase of 5,166 points in less than 4 years, more growth than the market had ever known before. It clearly illustrates that these little Santa Claus Rallies at the end of the year can have far-reaching results.

By any and all descriptions, this has been the most incredible bull market in history. In the old days, many would have called it the "frenzy at the top" and prepared to sell. The Dow Industrial Average has been like a train, heading for that 10,000-point level.

Although the charging Dow has hesitated at each major 1,000-point level, most hesitations were short-lived. The market stopped to see if anyone wanted to sell and headed upward again. Each year, 1995, 1996, and 1997, showed a small Santa Clause Rally, but they were minor when compared to the larger bull market rally for each year:

1995	up	1,282.68 points
1996	up	1,331.15 points
1997	up	1,459.98 points

The stock market has been fueled by a slow growth, low interest rates, stable economy. Money has also flowed into the U.S. stock market from weaker markets around the world, most notably the Asian markets. As the money has come in to buy stocks, the prices have risen and continue upward.

ALWAYS A SANTA RALLY

For the past few years, it would seem that there is always a Santa Rally, but there's no such thing as "always" for the fluctuations of the stock market. Because the market trades on anticipation of higher or lower prices, it frequently surprises investors with rallies or corrections. Although it is possible to have a bearish trend in the last two months of a year, there will likely be some kind of rally. Some of these rallies will be significant, others quite modest.

CHAPTER 53

There's Always a
Year-End Sell-off

The word *always* is a tip-off—things are seldom described as "always" in the stock market. The fact is, most years see some kind of selling near the end of the year, but "most" is not the same as "always". Sometimes the selling is significant; other times it's minor, and once in a while a year-end sell-off is nonexistent.

A sell-off at the end of the year is also referred to as *tax loss selling*, based on the belief that some investors are selling stocks that are trading at losing prices. Additionally, other investors might also be selling stocks with disappointing price performance records. Whatever the reason, the event does occur with some regularity.

To place some consistency on a definition of *year-end*, we will look primarily at selling during the final week of the year, basically December 26 through 31. Some consider only the final trading day of the year as a true year-end sell-off.

WHAT GOOD IS IT?

If an investor has a poorly performing stock, it is probably best to unload it before the year-end selling begins, possibly in a Santa Claus Rally. If an investor is looking for bargains, they might be available near the end of the year. One of the basic concepts of investing in stock is to buy when others are selling.

Some speculative investors might look at the year-end sell as a short selling opportunity; however, the targets must be carefully selected, and the opportunity doesn't seem to last for long period of time.

THE DOW INDUSTRIAL AVERAGE AND
THE STANDARD & POOR'S 500 INDEX: YEAR-END SELL-OFFS

Both the Dow Industrial Average and the Standard & Poor's 500 Index appear on the following charts in Figures 53–1 through 53–3. The left scale is for the Dow, and the right scale is for the S&P 500. One trading day of November is included with the daily closing levels of December for the years 1990 through 1997.

Although both indicators showed a sell-off in the final week, it wasn't much. The surprise is in how small the sell-off was after such a volatile month. However, the trends of both indicators were solidly up, ending the month with a nice advance. The Dow Industrial Average was up 68.07 points, and the S&P 500 Index up 6.12 points for the month. Those are both good gains, considering that the Dow still ended the year down more than 119 points, with the S&P Index down just over 23 points.

FIGURE 53–1

Year-end sell-off, Dow Industrial Average, S&P 500 Index, 1990.

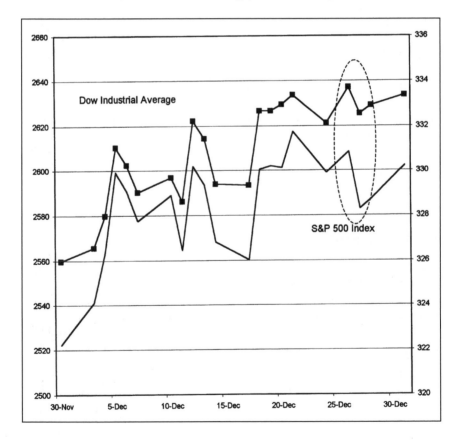

F I G U R E 53–2

Year-end sell-off, Dow Industrial Average, S&P 500 Index, 1991.

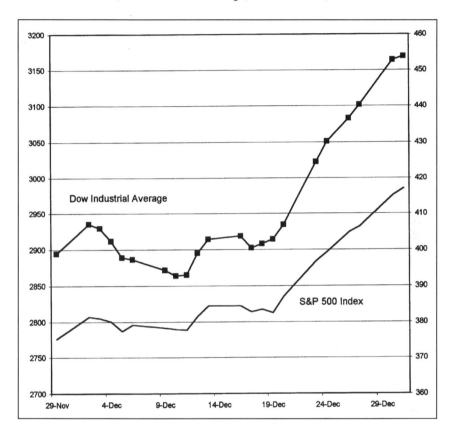

1991

Although some weakness appeared earlier in December, there really wasn't much of a year-end sell-off in 1991:

Dow Industrial Average up	535.17
Standard & Poor's 500 Index	86.87

1992

After ending a difficult 1992, the Dow dropped 32.15 points from December 28 through December 31. The S&P 500 Index dropped a more modest 3.44 points in the same time period, but the sell-off began earlier, with a total drop of 5.57 points. The Dow Industrials were up 132.28 points for the year 1992, with the S&P Index being up 18.62 points.

F I G U R E 53–3

Year-end sell-off, Dow Industrials, S&P 500 Index, 1992–1997.

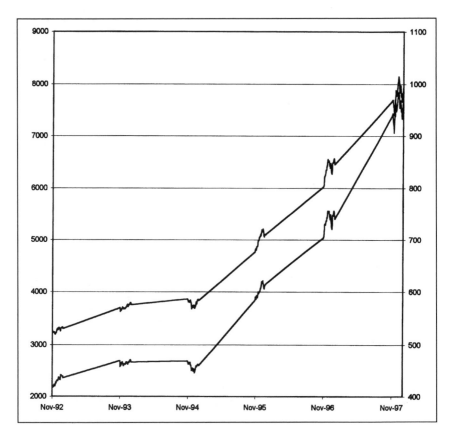

1993

The year was a rocket, with a sell-off at the end. The high for the Dow was 3,794.33, a 493.22-point gain. It ended the year up 452.98, still excellent. For the S&P 500 Index the top was 470.94; that's up 35.23. It then fell back to 466.45 with a gain of 30.74. There's no doubt that 1993 was a decent year for the stock market.

1994

Indecisive—that's the word for 1994. The stock market ran into a brick wall between 3,900 and 4,000 on the Dow Industrial Average. The wall for the S&P 500 was between 470 and 480 points:

Dow Industrial Average up   80.35
Standard & Poor's 500 Index   −7.18

A Significant Rally in 1994

The important rally at the end of 1994 continued to more than double the Dow Industrial Average and come within 50 points of tripling the S&P 500 Index by 1988. Even so, there was a year-end sell-off at the end of 1994.

1995

Dow Industrial Average up	1,282.68
S&P 500 Index up	156.66

Both indicators had a small sell-off at year-end.

1996

Dow Industrial Average up	1,331.15
S&P 500 Index up	124.81

A 100-point sell-off on the Dow Industrials occured at year-end. A 15.08-point sell-off on the S&P 500 Index occurred at year-end.

1997

Dow Industrial Average up	1,459.98
S&P 500 Index up	229.69

Both indicators had a minor sell-off at year-end.

WHAT CONCLUSIONS CAN BE DRAWN?

Based on the major indicators of the Dow Industrial Average and the Standard & Poor's 500 Index from 1990 through 1997, selling at the end of a year is often light and insignificant. Such selling is apparently unrelated to how well or poorly the market performed during the year.

Although some selling can be expected in late December, taking investment advantage of the situation is either to sell before the final week of December or be prepared to buy if the sell-off is deep and widespread.

CHAPTER 54

The First Week Determines the Year

Some say it's the first six days that determine what will happen at the end of the year. The idea of six days may go back a few years to when the stock exchanges were open on Saturdays. Others say the first week of the year determines what will happen for the rest of the year. Still others believe the month of January is the great market forecaster. As goes January, so goes the year.

Some people measure the year using the Standard and Poor's 500 Index, and others use the Dow Industrial Average as the stock market. To analyze this beginning-of-the-year phenomena, we will look at both the S&P 500 Index (SPX) and the Dow Industrial Average (INDU) as shown in Table 54–1.

Looking at the figures (Table 54–2) for the first week, forecasting for the Standard & Poor's 500 Index shows results that are 50-50. The index correctly forecast four of the eight years, where both the first week and year-end showed similar plus or minus results. Obviously, this sampling is too small to place much significance on these results. Further, only up markets were correctly forecast.

The Dow Industrial Average did only slightly better in forecasting the year-end results. It was correct five out of eight years, but again all of the correct years were up years. Although extending the study to a larger base number of years could be interesting, the accuracy of a forecast based entirely on the first week of the year is questionable, as can be seen in Table 54–3.

Wrong only twice in eight years (minor differences) is not a bad record, even for this small sampling of years. Additionally, the January forecaster for the S&P 500 Index correctly predicted 1990 as a down year. The S&P 500 Index had an up first month for 1994, (up 15.16), but the index closed the year actually down 7.18 points; which is a minor difference.

T A B L E 54–1

The First Week, Standard & Poor's 500 Index

Date	SPX	First Week	Year
12/29/89	353.40		
1/8/90	353.79	0.39	
12/31/90	330.22		**−23.18**
1/8/91	314.90	−15.32	
12/31/91	417.09		**86.87**
1/8/92	418.10	1.01	
12/31/92	435.71		18.62
1/8/93	429.05	−6.66	
12/31/93	466.45		**30.74**
1/7/94	469.90	3.45	
12/30/94	459.27		**−7.18**
1/9/95	460.83	1.56	
12/29/95	615.93		156.66
1/8/96	618.46	2.53	
12/31/96	740.74		124.81
1/8/97	748.41	7.67	
12/31/97	970.43		229.69
1/8/98	956.04	−14.39	

According to the January forecast with the Standard & Poor's 500 Index, 1998 would be an up year. It should be interesting to see the end result. The Standard & Poor's 500 Index ended 1997 at 970.43 points. On December 31, 1998, the index closed at 1,229.23 points, up a significant 258.8 points. The January forecast was correct.

The Dow Industrial Average got all the years correct, as shown in Table 54–4. The only down year was 1990 on the Dow. January was down 162.66 points for the month, and the year closed less than that at a negative 119.54 points. That crazy year 1994 had January up 224.27, but the year ended up only 80.35, and that was thanks to a Santa Claus Rally. There doesn't seem to be any consistent relationship between amounts. The 1995 January increase was only 9.42 points, but the Industrial Average finished the year up 1,282.68 points.

T A B L E 54–2

The First Week, Dow Industrial Average

Date	INDU	First Week	Year
12/29/89	2,753.20		
1/8/90	2,794.37	41.17	
12/31/90	2,633.66		**–119.54**
1/8/91	2,509.41	–124.25	
12/31/91	3,168.83		**535.17**
1/8/92	3,203.94	35.11	
12/31/92	3,301.11		132.28
1/8/93	3,251.67	–49.44	
12/31/93	3,754.09		**452.98**
1/7/94	3,820.77	66.68	
12/30/94	3,834.44		80.35
1/9/95	3,861.35	26.91	
12/29/95	5,117.12		1,282.68
1/8/96	5,197.68	80.56	
12/31/96	6,448.27		1,331.15
1/8/97	6,549.48	101.21	
12/31/97	7,908.25		1,459.98
1/8/98	7,802.62	–105.63	

Again, it must be stressed that this is an extremely modest sampling. Also, the Dow's performance since 1990 has been rather incredible.

A LARGER SAMPLING OF THE "JANUARY BAROMETER"

In his annual book *The Stock Trader's Almanac*, the noted statistician Yale Hirsch has no less than four interesting sections on the "January Barometer":

> "The Incredible January Barometer—Only Three Significant Errors in 48 Years"

> "January Barometer in Graphic Form"

T A B L E 54–3

The One-Month (The First Month) Picture, Standard & Poor's 500 Index

Date	SPX	January, +/–	Year, +/–
12/29/89	353.4		
1/2/90	359.69		
1/31/90	329.08	−24.32	
12/31/90	330.22		−23.18
1/2/91	326.45		
1/31/91	343.93	13.71	
12/31/91	417.09		86.87
1/2/92	417.26		
1/31/92	408.79	−8.3	
12/31/92	435.71		**18.62**
1/4/93	435.38		
1/29/93	438.78	3.07	
12/31/93	466.45		30.74
1/3/94	465.44		
1/31/94	481.61	15.16	
12/30/94	459.27		**−7.18**
1/3/95	459.11		
1/31/95	470.42	11.15	
12/29/95	615.93		156.66
1/2/96	620.73		
1/31/96	636.02	20.09	
12/31/96	740.74		124.81
1/2/97	736.99		
1/31/97	786.16	45.42	
12/31/97	970.43		229.69
1/30/98	980.28	9.85	

T A B L E 54–4

Dow Industrial Average, First Month

Date	INDU	January	Year
12/29/89	2,753.20		
1/2/90	2,810.15		
1/31/90	2,590.54	−162.66	
12/31/90	2,633.66		−119.54
1/2/91	2,610.64		
1/31/91	2,736.39	102.73	
12/31/91	3,168.83		535.17
1/2/92	3,172.41		
1/31/92	3,223.39	54.56	
12/31/92	3,301.11		132.28
1/4/93	3,309.22		
1/29/93	3,310.03	8.92	
12/31/93	3,754.09		452.98
1/3/94	3,756.60		
1/31/94	3,978.36	224.27	
12/30/94	3,834.44		80.35
1/3/95	3,838.48		
1/31/95	3,843.86	9.42	
12/29/95	5,117.12		1,282.68
1/2/96	5,177.45		
1/31/96	5,395.30	278.18	
12/31/96	6,448.27		1,331.15
1/2/97	6,442.49		
1/31/97	6,813.09	364.82	
12/31/97	7,908.25		1,459.98
1/31/98	7,906.50	−1.75	

"January's First Five Days: An Early Warning System"

"1933 Lame Duck Amendment Reason January Barometer Works"[1]

Hirsch has spent many years analyzing stock market statistics and drawing conclusions from trading patterns that developed. The old saying "Buy on Monday, sell on Friday" addressed earlier (see Chapter 39) is probably attributable to his work. His almanac has been published for the past 31 years.

CHANGE, THE ONLY CERTAINTY

The stock market changes constantly—the minute someone comes up with a trading pattern and calls attention to it, a change occurs. Chapter 39, "Buy on Monday, Sell on Friday," showed how the pattern has changed in the 1990s. Brokers of securities are taught that "past performance is not necessarily a predictor of future events."

THE ONLY THING THAT DOESN'T CHANGE

The investor must always remember that the stock market or individual stock prices do not have to follow set patterns or traditional trends. Most trading in the market is based on anticipation. It is the anticipation of higher earnings or prices that drives the market up and the anticipation of lower earnings or prices that drives it down.

The anticipation factor is not likely to change. If it does, the stock market will no longer be fair and orderly. Ownership of public corporations would cease to exist under such conditions.

---

1. Information on *The 1999 Stock Trader's Almanac* can be found on the Internet at http://www.hirschorganization.com/almanac.htm.

CHAPTER 55

It's Always a Bull Market

In the longest of long runs, of course it's always a bull market. If it weren't, there wouldn't be anyone buying stock. It doesn't matter if you go back 5, 10, 20 years, or more. You can look at the Dow Industrials, Standard & Poor's 500 Index, or the NASDAQ Composite. From all these charts, a similar bullish acceleration curve will appear (Figure 55–1).

As long as the stock market—any stock market—remains "fair and orderly," with an essentially free trading system and the economy continues to grow, the market will follow.

Although it's always a long-term bull market, some of the short-term damage can be severe. And it is not always a bull market for every company that is publicly traded. Sometimes companies that have been leaders in the past lose their ability to compete in an ever-changing marketplace. Other companies are poorly managed, and some never have much of a chance; therefore selection is important and often difficult, but it is the essence of prudent investing. As the legendary Peter Lynch indicated:

> People should at least spend as much time selecting a stock as they do when buying a new refrigerator."

F I G U R E 55–1

Always a bull market, Dow Industrial Average, 1981–1998 (monthly).

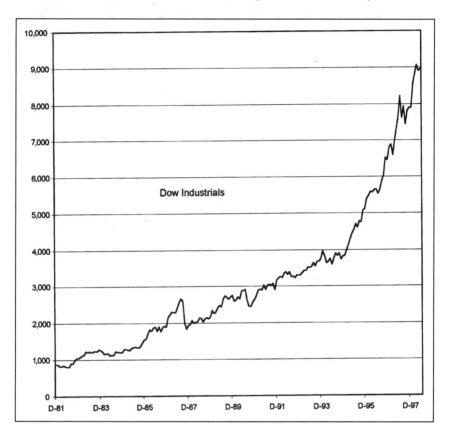

Watch the Bellwethers

bellwether 1. A wether, or male sheep, which leads the flock, with a bell on its neck. 2. A leader of a thoughtless crowd. *Webster's New Collegiate Dictionary*

Merriam-Webster possibly had the stock market in mind when adding the number 2 definition of *bellwether*. Stock market bellwethers are individual company stocks that are believed to lead the market. If a turn in the market is coming, those who watch these stocks believe the bellwether will turn first.

INDUSTRY BELLWETHERS

Bellwethers can relate to the entire market, to a sector, or to an industry group. They might be leaders in Internet stocks or technology stocks.

> Technology stocks stabilized after Tuesday's slide on growing worries about slack demand in the computer industry. The technology-laden NASDAQ composite index, which tumbled nearly 25 points on Tuesday, fell 3.81 to 1,179.27, but several computer-industry bellwethers rebounded. Intel rose 1 to 71 & 3/8 and Cisco Systems rose ½ to 53 & ⅜.[1]

The above quote lists Intel and Cisco Systems as bellwethers for the computer industry. When the term *bellwether* is used in this way, it is with a loose interpretation. More than a stock price that turns before the others, it is a descriptive term synonymous with *sector*, *industry*, or *market leader*.

---

1. "Most stocks fall but Dow gains," copyright 1996 *Houston Chronicle News Services*, 8:16 PM, June 19, 1996, http://www.chron.com/content/chronicle/business/96/06/20/markets-6-20.2-0.html.

If we look at the charts of Cisco Systems and Intel as compared to the NAS-DAQ Computer Index, we easily see that the prices of the two stocks track the index (Figures 56–1 and 56–2). Only on a few minor occasions does either price turn before the index.

One notable bellwether turn appears on the Cisco chart in October 1996, when the price of Cisco turned down before the NASDAQ Computer Index.

Big Blue

For many years the computer industry bellwether was the giant "Big Blue," that is, IBM. IBM is still considered a bellwether by many, not only for the computer

F I G U R E 56–1

Index tracking, Intel Corp. (NASDAQ: INTC), 1996.

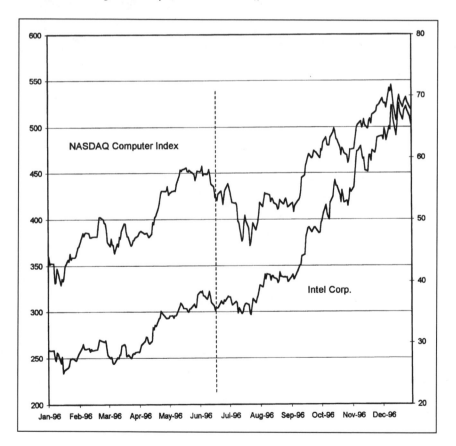

F I G U R E 56–2

Index tracking, Cisco Systems, 1996.

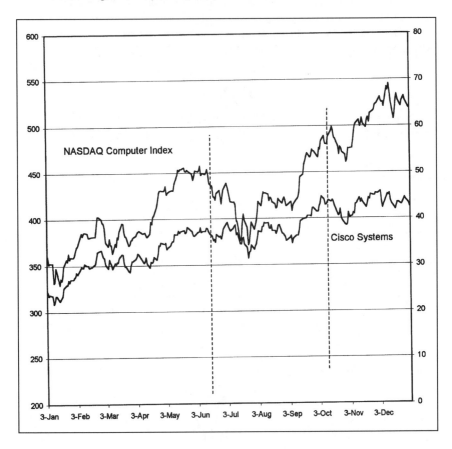

industry but also for the entire stock market. Since IBM ran into the realities cre-ated by the business use of personal computers, its bellwether quality changed in the mind of many investors. In fact, during the first half of 1998, it looked as though IBM wasn't even part of the stock market (Figure 56–3).

Sometimes Yes, Sometimes No

IBM corrected sharply in January 1998, and then it wandered off by itself (circled area). A rally in April through the first part of June turned into a technical head-and-shoulders pattern, and the price dropped, with a corresponding drop in the Dow Industrials. A conclusion that can be drawn from Figure 56–3 is that some-times IBM tracks the Dow Industrials closely, and sometimes it does not. It is a bellwether in the sense of being a strong market participant, strong enough to be watched closely for market changes, but it is not a reliable forecaster of turning points. Even if it had such a tendency, it would probably not last long because stock traders would base trades on the direction of IBM, and it would therefore no longer behave as a bellwether.

General Electric

A similar case can be made for General Electric, the only original member of the Dow Industrial Average still having the same name (Figure 56–4). At least with GE we have three visible points where the stock price turned before the rest of the market. The first time was in August 1997, the second in April 1998, and the third

F I G U R E 56–3

Dow Industrial Average and IBM, 1997–1998.

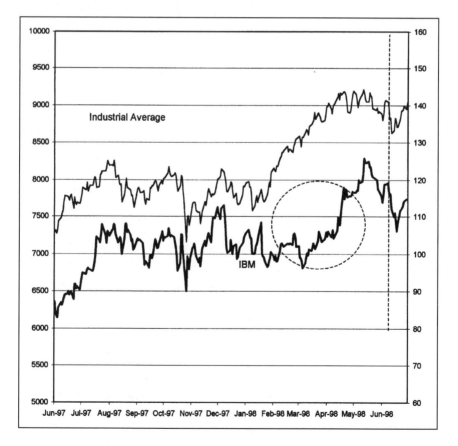

FIGURE 56–4

Bellwether, General Electric (NYSE: GE), 1997–1998.

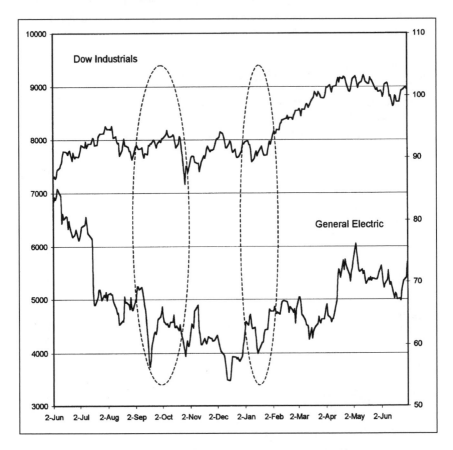

in June of the same year. But the fact remains, these so-called bellwether stocks tend to track the market direction rather than forecast turning points, at least for the long term.

LOOK INTRADAY

As the stock market trades larger volumes of shares, intraday price movements become more important. Computerization has enabled securities trading to do things that were impossible only a few years ago. Major moves can occur in a single trading session. Keeping this in mind, let's take a look at some intraday bellwether trading.

On July 15, 1998, the Dow Industrial Average had been trading near new highs and closed with a minor correction of 11.07 points (Figure 56–5). The

Standard & Poor's 500 Index, also trading near new highs, closed down 2.77 points.

General Electric

Although the price fluctuations of GE were within a narrow range of less than a dollar and a half, there were four times where the stock price appears to have turned before the Dow Industrial Average. General Electric is an important part of the Dow so we expect it to track the average closely, but the turning points are interesting. The downtrend in the morning is well defined, whereas the Dow Average appears to be attempting to rally.

Also of interest is the small price bubble in GE, near the close. One might call it a positive signal; the following day would see the price of GE close at

F I G U R E 56–5

Intraday bellwether, General Electric (NYSE: GE), July 15, 1998.

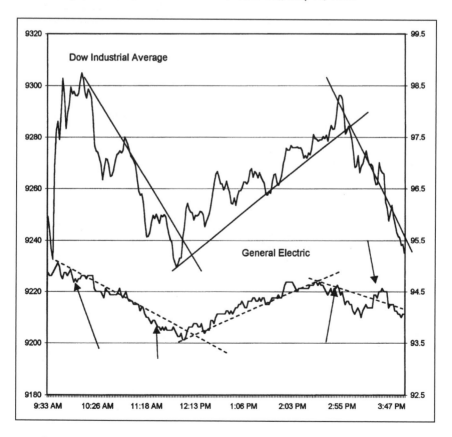

$95.75 a share. Obviously, the constant question is whether one can take trading advantage of turning points. Perhaps the greatest use of the information is a check of strength of the current trend. The early downtrend of GE showed market weakness. When the price turned, strength returned to the market.

IBM

IBM showed a weakness similar to that of General Electric on the morning of July 15, 1998 (Figure 56–6). The price stopped falling just above $118 a share. It found solid support. The Dow Industrials continued to drop. IBM tried a small rally, and the two moved upward together.

In midafternoon, IBM clearly turned south before the Dow Industrial Average. The small bounce at the end of the day seems to be a positive flag. IBM

F I G U R E 56–6

Intraday bellwether, Dow Industrials and IBM (NYSE: IBM), July 15, 1998.

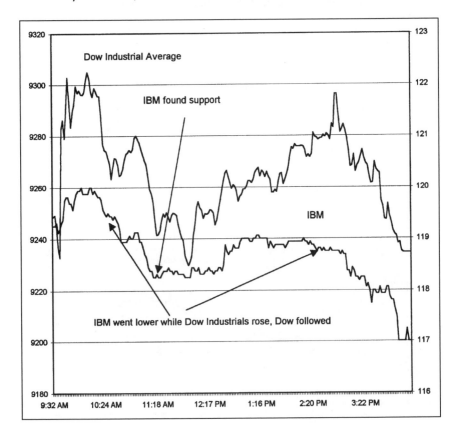

closed the following day at 118.375. Probably the two most useful strength signals for July 15 were the early downtrend and the support achieved by IBM's price in late morning. The first signaled weakness, and the second showed strength.

THE PROBLEM IS TIME

Many wheeling-dealing stockbrokers and portfolio managers actively watch bellwethers. Their computer screens constantly display the stock quotes, blinking with each trade and changing color with each uptick or downtick in price. They believe the bellwether stocks give them one more indicator of the strength and direction of the stock market.

It's not as easy for the individual investor to take advantage of bellwethers. Although some stocks appear to be ahead of the market, the market doesn't wait long before making the change. An investor can't wait for an hour or two to decide whether the market will follow a change in the bellwether. Change tends to happen quickly.

THE BEST USE OF BELLWETHERS

For most investors, the best use of stock market bellwethers is as another indicator of market strength. If the trend of the stock market has been up and the bellwethers appear to be stable in their uptrend, a turn is less likely. However, if the bellwethers become less stable and more volatile or start a downtrend, the stock market can quickly follow.

CHAPTER 57

Buy the Dips

Stock prices move as a group, which causes the stock market to fluctuate. The market virtually never moves in a straight line. As anticipation wavers based on economic developments or announcements, the stock market moves accordingly. Although in 1929, the market stayed down for four years and in 1977 it stayed down five years, most market declines are more short term. Many last only four to six months:

> For 10 straight years, every time the stock market has taken a hit, you've made big money if you jumped in with both feet. A "buy the dips" philosophy has outperformed any other strategy imaginable.[1]

James Cramer, a renouned hedge fund manager on Wall Street, goes on to say how the one exception to this was the market crash of 1987. But the biggest difference between then and the 1990s is the fact that interest rates were rising in 1987.

SELLING ON THE RALLIES

Buying on the dips can be used by the short-term speculator or the long-term investor. Some speculators follow a strategy of buying on the dips and selling on the rallies. Obviously, the ideal stock for this trading is one that tends to fluctuate on a regular basis (Figure 57–1).

Medtronic shows some dips that could have been good speculative trades for 1997 and 1998. The 554-point Dow correction in November 1997 knocked the price

---

1. James J. Cramer, "Stick with the Dips Crash or Not," *Business*, October 20, 1997, vol. 150, no. 16, http://www.pathfinder.com/time/magazine/1997/dom/971020/business.stick_with_th.html.

F I G U R E 57–1

Dips and rallies, Medtronic, Inc. (NYSE: MDT), June 1997–1998.

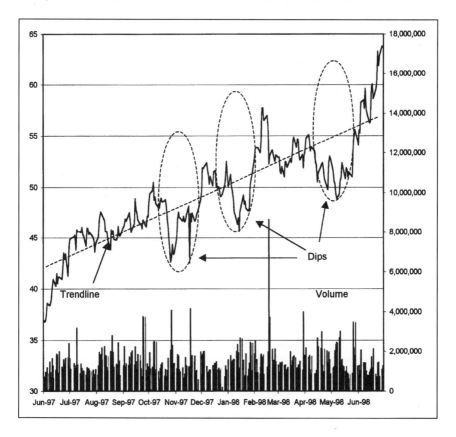

down significantly. The price dropped from $48 to $42. After the correction stabilized and sorted things out, the stock price returned to its previously established trend line. There is a tendency for stocks to follow that pattern when their price weakness is due to a market correction rather than a weakness in the company.

BUY STOP STRATEGY

All of the dips shown in Medtronic's price are caused by market corrections. A speculator buying on these dips could have profited $10 or more per share. The major difficulty with such a strategy is knowing when to make the move. A possible strategy to use, once the price drops, would be to place a buy stop order (on exchange traded stock) above the current price. That way the buy wouldn't be made until the stock moved upward. The stop could be lowered if the price continued to drop. A limit placed on the buy stop could give protection from an extreme upsurge.

OPPORTUNITY FOR LONG-TERM INVESTORS

The dips here could also be good for the long-term investors. Price weakness, caused primarily by market weakness, can provide excellent opportunities to add stocks to a portfolio position.

Wal-Mart Stores

Now the largest retailer in the United States, Wal-Mart's chain of discount department stores has been a strong performer for the past few years. Those who bought the stock years ago have undoubtedly been pleased with the price performance (Figure 57–2). The short-term speculators did not have as much profit potential as they had with Medtronic, but there were a few plays possible. Again, these areas of weakness correspond with market corrections and do not reflect any weakness in the company's stock. Buying the dips on Wal-Mart Stores can give the long-term investor somewhat better prices.

Ralston-Ralston Purina Group

After the bakery products business (Ralston-Continental Baking Group: CBG) and consumer foods and resorts businesses (Ralcorp: RAH) were spun off in 1993 and 1994, RAL became a company of mostly pet foods (Purina) and battery products (Everyready and Energizer). It is the world's largest producer of dry dog and dry or soft-moist cat foods. It is also the world's largest producer of dry-cell batteries. The June 1997 through 1998 chart shows a nice steady uptrend with several modest price dips. Professional speculators would have had interest in these dips, as they would not have needed much of a price move to have made a profitable trade (Figure 57–3).

IT'S A NO-BRAINER

To buy stock on price dips is a sound strategy, especially when those dips are caused by stock market corrections. Certainly the stock market might keep correcting and enter a bear market, but this is not what usually happens. Most corrections stop quickly, and the market recovers.

The following statement appeared in the *Christian Science Monitor* just after the October 1997 Dow Industrial Average fell more than 554 points in one day:

Monday's tumble, for example, took the Dow about 13 percent below its August high. That's the first retreat of more than 10 percent in seven years.

And since reaching that record high, the Dow has tried, and failed, to grasp those heights again. A giddy rally two weeks ago turned into the rout that gained speed last Monday.

And the small investor has been well trained to finance the professional investor's exit. "Buy on the dips" goes the chant. Downturns are temporary.

And that's been true for 15 years, even through the crash of October 1987. Maybe this is one of those times.[2]

F I G U R E 57–2

Dips and rallies, Wal-Mart Stores (NYSE: WMT), 1997–1998.

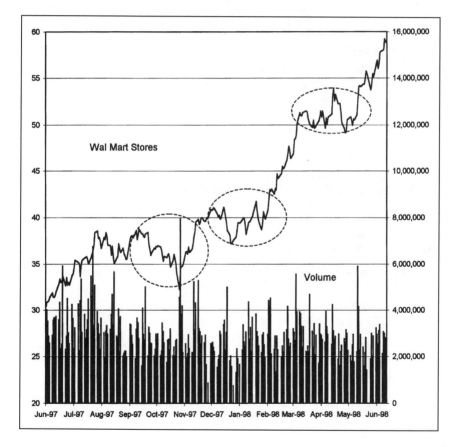

2. Lynde McCormick, "Dow-tful," *The Christian Science Monitor*, November 3, 1997, http://www.csmonitor.com/durable/1997/11/03/econ/econ.1.html.

F I G U R E 57–3

Dips and rallies, Ralston (NYSE: RAL), 1997–1998.

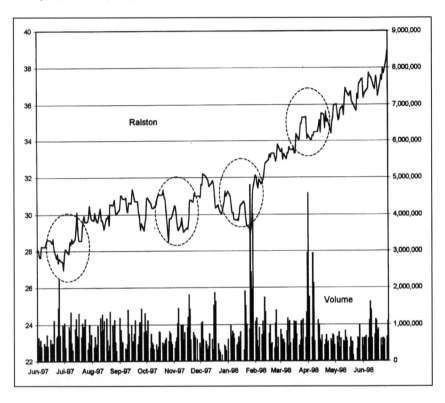

BUYING OPPORTUNITIES

Individual stock prices that are influenced by the market create buying opportunities for both the speculator and the long-term investor. These opportunities do not usually last for a long period; therefore, the investor should have targets selected in advance and move swiftly.

CHAPTER 58

Buy the Dow Dogs

Investing in the "Dogs of the Dow" (also called the *Dow dividend strategy*) is simple. When the stock market closes on the last trading session of the year, of the 30 stocks in the Dow Jones Industrial Average, find 10 with the highest dividend yield. Buy them.

Call your broker and invest an equal dollar amount in each of these 10 highest-yielding stocks. Hold the 10 Dogs of the Dow for one year. Repeat these easy steps every year.

On the Internet, several sites work with the dogs strategy. This is what they say about its potential, based on history:

> Of the 30 stocks that comprise the Dow Jones Industrial Average, select the top ten yielding stocks. Invest evenly in these stocks for a period of one year. In the past twenty years, the average return for the Top-Ten Strategy has been 19.62%. This would have allowed a $10,000 investment in 1978 to grow to over $350,000 (barring fees and tax considerations).[1]

HISTORY OF THE THEORY

Actually, the strategy is not all that new. Apparently, it moves in and out of popularity, as do many stock trading strategies. Benjamin Graham's *The Intelligent Investor* contains a reference to a study by H. G. Schneider published in the June 1951 issue of the *Journal of Finance* documenting a strategy of investing in unpopular DJIA issues from 1917 through 1950. A second study noted in the book covers the years 1933 through 1969.

1. *Buttonwood Investment Strategies*, http://www.buttonwood.net/dogs.htm.

T A B L E 58–1

Performance

Year	Top 10, %	Dow Industrials, %	S&P 500 Index, %
1990	−7.60	−0.40	−3.20
1991	34.30	23.90	30.00
1992	7.90	7.40	7.60
1993	27.30	16.80	10.10
1994	4.10	4.90	1.30
1995	38.90	38.60	37.70

Source: Barron's, "Beating the Dow."

The studies looked at strategies of buying either the 6 or 10 issues in the DJIA selling at the lowest earnings multiples and rebalancing at holding periods ranging from one to five years. As shown in Table 58–1, although it was unprofitable from 1917 through 1933, from 1937 through 1969, the strategy consistently beat the high multiple 10 and the Dow Industrial Average.[2]

The performance obviously varies. Commissions for trades and tax liabilities are not taken into consideration for Table 58–1. How well or how consistently the strategy works in the future cannot be determined by this information.

VARIATIONS OF THE THEORY

It seems as though the minute a new investment strategy appears, someone comes up with a variation. Here are some variations of the Dow dividend strategy to meet the needs or interests of individuals.

Lowest Prices

Beating the Dow, by Michael B. O'Higgins and John Downes, was published in 1991, with a paperback edition in 1992. Buy only 5 stocks in the list of the 10 highest yields, the 5 with the lowest prices per share.

The book also discusses alternative strategies. One, for example, is to buy a single stock, which would be the second-lowest-priced stock of the 10 with the highest yields. The choice of the second-lowest-priced stock is made because the lowest-priced stock may be a troubled company. A caution here: Obviously a one-stock investment always has greater risk than diversification.

---

2 "Dogs of the Dow" and the "Foolish Four," *Investor Home*, June 15, 1998.

Fund Variations

Mutual funds and unit trust aren't being left out on this strategy. Various broker-age firms have established such funds geared to the Dow dividend strategy. The mutual fund approach is convenient and affordable for most individuals. Also, the fact that the funds are more diversified makes them somewhat lower in risk. However, they are not all pure plays.

Because of regulations, mutual funds must have considerable diversification.

Therefore, they might invest half the assets in the Dow dogs and the remainder in U.S. Treasury issues. Others invest half the assets in the dogs and the rest in high-yielding stocks from the Standard & Poor's 500 Index.

A NEED FOR CAUTION

The buy-and-hold investor is annually forced to sell and take taxable profits. Depending on an individual investor's tax situation, this could be a problem. Logic dictates the usual caution about future results not being guaranteed by past performance. The problem with most trading strategies is the attention they attract. If too many investors begin to use the strategy, their activity affects the results. Sometimes results are enhanced, but other times they are either lowered, or trading changes the market too fast for the individual to participate.

There are other considerations to keep in mind as well. Recent changes in the tax law raise another issue that Dow dividend strategy investors should consider. The capital gains tax rate of 20 percent will apply to holding periods of 18 months. Lengthening the holding period of any strategy in order to take advantage of the new tax rate could be worthwhile for many investors. The question then becomes, how will such an adjustment change the Dow dividend strategy?

CHAPTER 59

A Trend Remains in Force until It Changes

A *trend* is a line drawn on a graph by connecting the points representing the closing price levels of a stock or point levels of an average or index. Trends of the stock market and of individual prices are an important part of investment analysis. Technical analysts and stock traders follow trends religiously. Even fundamental analysts keep an eye on trends for some idea of strength and direction (Figure 59–1).

CHARLES DOW

More than 100 years ago, Charles Henry Dow, founding father of Dow Jones and Company, as well as *The Wall Street Journal*, placed great importance on the study of trends and trend lines. He compared stock market trends to the ocean tides washing up on the beach. By placing a stick in the sand, one can tell if the tides are coming in or going out. His analysis of the stock market was developed further by journal editor William Hamilton and was eventually called the *Dow theory*. Some analysts still follow the theory or at least make use of some of its components.

THE THREE TRENDS

Dow said there were three important types of trends:

Primary trend: The long-term trend of the market over months and years

Secondary trend: Short-term trends of a few days or weeks, running contrary to the long-term trend

Tertiary trend: The daily movements of the market

FIGURE 59-1

Trends, Dow Industrial Average, 1997–1998.

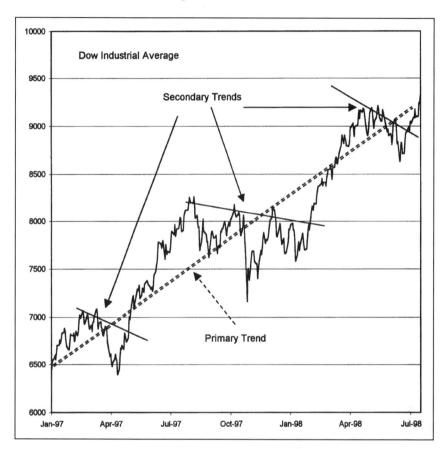

THE STRONGEST TREND

The strongest trend is the primary trend. The market can have expected or unexpected weakness, where the Dow Industrial Average drops 10 or more than 500 points but then recovers. In these situations, the primary trend remains strong.

When it changes direction and breaks through the trend line, it is a signal of stock market weakness that could become a trend reversal. Breaking through the trend line alerts market observers to a possible reversal. Market reversals don't always happen, however. Sometimes false signals are given, and the market resumes its former trend.

WHERE TO DRAW THE LINES

When a person first begins drawing trend lines on a market chart, the question occurs as to where the lines should be drawn. The inadequate (although accurate) answer is to "draw them where you want—they're your lines." Here are some more useful guidelines:

> *Uptrend*:   Draw the trend line underneath the data point lows.

> *Downtrend*:   Draw the trend line on top of the data point highs.

The main reason for these two locations is that they will clearly show where the trend changes direction and breaks through the line.

A look at Figure 59–2, shows a well-defined primary uptrend. Notice the market weakness at the three breakout points, where the market dropped through

F I G U R E 59–2

Uptrend, Standard & Poor's 500 Index, 1997–1998.

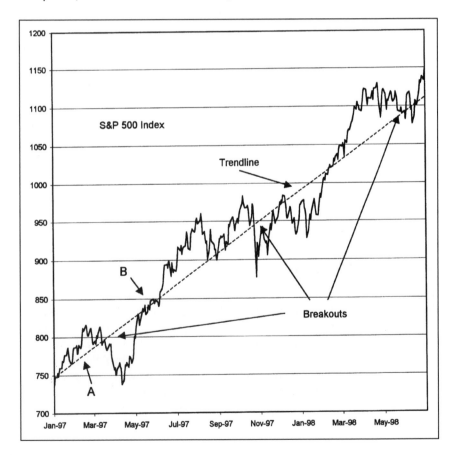

the primary trend line. Also notice how the trend line is like a platform, at times supporting a weaker or volatile market (point *A*) and at other times resisting a rising market (point *B*). These areas are important because they often help the analyst decide where to draw the trend line.

A Best-Fit Approach

There are many opinions as to where trend lines should be drawn. The ideal is to figure out where the professionals think the trend lines are located. Interestingly enough, this tends to be where the trend line fits best. Several data points are connected by the trend line. The line shows examples of support when the market is trading above the trend and resistance when it's trading below. If there are secondary trends, it's easy to see the market usually correct sharply if the trend line is penetrated (Figure 59–2). It takes some practice and experimentation to see which location is most effective.

Data Point Extremes

Some say to draw trend lines at data point extremes. This does not work because doing so totally bypasses the secondary trends. Although the trend line will show some areas of support, it will not show resistance. Drawing lines at extreme ends of data may work for technical patterns, but it isn't effective for trend lines.

Length of Time

Here again, the length of time is up to the person making the charts. However, 12 to 18 months are usually good for determining the primary trend. Once that is established, secondary trends are usually easy to see.

A longer-period chart can be an interesting reference for the analyst to see where the current trend is coming from. If we look at the long-term chart from 1990 through 1998 in Figure 59–3, we see some interesting points.

The primary trend for Figure 59–1 is virtually identical to the long-term chart, which goes all the way back to late 1994. It confirms the accuracy of the 1997 through 1998 trend line, although sometimes that doesn't happen because of changes in the market. But notice the change in angle from the 1990 through 1994, to the 1994 through 1998 line. The market shifted into high gear and decided to go up, attracting money like a high-stakes lottery. New money and lots of anticipation came into the stock market. Pressure to keep interest rates down is reflected in what happened with the trend.

F I G U R E 59–3

Long-term trend, Dow Industrial Average, 1990–1998.

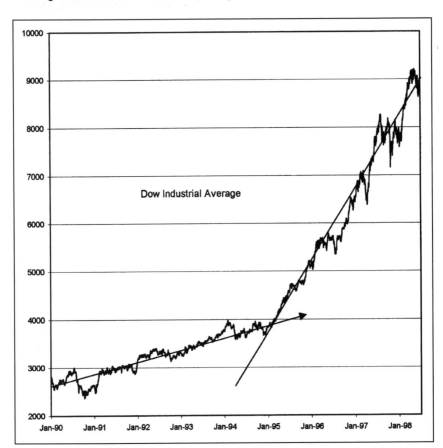

FINAL NOTES

Although plotting trends can help an investor understand the stock market, it is important to remember the factor of anticipation. The stock market constantly attempts to anticipate what will happen next. Anticipation is often unfulfilled or entirely incorrect. The trend remains in force until a trend changes. The difficulty is in knowing if the trend has changed or a correction is just a secondary trend. That's why the market tends to correct sharply if the uptrend line is penetrated. Although trends are an important indicator, they can be overridden by other events.

CHAPTER 60

It Depends on Support and Resistance

In Chapter 59, we discussed support and resistance in relation to a trend line. Here we will consider other aspects of support and resistance.

THE DOW THEORY

The idea of market support and resistance goes back to the Dow theory, originated by Charles Dow and further developed by a later editor of *The Wall Street Journal*, William Hamilton.

Support is a point in a declining stock market where buyers start buying. *Resistance* is the point where sellers start selling. When a market declines, analysts look lower for the next area of support. The strength of an area of support is determined by how many times the level stopped former declines. If it stopped only once, it is weak support. If market declines stopped at the same level more than once, it is stronger support. When the market falls through strong support, it has a tendency to drop much further.

Resistance is the opposite of support. It is a level where stock market advances stopped in the past. If advances were stopped only once or maybe twice, it is weak resistance. If several advances were stopped, it is stronger resistance. When the market breaks through resistance, it tends to rise much higher. Sometimes support or resistance levels are at precisely the same point. Other times they are not so exact but rather are a range of support or resistance.

Keep in mind, these are tendencies, not guarantees. The stock market does what buyers and sellers determine, not necessarily what someone thinks it's supposed to do.

AN IMPORTANT SWITCH

Resistance becomes support, and support becomes resistance. The two conditions of support and resistance switch roles (Figure 60–1). When resistance is penetrated, resistance becomes support. If the Dow Industrial Average stops a few times at the 9,000 level, then rises to 9,100, the former level becomes support. On the other end, if the market falls through a support area, that area becomes new resistance.

In June 1998, the Dow Industrial Average encountered previously established resistance between 9,000 and 9,100 points. It was an area that had served as support in previous months. From there it dropped to just above the 8,800 level, had a small rally, then continued to drop to the next support level. It finally found support at the 8,600 level. The ensuing rally finally broke through resis-

F I G U R E 60–1

Support and resistance, Dow Industrial Average, 1998.

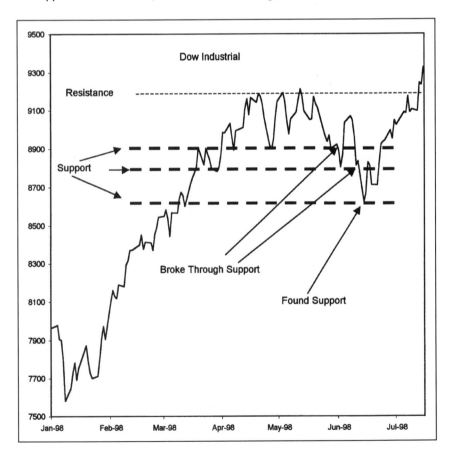

FIGURE 60–2

Support and resistance, Infoseek, 1997–1998.

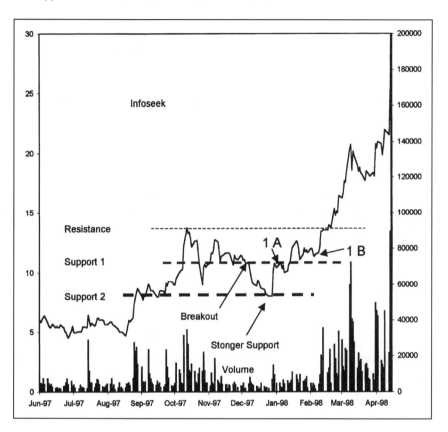

tance in mid-July 1998, after having enough momentum to break through the two major areas of resistance, which were formerly support.

STOCK PRICES

Stock prices also show areas of support and resistance. In fact, they are a key element in technical analysis and are frequently observed by the fundamental analyst. As with indicators, the areas show where buyers or sellers enter the market.

INFOSEEK

Infoseek (NASDAQ: SEEK) is a company that maintains one of the major search engines on the Internet. In August 1997, the stock price shifted into a strong uptrend (Figure 60–2). Between August and October, the price nearly tripled, going from just under $5 a share to nearly $15. The price then dropped to the first support level (formerly resistance) at about $9 a share. In November, it started upward again, this time meeting resistance first at $10.50 and higher at just above $12.50. A mostly sideways price movement (consolidation) then fluctuated between $11 and $11.50 a share.

Coming up on the end of the year, the price looked as though it wasn't going anywhere. A sell-off caused the price to break through a strong support area and drop from $11 to $8 a share. Notice how the price found support at a previously established (September 1997) level.

With the sell-off out of the way, Infoseek looked like a bargain, and the buyers came back. January saw resistance at the $11 level (point 1A—it was formerly a support level), had a consolidation, a minor correction, and moved up again. In late January the trading range moved higher. Notice how the resistance levels are just a small amount lower than previous levels and the support levels are a bit higher. Many investors likely viewed this as a strength signal.

At point 1B former resistance becomes support and the price rallies, breaking through strong resistance on its way to new highs. By April 1998, Infoseek had climbed to more than $34 a share.

IMPERFECT PREDICTORS

Support and resistance do not really predict or forecast what will happen next. All they do is indicate what happened in the past and could happen again. The anticipation and subsequent actions of buyers and sellers will determine what happens. However, the knowledge of support and resistance can give the investor an indication of what is likely to happen.

CHAPTER 61

The Stock Market Predicts the Economy

Invariably, when the stock market experiences a sharp correction, one or more of the nightly newscasters will say something like the following:

> The Dow Industrial Average had a hard time on Wall Street today. The average dropped more than 554 points, a new record one-day decline. The stock market is believed to predict what will happen in the economy six months from now. We could be looking at hard times.

Although it's very nice, the newscasters' telling us about the future of the economy, it comes under the category of "gimme a break—please." Think about it for a moment. Imagine yourself, in charge of a $23 billion mutual fund, with the Dow down—only 300 points at midday. Your reputation and your job are on the line. Are you going to be concerned with the economy status six months from now? I don't think so. The main focus of your attention is on what happens in the next 10 minutes, not what might happen in six months. In fact, you are probably watching the next support level to see if it holds and stops the decline. If the market stops declining, you will likely become a buyer.

Yes, what happens in the stock market does have some—*some*—relationship to the economic developments of the future. But it is always more concerned with the hear and now. What's happening and how can I take advantage of the situation?

The predicted recession/depression after the 1987 collapse did not materialize. The weak economy after the October 1997 correction didn't get any worse. It was already slow, but that was positive in a growth sense.

Ever notice that newscasters never say that the economy will be better because the Dow Industrial Average reached new highs? If the market "predicts the economy," it would seem that a new high would be great news. Instead, you can almost hear them suck in air of skepticism, as if they believe the Dow is on its way back to the 2,000-point level. Some journalists go even further and make bold statements:

> Unfortunately, although a high Dow does not necessarily signal a good economy for all, a bust is bad for almost everyone. If the Dow drops drastically and stays down, it is usually following some fundamental economic crisis that hurts working people.
>
> If experience is any guide, the current boom of the stock market will be followed by another drop.[1]

Looks like a safe statement, since drops happen in even the best of years.

The most important point is that corrections in the stock market force professional investors to make adjustments. When the market is in free fall, they aren't thinking about the economy; they are thinking about the stock market and making those adjustments. In most cases, a one-day drop doesn't have any discernible impact on the economy. Rather it's the trend over weeks and months that is important. Although a big drop may send a signal of stock market weakness, its impact on the economy will be more dependent on what happens in the next few weeks and months. Don't panic, and get ready to buy.

---

1. Arthur MacEwan, "U.S. Stock Market vs. the Economy," *Dollars and Sense*, September/October 1997, http://www.infoasis.com/people/stevetwt/Economics/StocksvsEconomy_DS.html.

There Is a Bear Market Coming

Of course, there is—there is always the specter of a bear market on the economic horizon. It's as true as the fact that there are some investors who believe the Dow Industrial Average will drop below 2,000 again. Many who believe the bear is hiding around the corner don't even have a clear definition of what makes a bear.

WHAT IS A BEAR MARKET?

Actually, there are several definitions of a bear market.

A Classic

A bear market is a time when securities prices are steadily declining for a period of weeks, months, and sometimes years.

Trader Vic's Bear Market

A long term downtrend (a downtrend lasting months to years) in any market, especially the stock market, characterized by lower intermediate lows (those established in a time frame of weeks to months) interrupted by lower intermediate highs.[1]

---

1. Victor Sperando, *Trader Vic—Methods of a Wall Street Master*, http://www.lowrisk.com/bull-bear.htm.

Marty Zweig's Bear

A bear market is a decline of at least 15% in each of three important stock averages: the Dow Jones Industrials, the S&P 500 Index, and the . . . Value Line Index.[2]

Another Classic

A bear market is a decline in the Dow Industrial Average of 20% or more. It can also be a time when the Dow Industrial Average is down (from established highs) for more than two consecutive months.[3]

Keep in mind that newscasters and analysts will talk of "bearish" moves in the stock market. They do not necessarily mean that the stock market has become a bear market. Virtually all corrections or secondary market downtrends are referred to as "bearish".

WHAT'S THE TREND?

A bear market represents a downturn in the long-term trend. Most of these trends are short-lived. They might last from three to six months. Only a few last more than a year, the most notable being the bear market from October 1929 to July 1932.

One of the problems with the crash of 1929 was the fact that many companies went out of business, either because of the bear market or the economic climate that followed. Most, in 1998, have viewed the economic climate as positive with this most recent market acceleration. However, there is a problem with the Asian economic crises.

A WORD OF CAUTION IN MID-1998

In 1998, economic problems appeared in Asia—importantly in Japan with a serious recession, negative GDP growth, and problems with the banking system. As economic problems continue to grow, they affect a country's ability to buy our products, until we also begin to have trouble:

> Without a change in FED policy or a miracle in Asia my guess for the start of a recession is this time next year. Usually the Stock Market anticipates a recession by three to nine months.[4]

---

2. Martin Zweig, *Martin Zweig's Winning On Wall Street*, http://www.lowrisk.com/bullbear.htm.
3. The Standard & Poor's 500 index can be substituted here for the Dow Industrial Average.
4. Victor Weintraub, "Midyear Economic Review," FirstCapital Corporation, July 5, 1998, http://www.firstcap.com/smt/erq298.html.

THE MARKET DOESN'T USUALLY WAIT

If there is a strong enough belief that a recession is coming, the stock market probably won't wait to send a signal. For that matter, the recession probably won't wait either. Recessions have a tendency to move just ahead of the current economic situation. Although they seem to be always looming in the future, if the right moves are made, the recessions often don't materialize.

THE BEAR GROWLS

Comments from an important figure like Federal Reserve Chairman Alan Greenspan can throw the stock market into turmoil. In July 1998, Greenspan's comments did not exactly inspire investors with confidence.

> Sounding like a Wall Street guru, Greenspan returned to the bully pulpit to preach, saying the market could be ripe for a big correction.
> His words ignited a sell-off that drove the Dow Jones industrial average to its biggest weekly loss ever, pushing the blue-chip index below the 9,000-point level.
> Stocks reeled because Greenspan threatened a bear market if things do not simmer down.[5]

Although the Fed's chairman has an undeniable impact on the stock market, there tends to be a great deal of skepticism as to the accuracy of any forecasts he makes. Many believe he periodically throws out a warning of doom and gloom, just in case he might be right some time.

> Who benefits from the warnings?
> Greenspan may scare the small speculators and short-term traders, but the long-term investors will stay put because they are looking at the value of individual stocks," said John Geraghty at North American Equity Services, a consulting firm.
> He said Greenspan's credibility is waning among professional traders.

When the Fed acts by raising or lowering interest rates, everyone listens. Actions speak louder than words, and the stock market is most sensitive to changes in interest rates.

BEAR MARKETS—BUYING OPPORTUNITIES

They certainly have been buying opportunities in the past, with some notable exceptions. The 1929 bear saw several companies go out of business. The way to

---

5. Pierre Belec, "The Man Who Would Be the Nation's Chief Investment Strategist," Reuters, July 24, 1998, http://www.pathfinder.com/money/latest/rbus/RB/1998Jul24/608.html.

avoid such difficulties is to choose stocks carefully and wait for some signs of stability. However, a wait can be difficult because of the speed the market can recover. Waiting too long leads to missed opportunities. See Chapter 63 (next chapter) for some excellent bear markets.

There Are More Advances in a Bear Market Than There Are Declines in a Bull Market

Well, of course there are—the stock market tends to have more optimism than pessimism. When it's sliding into that bear market, buyers become active, believing the slide will stop. Many buyers will enter the market, usually at previously established support levels, but they quickly exit again if there isn't enough buying pressure to sustain the rally. Here we'll look at some classic bulls and bears.

1928

A wonderful bull market, the Dow Industrial Average rose nearly 100 points. That's not so great you say; in 1998, the Dow can make a move like that in one day. But, it was a 50 percent increase in the Dow—for a one-year gain, that's tremendous (Figure 63–1).

There were dips and secondary trends along the way, allowing new investors to enter the market at reduced prices. It was a boom-time for the stock market. Things were rolling along nicely, even into 1929, when things changed (Figure 63–2).

F I G U R E 63–1

Bull market, Dow Industrial Average, 1928.

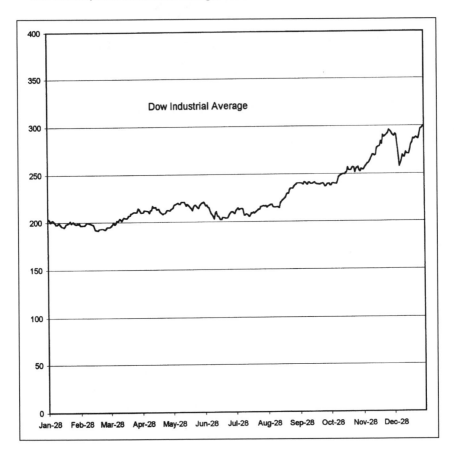

1929

The first half of 1929 saw some price consolidation with the Dow Industrials trading between 300 and 320 points. Strong support was established at the 300-point level. In late May, the market began to rally. It rose higher and higher in a buying frenzy. On September 3, 1929, it reached a high of 381.17, then turned. In October, it crashed through the 300-point support level and went into a free fall.

Small and large rallies happened all the way down. Comparing Figure 63–2 to 63–1 easily shows the title of this chapter to be true. There appear to be more rallies in a bear market than corrections in a bull market, at least in this bear market. The trend turned in 1932.

1987

Obviously, this example does not fit the axiom. When the market drops more than 20 percent in one day (by itself, the October 19 drop qualified as a bear market), what else can be expected? The stock market drop of 1987 shook the financial world. Although the causes of the severe and sudden decline can be continually debated, one thing is certain: 1987 saw a bear market with panic selling (Figure 63–3).

The 1987 peak was actually reached on August 25, at 2,722.42. The Dow bottomed out at 1,738.74, on October 19, when the Dow set a record by dropping 508 points. The market rallied, moved sideways, and fell again in early December. At this point, the next bull market began.

F I G U R E 63–2

Bear cycle, Dow Industrial Average, 1929–1933.

F I G U R E   63–3

Panic selling, Dow Industrial Average, 1987–1988.

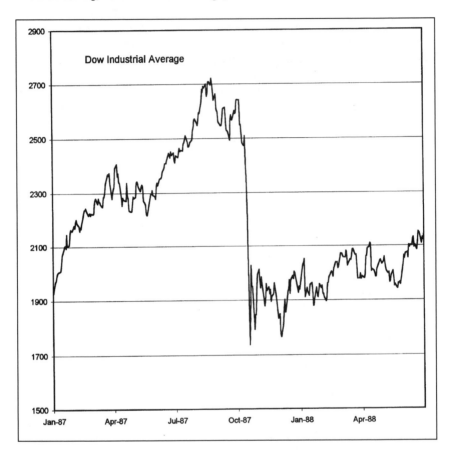

1990

Military and political troubles in the Persian Gulf sent the advancing market into a tailspin. The trend turned in mid-July, where the Dow met resistance at the 3,000 level. It continued to decline until mid-October at the 2,365.1 level, a 27 percent drop (Figure 63–4). Again, there were not many rallies in the 1990 bear market.

1994

In 1994, strong resistance was encountered at the 4,000-point level (Figure 63–5). Then we entered a somewhat controversial area. In the area from

February to November 1994, the market acted like a bear. In fact, it was sort of a bear market, followed by a bull market, and then another bear. It does not meet most of the classic definitions of a bear, as the drop was only 10 percent. However, the Dow Industrial Average was down for more than two months on both occasions. Down for more than two consecutive months is one of the bear market definitions.

Whether the areas in 1994 are called "bear markets" or not is unimportant. What is important is that they were both buying opportunities for the bull market or bull resumption that followed.

The chapter title does not hold up again. Market declines tended to be sudden and severe with a few rally attempts.

FIGURE 63–4

Bear crisis, Dow Industrial Average, 1990.

F I G U R E 63–5

Bear or consolidation, Dow Industrial Average, 1993–1995.

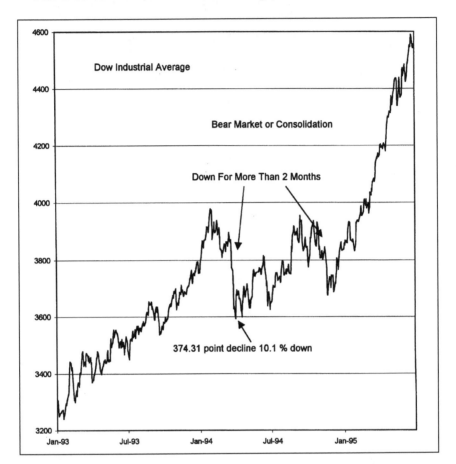

CHANGING MARKET

It seems that the increased speed of the stock market in the late 1990s has changed the axiom for this chapter. The market moves considerably faster now than in 1929, 1973, or even 1987. Severe corrections currently last a day or a few days and could moderate the time and depth of market declines. When they happen quickly, there is no time for all those daily or weekly rally attempts on the way down. Any rally attempts will show up in the intraday view.

CHAPTER 64

Use Protective Puts in Volatile Markets*

A *put* is an option to sell a specified number of shares of a stock at a predetermined price, until the put expires. If an investor owns 100 shares of stock, currently selling at $51 and buys a put contract at 50, before the expiration the investor can put the stock and receive $50 a share, no matter what the current stock price situation. For this privilege the investor pays a per share premium that is based on the stock's current price and time left to expiration. In this way, puts are used to protect profits or limit losses.[1] It's like buying an insurance policy on the stock.

WHO USES PROTECTIVE PUTS?

Protective puts are most often used by investors who are holding stock that they prefer to not sell. They believe the price will rise, but are wary about risking the profit. Also, investors who wish to limit downside risk on stock they plan to buy will consider buying a put.

Essentially, investors concerned with the uncertainties of the stock market are those who most often buy puts. During bull markets, they worry about market corrections, and in bear markets, they are concerned that their stock prices could fall further. This uncertainty can lead to a hesitation to invest, and strong upward

---

* Information source Chicago Board Options Exchange.

movements can be missed. Buying puts against an existing stock position or purchasing stock and puts at the same time can supply the confidence to overcome the uncertainty of the stock market. Although people don't hesitate to insure other valuable assets, most investors are not aware that many of their stock positions also can be insured. That is exactly what a protective put does. Normally, by paying a relatively small premium (small in comparison to the market value of the stock), an investor insures that no matter how far the stock drops, it can be sold at the strike price of the put any time up until the put expires.

A protective put may not be suitable for all investors. However, the strategy can provide the protection needed to invest in individual stocks in volatile markets because it provides limited downside risk and unlimited profit potential until the option's expiration.

HOW DO THEY WORK?

Buying a protective put involves the purchase of one put "contract" for every 100 shares of stock already owned or purchased. A put gives the owner the right, but not the obligation, to sell the underlying security at a set price (the strike or exercise price) up to the expiration date. Puts (and calls) are available with expirations of up to eight months on over 1,700 stocks, and three years for more than 200 stocks. The three-year options are known as LEAPS: Long-term Equity AnticiPation Securities.[2]

Let's take a look at what happens to a protective put position as the underlying stock price moves. Commissions have not been taken into consideration in these examples. The following explains how to use a protective put as insurance. We will look at some possible results at expiration.

A. Stock Alone: Buy 100 shares XYZ at $50

If XYZ stock is bought at $50 per share, as soon as the stock drops below the purchase price, the investor begins to lose money. Essentially, the entire $50 per share price is at risk. Accordingly, if the price increases, the investor gains the entire increase without having the cost of the put premium. The investor is at risk of losing the total investment.

B. Buy 100 shares XYZ at $50; Buy 1 Share XYZ at $50 Put

Compare buying XYZ stock alone to buying XYZ with a protective put. Here also buy the stock at $50 per share. Buy a six-month put with a strike price of 50 for 2¼ or a total of $225 per contract ($2¼ times 100 shares in the contract).

---

2. LEAPS and Long-term Equity AnticiPation Securities are registered trademarks of the Chicago Board Options Exchange, Inc.

This put is insurance "without a deductible" because the stock is purchased at $50 and an "at-the-money" put (current stock price and put strike price are identical) with the same strike price of $50 is purchased.

If the stock drops below $50 a share, the put or insurance will begin to offset any loss in XYZ (less the cost of the put). A breakeven point would be the sum of the stock price, the premium price, and the commission costs. Obviously, it would be higher than the $50 a share, at least initially.

It doesn't matter how low the price of XYZ falls; buying the put with a 50 strike price gives the investor the right to sell XYZ at $50 up until the option expires. The risk is only $2¼: the total cost for the stock and option position, $52¼, less $50 (strike price).

The investor has the advantage of having downside risk protection without limiting upside potential above the total cost of the position ($52¼). A disadvantage is that the investor will not begin to profit until the stock price moves above the $52¼ cost.

If XYZ remains at $50 a share or higher, the put will expire worthless and the premium will be lost. If just the stock had been bought, the investor would begin to profit as soon as the stock rose above $50. However, the investor would have no protection from the risk of the stock's declining in value.

C. Buy 100 shares XYZ at $50; Buy 1 Share XYZ at $45 Put

If an investor wants risk protection on a stock position and is willing to have a "deductible" in exchange for the lower "insurance" cost, buying an "out-of-the-money" put (the option strike price is below the stock price) can be the strategy.

XYZ is purchased at $50 with a six-month put at a $45 strike and a premium cost of 1, making it $100 per contract. The put gives the owner the right but not the obligation to sell XYZ at $45 a share, no matter how far the stock price drops, until the option expires. Buying the put with a 45 strike and purchasing the underlying stock at $50 is effectively insurance with a $5 deductible.

If XYZ declines, the put will partly offset the loss in the stock below a price of $45. The investor has two choices: exercise the put to sell the stock or sell the put. If the investor believes XYZ has stopped declining, the choice might be to sell the put. Below 45, the put will at the very least be worth the difference between the current stock price and the strike price.

The profit earned from the put sale can offset some of the decline in the stock price. The investor still holds XYZ shares in anticipation of the stock price's rising again. However, once the put has been sold, the investor no longer has risk protection on the stock position.

A disadvantage is that the investor will not profit until XYZ rises above $51 a share. Had just the stock been purchased, the investor would begin to profit as soon as the stock moved above $50. However, purchasing the put has limited the loss (until expiration) to $6 a share, and the investor still retains all the gain in the stock above the $51 level.

PROTECTIVE PUTS OFFER OTHER STRATEGIES

If XYZ has been purchased at $50 without a put and the investor was correct (if XYZ rose to $70), what choices are available? Without knowledge of the protective put, there are two choices: either hold onto XYZ hoping it will continue to go up or sell it and take the profit. Now a third choice is available: buy a protective put.

REMEMBER THE EXPIRATIONS

Protective puts do expire, at times before they provide any insurance value. To benefit from a protective put strategy over a longer period of time, investors can either buy LEAPS, long-term stock and index options, or, if uncertain how long they will want insurance, they could repeatedly buy short-term puts. Repeatedly buying, or "rolling," short-term puts gives the owner the flexibility of easily adjusting the strike price as the stock moves, but obviously it results in higher costs, costs that push the breakeven price up.

SUMMARY

The volatility of the stock market is a concern to many investors. However, the purchase of a protective put can give the comfort level needed to continue purchasing stock. This strategy is considered more conservative than purchasing stock by itself. Remember, as long as a put is on a stock position, it has limited risk; the investor knows the price at which the stock can be sold. The only disadvantages are that profits cannot be made until the stock moves above the combined cost of the stock and the put (also commission costs) and that the put has an expiration date. Once the stock rises above the combined cost of the position, the investor retains a potential for unlimited profits.

CHAPTER 65

The Stock Market Is a "Random Walk"

The Random Walkers are quite serious in their belief. To them, the past never predicts, forecasts, or indicates the future; therefore, any study of previous events in the stock market is not meaningful. Along with the Random Walk enthusiasts are the Dart Throwers, those who believe you can put a newspaper stock quote page on the wall and throw darts to choose the best investments. Both groups do well in strong bull markets. But then, nearly everyone does well in strong bull markets. Although some of these groups hedge their strategy by narrowing the field, many continue to believe in total randomization.

Although there is a random quality to the stock market, because most investors have similar desires and fears, the actions are not completely random. Probably the best examples of random numbers are the interstate Powerball lottery results. When placed on a chart, Powerball selections give a good example of a random selection (Figure 65–1).

TIME DOESN'T MATTER

It doesn't matter what period or how long a time segment is used; the results always look like a random selection. Although the lottery can pay a higher return than the stock market, it is necessary to come up with a winning number at 80 million-to-1 odds. The odds in the stock market are definitely better; individual stock prices aren't nearly as random (Figure 65–2).

IT'S OBVIOUS

An easy comparison of Figures 65–1 and 65–2 shows the difference between a random walk and price patterns. The Powerball is an obvious random grouping, while the Dow Industrial Average doesn't look as random. It has trends, support, and resistance, as well as other pattern formations.

Also, the stock market is influenced by economic forces. News of earnings, inflation, or interest rate changes can cause strong rallies as well as severe declines. The news never impacts Powerball numbers and never will.

Whether one uses fundamental technical analysis is a matter of personal preference based on experience. But, if the stock market were a true random walk, it would be up about the same amount as it would be down. Investors could quickly lose interest in such a stock market; they'd probably all invest in bonds.

F I G U R E 65–1

Random selection, Powerball lottery, 1997–1998.

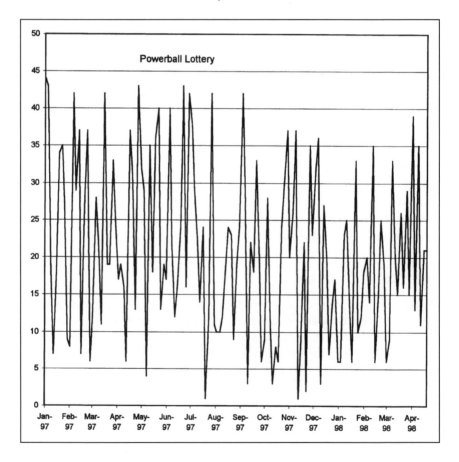

FIGURE 65-2

Nonrandom price movement, Dow Industrial Average, 1997–1998.

CHAPTER 66

Use the Rule of 72 to Double

So, if you're saving for a specific goal, like your child's education, once you have figured out an estimate of how much money you'll need, how much does your current investment have to grow to be there? Or possibly you simply want to know how much growth each year you need to expect from your stock purchase for it to double in 5 years or 10 years.

A quick, easy method of calculation is to use the *rule of 72*, which essentially estimates the number of years it will take for your investment to double at a given rate. Don't rush out and buy a new computer; in fact, many times even a calculator is unnecessary.

FORMULA FOR THE RULE OF 72

The rule of 72 allows you to calculate, in your head, the approximate number of years required for your investment to double with varying growth rates. Consider your investment portfolio. Maybe you want to know when it'll double if it grows annually at 20 percent. Simply divide 72 (a magic number) by 20 (percent growth rate), and round off to the nearest number. You know right away that 72 divided by 20 is 3.6, rounded up to the whole number 4. It will take approximately 4 years for your portfolio to double at a 20 percent annual return.

O.K., YOU WANT LESS RISK

What if you earn "only" 15 percent a year, because you decide that 20 percent is too risky? Decide for yourself. Again, divide 72 by 15 and round the answer to the nearest number. It comes to 4.8 (round up), that is to say, 5 years to double. So, what do you get in money market savings, 3 percent? O.K. 72 divided by 3: The money will double in 24 years. There might be a better investment, without high risk but a better return.

The number of years to double equals: the number 72 divided by the percent growth rate (rounded):

Percent growth rates	5	6	7	8	9	10	11	12	20	25
Years to double	14	12	10	9	8	7	7	6	4	3

YOU CAN ALSO CALCULATE A RATE

The rule of 72 also can be used to figure the rate of growth needed to double an investment in a certain number of years. For example, the investor wants to estimate the rate at which an investment must grow to double by the time a child goes to college, say, 11 years from now. It's a similar formula: Divide 72 (the magic number) by 11 (the number of years to college) and also round to the nearest whole number. No genius required: 72 divided by 11 equals 6.545, or 7 percent, to double in 11 years when the tuition payments are due to begin.

The rate equals the number 72 divided by the number of years to double (rounded):

Years to double	5	7	9	11	13	15	17	19	20	25
Percent Growth Rates:	14	10	8	7	6	5	4	4	4	3

Of course, the results with the rule of 72 aren't precise. However, they are close enough to count and quickly and simply calculated. The formula is intended to be a fast and easy way of estimating.

WHAT CAN GO WRONG?

The biggest problem encountered by virtually all savings and investment programs is the old Murphy's law: If anything can go wrong, it probably will. Emergencies or other situations requiring funds often interfere with keeping savings or investments. Although some emergencies require dipping into savings, it should be considered a loan of last resort. Just as you should pay yourself first, try not to borrow money from yourself. If it cannot be avoided, treat the savings withdrawal as a loan, and repay the funds as soon as possible.

PERIODICALLY RECALCULATE

It's a good idea to recalculate the doubling time annually, based on the return for the previous year. In the stock market, returns tend to continually change, and the investor might get 20 percent one year and 5 percent the next. The recalculation will help an individual stay on track to the college education or other goal.

CHAPTER 67

A Stock Price Splits
When It Gets Too High

Warren Buffett doesn't think so. Look at the chart in Figure 67–1, which is not a chart of the Dow Industrial Average—obviously it's much too high. Rather, it's a chart of Berkshire-Hathaway's price.

The stock has always tended to do well, but give it a good bull market and away it goes. At the end of July 1998, Berkshire-Hathaway was trading just above $17,000 a share (Figure 67–1). So, just what is a price that's too high and should split? This type of action is primarily under the control of the legendary Warren Buffett, who doesn't much believe in the idea of splitting a stock because it gets "too high."

Many believe the too-high idea was fostered and is still nurtured by companies who split their stock because they want to see the price go up. Splitting a stock when they are forward splits tends to bring confidence to a company. The common belief is that the company must have a lot of confidence in their future or they wouldn't go to the trouble and expense of splitting the stock. However, a lack of confidence in the future can sometimes be the reason behind a stock split. Sometimes a company announces a stock split just before reporting weaker earnings.

When Buffett issued Class B stock back in 1996, it wasn't really a split. It hit the market at what many would consider to be a price that was too high and that should be split, which was $1,000. The price was well ahead of the next-highest price, that of the Washington Post Co., which was trading at $291.50 per share. The price of Class B immediately hit $1,200 dollars and declined to 1,000, and that was the bottom. After the $1,000 support level was briefly touched, the stock price rallied and didn't look back (Figure 67–2).

FIGURE 67–1

High price, Berkshire-Hathaway (NYSE: BRK-A), 1990–1998.

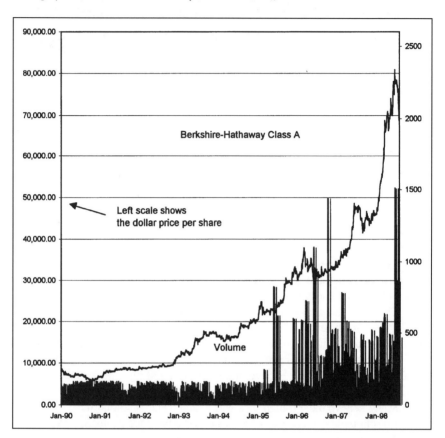

The price of Berkshire-Hathaway Class B hit strong resistance at the $1,600 level, dropped back to 1,400, and rallied again. Illustrating that there might not be any such thing as too high, the price continued to climb. All the way up to 2,705 it went before turning the trend. That's up more than $1,100 in less than a year, up 1,300 from the lowest price of that time segment.

Although some might consider the Class B stock a split, it really wasn't. Here are some of the diffferences.

Berkshire-Hathaway, Inc., has two classes of common stock designated Class A and Class B. One share of Class B common stock has the rights of 1/30th of a share of Class A common stock with these exceptions: First, a Class B share has 1/200th of the voting rights of a Class A share (rather than 1/30th of the vote). Second, the Class B shares are not eligible to participate in the Berkshire-Hathaway, Inc., shareholder designated contributions program.

Each share of a Class A common stock is convertible at any time, at the holder's option, into 30 shares of Class B common stock. The conversion privilege does not extend in the opposite direction. Holders of Class B shares are not able to convert them into Class A shares. Both Class A and B shareholders are entitled to attend the Berkshire-Hathaway Annual Meeting held the first Monday in May.[1]

Since the Class B allows other investors to be able to afford shares of Berkshire-Hathaway, it has at least that quality, which is similar to a split.

The Berkshire-Hathaway home page indexes several interesting pages containing the investment philosophy of Buffett and his colleagues. Although part of

FIGURE 67-2

New stock, Berkshire-Hathaway, Class B, 1996–1998.

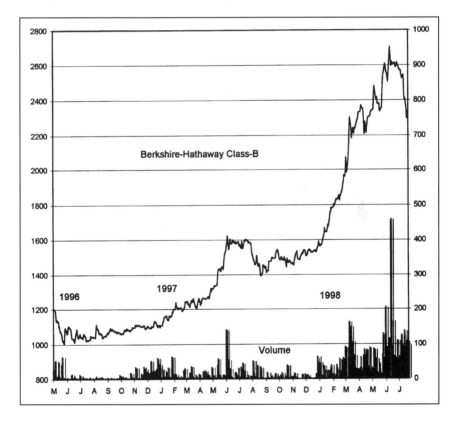

1. Information based on *Comparison of Berkshire Hathaway Inc. Class A and Class B Common Stock*, http://www.berkshirehathaway.com/classab.html.

his investment strategy is determined by incredibly large assets, much of what he believes about investing can be useful to the individual investor.

A stock does not have to split because the price gets too high. As Berkshire-Hathaway has shown for some time, there's no such thing as too high. Often the implication of being too high is suggested by companies who split their stock. The real reason behind the split is likely to be something they aren't immediately announcing.

CHAPTER 68

Join the Club

We could start a club. Get a bunch of people together, pool our money, and get rich together. That's often the way it starts; someone suggests a club, talks up the idea to friends, neighbors, and acquaintances, who then meet monthly. Some clubs do well, some become famous (e.g., Beardstown Ladies), others fall apart the first year. The Internet is becoming a large source of investment clubs that supply research and other information to members. Although investment clubs aren't for everyone, they can be a valuable source of information and education for the individual investor.

THE NAIC

Investment clubs generally aren't a phony pyramid or other scheme created for someone to get rich quick. The National Association of Investors Corporation (NAIC) is a not-for-profit organization devoted to individual investors and to assisting individual investors form and operate investment clubs. Currently there are more than 37,000 clubs that are members of the NAIC, with around 700,000 individual and club members.

The NAIC provides services and advice for individual investors and investment clubs. The organization also has a low-cost stock purchase plan to further facilitate members' purchase of common stock. Some clubs have been in operation for 40 years, and today the majority of investment clubs that belong to NAIC do better with their portfolios than the Standard & Poor's 500 Index.

HOW DOES A CLUB FUNCTION?

Most clubs have simple rules that can be changed as necessary. Normally groups of 10 to 20 people, often organized as a legal partnership (for tax purposes), meet on a regular basis, usually monthly. Club officers are elected, and members are asked to actively participate through the following activities:

1. Attending the monthly meetings
2. Making a monthly contribution, often a $20 minimum with no maximum
3. Researching and following the progress of a specific company's stock or group of stocks that the club owns or has targeted for investment

Based on their strategy and plan, the club invests money in the stock market, and usually one or two members are authorized to place trades with a stockbroker. Each member has shares of the investment portfolio, based on the amount of money he or she contributed (i.e., the $20 monthly minimum and any other contributions). With a low monthly minimum, virtually anyone can afford to belong to the club. From then on, the main requirements are a willingness to work, learn, and get along with the other members. Obviously, a mutually agreed upon system of resolving differences is a good idea.

In Business Together

Since the club is a legal partnership, all the members are effectively in business with each other with all the advantages and problems that can cause. Trust is essential. The organization sets broad goals of education, to learn about investing in the stock market and capital gains, to make a profit. Club members need to understand that gains could be minimal or even nonexistent for the first couple of years. Often clubs place restrictions on withdrawals considered to be early.

Eventually club members start their own individual portfolios, supported with the knowledge and skills they learned by being an investment club member.

Federal Taxes

Here is a brief summary of some of the Internal Revenue Service's tax requirements.

Identifying Number

Each club must have an *employer identification number* (EIN) to use when filing its return. The club's EIN also may have to be given to the payer of dividends or other income from investments recorded in the club's name. If your club does not have an EIN, get Form SS-4, Application for Employer Identification Number, from your nearest Social Security Administration office or call 1-800-TAX-

FORM (1-800-829-3676). Mail the completed Form SS-4 to the Internal Revenue Service Center where you file the club's tax return.

Tax Treatment of the Club

Generally, an investment club is treated as a partnership for federal tax purposes unless it chooses otherwise. In some situations, however, it is taxed as a corporation or a trust.

Are Investment Clubs Regulated by the SEC?

Investment clubs usually do not have to register, or register the offer and sale of their own membership interests, with the SEC. But since each investment club is unique, each group should decide if it needs to register and comply with securities laws.

Two laws can relate to investment clubs:

1. Under the Securities Act of 1933, membership interests in the investment club may be securities. If so, the offer and sale of membership interests could be subject to Federal regulation.
2. Under the Investment Company Act of 1940, an investment club may be an investment company, and regulated accordingly.

States Regulations

State securities laws can differ from federal securities laws. To learn more about the laws in your state, call your state securities regulator. Look under state listings in your telephone book, or to get the telephone number for your state, call the North American Securities Administrators Association (NASAA) at 202-737-0900 or visit their Web site at www.nasaa.org.

For Further Information

Call 1-800-SEC-0330 for more information or to request other publications for investors, such as the following:

- *Invest Wisely: Advice From Your Securities Industry Regulators*
- A copy of federal securities laws, such as the Investment Company Act of 1940
- The Investment Company registration package, which contains more information about exceptions to the laws
- Visit the SEC's Web site at www.sec.gov[1]

---

1. *Investment Clubs and the SEC*, April 1998, http://www.sec.gov/consumer/invclub.htm, last updated June 16, 1998.

TRUST, BUT AUDIT RESULTS

Trust is obviously important. Establish the club with safeguards to protect both the investors and the person in charge of the money. Remove the opportunity for mistrust as much as possible. Decrease the chances for temptation. Make it difficult for those who might take the money. Also, check to see that the agreed-upon investments are being made. Sometimes those authorized to do the investing wrongly decide to buy their choices rather than those of the club. When people know from the beginning that they are going to be audited, they are less likely to be bothered by the fact. It's the unexpected, surprise audits that make them feel not trusted.

SUCCESS IS IN THE SETUP

The most difficult thing for a group of people to do is make a decision. Because the initial setup is so important to the successful operation of a club, remove or moderate the decision-making process by relying on experience. Contacting an organization like the NAIC at 1-248-583-6242 or www.better-investing.org for their suggestions accomplishes much of the difficult organizational work and simplifies the decision process.

CHAPTER 69

Small Stocks Make the "January Effect"

Investors have traded the "January Effect" for many years. The effect is a noticeable tendency for smaller-company share prices to rally in the first month of the year:

> THE JANUARY EFFECT, for those few investors who haven't already heard about it, is the pronounced tendency for all stocks, but especially those of small-cap companies, to perform well during the first few weeks of the new year.[1]

WHY DOES IT HAPPEN?

Although somewhat debated, the consensus seems to be that tax loss selling at the end of the year leaves individual investors with cash. In January, they rebuild their portfolios, often in the smaller companies. There also appears to be some positive influence after a Democrat is elected president, possibly because of an antitrust leaning.

---

1. Mark Hulbert, "The Case for Small Caps," "Wall Street Irregular," *Forbes*, December 1996, http://www.forbes.com/forbes/121696/5814392a.htm.

WHO'S SELLING AND BUYING?

Logic says, it's the individual investors, those who can take advantage of tax loss selling. Institutions generally don't need the strategy:

> Only individual investors—the bulk of small stock owners—worry about taxes since institutional investors are exempt. That fact has made small stocks perform better than larger ones since at least World War II.[2]

Often, small issues return 6.8 percent in January, with the larger-company shares returning less than 2 percent. Small stocks are commonly determined as having a market capitalization of $150 to $200 million. Market capitalization is calculated by multiplying the market price times the number of shares outstanding.

The phenomenon is indirectly influenced by large institutional investors. The large portfolio managers are paid in relation to their performance. Near year-end they have a tendency to avoid the riskier small capitalization companies in favor of the large conservative ones.

The way Wall Street's largest institutional investors are paid reinforces the January Effect. Their bonus and salaries are based on how well they perform. Performance frequently uses the larger cap companies in the Standard & Poor's 500 Index as a benchmark. Whereas during the year they are willing to take more risk (especially in January), coming up on the end of the year is the time to be conservative:

> According to Professors Robert Haugen and Philippe Jorion of the University of California, Irvine, these compensation packages encourage managers in the last months of the year to lock in their relative gains by mimicking the S&P 500. Consequently, their incentives to purchase small-cap stocks outside the S&P 500 will be lowest in December and highest in January.[3]

Professors Haugen and Jorion further believe the growing dominance of institutional portfolio managers will perpetuate the existence of the January Effect.

Although opinions of experts are all well and good, the evidence suggests that the January Effect could be changing. Any time a consistent trading pattern receives publicity, there are many investors who will try to take advantage of the situation. Previously we saw how the "Buy on Monday" axiom has changed since 1990 (Chapter 39). Is it also possible the January Effect is going through some change (Figure 69–1)?

Keep in mind, the chart is showing only the percentage difference between the two indexes. The difference showed phenomenal success in 1968, at 15.4 percent. It also did well in the early and mid 1970s and 1991 through 1992. Although a quick look might suggest a decline in the January Effect from the mid 1970s to 1990, a similar occurrence took place in the 1955 to 1966 years.

---

2 Paola Banchero, "So-Called January Effect Is Looking Good for Investors," *Kansas City Business Journal*, December 30, 1996, http://www.amcity.com/kansascity/stories/123096/story4.html.
3. Paola Banchero, op. cit.

F I G U R E 69-1

January effect, difference (based on monthly averages) between S&P 500 Index and S&P low-priced stocks. (*Source:* Yale Hirsch, *The 1999 Stock Trader's Almanac*, The Hirsch Organization, Old Tappan, NJ, August 1998. Web address: www.hirschorganization.com.

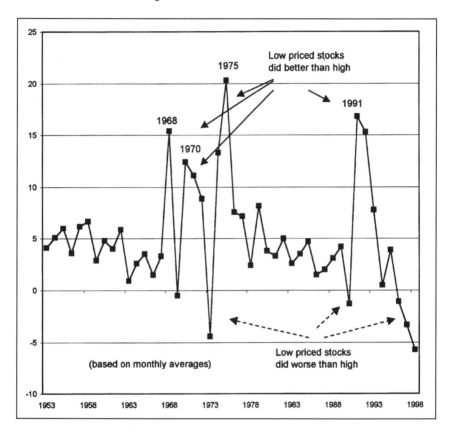

HAS IT GONE AWAY?

Of great concern is the 1996 through 1998 time period when the small companies were in negative territory. The last significant move was back in 1992. Could it be that the time honored January Effect has traded itself away? If it has taken a temporary hiatus, will it return?

It would be difficult for individuals to trade the January Effect. Selection of what to trade is only one of the major problems. Also, the profitability weakens with small quantities of stock, although an intent to sell a small cap stock might do well in the month of January. As shown by Figure 69–1, when the effect reappears, it does so in a dramatic way as it did in 1968 or 1991.

WILL IT REAPPEAR?

History will show whether the effect will reappear. It's part of the speculation that goes with smaller companies and trying to profit from short-term strategies. The individual investor should approach this strategy like all others, with knowledge and the realization that it might fail to occur. However, in the 45 years covered by the chart, only 6 years were below the gain on the large cap Standard & Poor's 500. The caution is based in the fact that 3 of the 6 were in the most recent years. The only certainty in the stock market is change.

CHAPTER 70

Invest According to Objectives

"I want to make a lot of money in the stock market, but I don't want to take risk."

Is it a wish or an objective? Since one of the synonyms for the word *objective* is *measurable*, the general statement is assuredly a wish. However, a wish can be redefined as an objective.

ESTABLISHING A GOOD OBJECTIVE

Often, such things as retirement, children's college education, a house, or a new car are stated as objectives for investing. Even they are quite general, although they are more specific than "a lot of money." What about a set time for achievement? Retirement and children's education have built-in time periods; however, it's a good idea to break these large (10 or 20 years) blocks of time into smaller segments like 1 to 5 years. Having shorter time for achievement helps to ensure that the investor is evaluating performance and making changes along the way.

DECISIONS THAT NEED TO BE MADE

In order to meet an investment objective, certain information is essential. What specifically will be done? What performance is reasonable? What kind of stocks will be purchased? How much diversification is necessary to moderate risk? What time frame should be used? How will success be measured? When the answers to these questions are decided, they need to be set down in writing.

An objective should have the following characteristics:

- *Be specific*:   What activities will be done to choose investments?
- *Be reasonable in expectations*:   Base expectations on observable performance.
- *Consider risk*:   Select stocks and diversify to a comfort level.
- *Have a time frame*:   One year, two years, five years, and so on.
- *Be measurable*:   Performance needs to be measured to be evaluated.

Categories of Stock

When stockbrokers open new accounts, they are required by Rule 144 of the NYSE to know their customer. That means they need to know certain details about the person's investing experience, financial status, and most importantly investment objectives. In order to standardize objectives into mutually understood concepts, they usually list four categories for investment:

- *Income*:   Investments that generate income from dividends or interest payments
- *Growth*:   Investments that demonstrate price growth—usually newer companies that pay no dividends
- *Total return*:   Investments that will see both price growth and income from dividends
- *Speculation*:   Investments for short-term trades that result in quick profits (e.g., new companies, companies in rapid growth areas, turnarounds, and other speculative situations)

Income, growth, total return, or speculation—all financial investments fit into these categories.

Income Stock

Traditionally, income stocks are most often utilities, especially electrical utilities. They are conservative investments usually with steady streams of income and are normally financially stable. Although there is always risk involved with common stock investing, income stocks should be some of the lowest risk. Sometimes they are colorfully referred to as the "widow and orphan stocks," meaning investments for people who can't afford to lose money.

Obviously, dividends are a priority when an investor's objective is income. Dividend growth and dividend stability are likewise important. Looking at the average annual growth of dividends over at least a five-year period can give the investor some idea of how much growth to expect in the future. In order for a company to pay out dividends, the growth of revenues and income are important.

The primary sources of income can be a concern in some areas. The Detroit area might have trouble if the automotive industry is in a slump. The Silicon Valley area of California might have trouble when the computer industry is slow. The source of income is a part of risk, more specifically the risk of slower growth.

Matching the General Objective

With income as a general objective, we will narrow the focus to looking at electric utility companies that have a current yield comparable to 5-year U.S. Treasury notes (for example, 8/7/98 at 5.375 percent). These companies should have somewhat consistent growth in dividend payments, revenues, and earnings.

Selecting Some Candidates

Once income becomes the objective, select some candidates (5 to 10), and choose what you believe to be the best opportunities. We will look at three examples, beginning with consolidated Edison (ED):

	Recent Price, 8/5/98	52 Weeks		Current Dividend Yield
		High	Low	
Consolidated Edison (NYSE: ED)	$42.69	$47.88	$30.25	5.0%

For an income objective, the most important information here is the current dividend yield of 5 percent. If the shares are purchased at the $42.69 a share, the investor locks in a 5 percent yield no matter what happens to the price. That yield will increase as the dividends are increased (usually annually), but that yield can only decrease if the amount of the dividend is lowered.

The data showing growth as presented below are based on information from Rapid Research, who used information from Media General Financial Services. EPS estimates are from *Nelson's Consensus Earnings Estimate Database*.[1]

Consolidated Edison (NYSE: ED) Electric service to New York City and most of Westchester County. Supplies gas to Manhattan, The Bronx, and part of Queens and Westchester. Also supplies steam to part of Manhattan.

Our second example is Northern States Power (NSP):

	Recent Price, 8/5/98	52 Weeks		Current Dividend Yield
		High	Low	
Northern States Power (NYSE: NSP)	$26.25	30.22	24.00	5.4%

---

1. http://www.rapidresearch.com.

NSP generates and transmits electricity, and it also transports gas to consumers in Minnesota, North Dakota, South Dakota, Wisconsin, and Michigan.

Our third example is Detroit Edison (ED):

	Recent Price, 8/5/98	52 Weeks High	52 Weeks Low	Current Dividend Yield
Detroit Edison (NYSE: ED)	$39.75	$42.00	28.06	5.2%

ED generates, purchases, transmits, and distributes electrical energy to southeastern Michigan. Table 70–1 gives the annual dividends per share for the preceding three companies.

First, there have been no drops in dividend payment amounts, nor have there been any missed payments. Second, from these three stocks we can set a reasonable income objective of 5 to 5.5 percent, with a 2 percent annual growth rate. With 5-year U.S. Treasury notes just under 5.5 percent, the expectations are reasonable. The strongest dividend growth is with Northern States Power, averaging 2.07 percent per year for the 5 years. The DET dividend growth rate is 0.32 percent, while ED is somewhat higher at 1.76.

The Northern States Power dividend yield (based on current price of $26.25, August 5, 1998) stood at 5.4 percent. Detroit Edison's yield was 5.2 percent, and Con Edison was 5.0 percent. At this particular time, NSP offered the highest current yield, based on price, as shown in Tables 70–2 and 70–3.

Although the earnings of NSP had a significant drop in 1997, the following year seems to have improved, and the stock does show consistent revenue growth. Further analysis could reveal the reason for the earnings decline of 1997. However, there is enough consistency here for this stock to be a viable selection for investment.

Stock analysis can be much more thorough than this, depending on how deeply the investor wants to dig into a company's financial situation. Debt, new projects, and future sources of revenues can also be examined. With electric util-

TABLE 70–1

Annual Dividends per Share

Years	1993	1994	1995	1996	1997	1998
ED, $	1.94	2.00	2.04	2.08	2.10	2.12
(%)		(3.0)	(2.0)	(2.0)	(1.0)	(1.0)
NSP, $	1.28	1.31	1.34	1.37	1.40	1.43
(%)		(3.0)	(2.0)	(2.0)	(2.0)	(2.0)
DET, $	2.04	2.06	2.06	2.06	2.06	2.08
(%)		(1.0)	(0.0)	(0.0)	(0.0)	(1.0)

T A B L E 70–2

Yield, Millions of Dollars

Years	1993	1994	1995	1996	1997	12 Months
ED	6,265.4	6,373.1	6,536.9	6,959.7	7,121.3	7,145.1
(%)		(2.6)	(6.5)	(2.3)	(2.3)	(0.3)
NSP	2,404.0	2,486.5	2,568.6	2,654.2	2,733.7	2,736.9
(%)		(3.4)	(3.3)	(3.3)	(3.0)	(0.1)
DET	3,555.2	3,519.3	3,635.5	3,645.4	3,764.0	4,012.1
(%)		(−1.0)	(3.3)	(3.0)	(3.3)	(6.6)

T A B L E 70–3

Yield, Earnings per Share, Dollars

Years	1993	1994	1995	1996	1997	12 Months
ED	2.66	2.98	2.93	2.93	2.95	3.07
(%)		(11.5)	(−1.4)	(−2.2)	(0.7)	(4.0)
NSP	1.51	1.73	1.96	1.91	1.61	1.65
(%)		(15.0)	(13.3)	(−0.5)	(−13.6)	(3.4)
DET	3.34	2.67	2.8	2.13	2.88	3.21
(%)		(−20.5)	(4.0)	(−23.8)	(34.8)	(11.8)

Note: Percents for earnings are based on total dollars.

ities, nuclear and coal issues can be an important area of examination. However, companies that have been consistent in the past will likely continue to be consistent unless an unusual situation arises.

Any of these stocks could be a good selection for the right investor, but for selecting purposes, we'll buy the NSP stock because of current yield, dividend growth, and revenue and earnings consistency. When other stocks are selected for diversification, the first selection of NSP can be used as a benchmark to select others. The portfolio can be as diversified as the investor wants, but each stock added increases the amount of time and analysis for selection and monitoring. Many investors would keep the diversification to three to five different utilities.

Complete Objective

For purposes of dividend income, the amount of $100,000 will be invested in the stock of at least three electric utility companies. The expected annual yield will be 5.4 percent with at least 2 percent annual growth rate in the dividend. Risk will be considered by evaluating the consistency of the growth in revenues, earnings, and dividends. Performance will be evaluated at least on an annual basis, with changes being made as necessary.

EVALUATION

When an objective is precisely detailed, evaluation is ever so simple. Either the objective is being met or it is not. If not, learn the reason why not, and make a decision to hold your position or sell the stock for a better-performing candidate.

Notice that the objective says nothing about price growth. That's because price growth is not a consideration for an income objective. The steady income is important. Any growth in price is just an extra benefit if the investor chooses to sell some or all of the stock. The price growth is often why income investors will choose stock rather than safer U.S. Treasury securities.

A SHORT ANALYSIS

The analysis used in this chapter is a brief form of "Fundamental Analysis," examining the revenues, earnings, dividends, and price growth of a company. Even a short analysis tells a lot about a company and its consistent growth. The purpose of this chapter is not to explain analysis but rather to illustrate how an analysis can be made based on the information readily available to investors.

OTHER OBJECTIVE CATEGORIES

Growth

Investors looking for growth should consider revenue and earnings growth as a higher priority than dividends. Price growth over the past five years essentially replaces dividend growth as a focal point. Growth companies are generally small to midsized, and they are leaders or are becoming leaders in their industry niche. A benchmark for performance can be an index such as the Russell 2,000 Index or the Wilshire 5,000 Index. However, because of the influence of growth stocks on the entire stock market, the investor should also look at the stock's performance within the Dow Industrial Average and the Standard & Poor's 500 Index for growth comparisons.

The price-earnings ratios (p/e ratio equals the price divided by earnings) can be an important part of determining risk in growth stocks, but the ratios should not be examined alone. A current p/e ratio in comparison to a company's five-year average p/e ratio can show whether a stock is currently more or less attractive to buyers. Although it's an oversimplification, a higher-than-average p/e is considered to indicate more risk, whereas a lower-than-average p/e means less risk. It is essential to look at the information behind the p/e ratio and ask why is it high or low. Comparing the p/e ratio to other companies in the same industry can also be helpful in determining risk and market appeal.

For growth stock objectives, look at:

■ Price growth

■ Revenue growth

■ Earnings growth

■ Price-earnings ratio

■ Analyst opinion (Why will the growth continue?)

Growth stock objectives should be evaluated at least annually, but they can also be evaluated quarterly or even monthly. A caution with monthly evaluations: Don't overreact and sell out too soon.

Total Return

Total return stocks are dividend-paying stocks that also have good price growth. The focus is usually on industry leaders, the "stalwarts" that also pay out dividends. These would include the so-called blue-chip stocks like AT&T, General Electric, American Home Products, and Eastman Kodak. They are considered lower-risk stocks, because they are well-established companies and because every time a dividend is paid out, the risk is lowered by that amount.

Analysis of total return stocks is similar to the analysis for growth stocks, but it will obviously include dividends and dividend growth. The objective statement needs to include both price and dividend growth.

Total return objectives can be evaluated annually, quarterly, or monthly—just be careful with sell decisions. Don't sell out too quickly when the market declines. Often that is the best time to buy more stock.

SPECULATION

The speculation category covers everything else. It can be the act of investing with "wild abandonment," or it can include some analysis to moderate risk. Although there is a belief among many that higher risk brings higher rewards, that is not usually what happens. Higher risk can also mean greater losses.

Rather than approaching speculative investing with wild abandonment, why not just extend the objective to a higher level? If the Standard & Poor's Index is growing at 10 percent, set the objective at 30 percent, or use a shorter time period for achievement. Use basic fundamental analysis to find companies that either have or are working toward strong revenues and earnings. Technical analysis is also used for short-term speculative investing, but the risk can be moderated by learning some basics about the company. No matter what type of analysis is used for speculative investing, the greatest difficulty is keeping up with the rapidly changing market. Opportunities appear suddenly and are gone within minutes. The individual investor can have problems trying to keep up with the professionals who watch the market change tick by tick.

Evaluation of speculative trading is often done on trade-by-trade basis.

WHAT AN OBJECTIVE DOES

Setting a well-defined objective makes investing easier for the investor. Decisions to buy or sell stock are easier because it is only necessary to determine if the stock fits the objective or is achieving the objective. If a stock doesn't fit, don't buy it; if performance is below standard with recovery unlikely, sell.

REVIEW

An objective should have the following characteristics:

Be specific: What activities will be done to choose investments?

Be reasonable in expectations: Base expectations on observable performance.

Consider risk: Select stocks and diversify to a comfort level.

Have a time frame: One year, two years, five years, and so on.

Be measurable: Performance needs to be measured to be evaluated.

Index

A

Addiction, to trading, 204–205
All or none (AON) qualifier, 143, 149
Announcements:
  of splits, 89–90
  of stock buybacks, 29–30
Anticipation:
  of earnings, 110–111, 114
  by market, 119
Asian economic problems, 270
Averaging down, 21
Averaging up, 15, 21, 22–23

B

Bad news, company stock buybacks and,
  27–28
Bear markets, 15, 225, 269–278
  advances in, 273–278
  buying in, 271–272
  definitions of, 269–270
Beating the Dow (O'Higgins and Downes),
  256
Bellwethers, 242–249
  best use of, 249
  industry, 242–246
  intraday price fluctuations of, 246–249
Bid, 154
Blue-chip stocks, 307
Blue sky, 80
Borrowed stock, short sales and, 59
Bottom, 121
Bottom fishing, 154, 159–162
  as speculation, 162
Brokerage account statements, saving, 197
Brokers:
  churning by, 205–206
  cold calls from, 104–105
Buffett, Warren, 289
Bull markets, 240
Buy high, sell higher strategy, 48–53
Buying:
  in bear markets, 271–272
  days of the week and, 182–184
  dollar cost averaging for, 221–224
  following market declines, 208–213, 250–254

Buying: (*cont.*)
  low, 43–47
  with moving prices, 88
Buy limits, 156
Buy low, sell high strategy, 43–47
Buy on the rumor, sell on the news strategy,
  54–57
Buy on weakness, sell on strength strategy,
  138–141
Buyouts (*see* Takeovers)
Buy stop orders, 22, 23–24, 83, 85–86
Buy stop strategy, 251–252

C

Chasing, 147, 175–176
Chop stocks, 104, 105
Churning, 205–206
Classifying stocks, 109
Company stock buybacks, 26–30
Competition:
  of companies, 220
  among investors, 152–153
Corporate takeovers (*see* Takeovers)
Corrections:
  buying following, 208–213, 250–254
  diversification to protect against, 189
  of October 1989, 119–121, 252–253
  of October 1997, 23, 216
  partial liquidation as protection against,
    192–193
  value and, 3–5
Cramer, James, 250
Crash of 1929, 208–211
Current events, market effects of, 172–174
Current trend, 215
Cyclical stocks, buy low, sell high strategy with,
  45–47

D

Daily price fluctuations, value and, 2–3
Day orders, 148
Discount rate, 127, 128
Divergences, 214–218
Diversification, 188–191